A Local Boy

A Memoir

David F. Gouveia, M.D.

First published by Dog Ear Publishing
4011 Vincennes Rd
Indianapolis, IN 46268
www.dogearpublishing.net

ISBN: 978-1-4575-5945-7

This book is printed on acid-free paper.

Printed in the United States of America

Table of Contents

Some Comments by the Author

Over the years while sitting, laughing, playing and talking with my children and grandchildren, I've been asked numerous questions - for example: what was life like when you were growing up? What was it like working in a family grocery store? What was school like? What was it like being a son of immigrant parents? Tell us that story again Papu about etc. etc. etc.

How to answer these questions? My family encouraged me to write down my story. Writing this memoir was easier than I anticipated. I found that the more I thought about a topic, my mind became filled with more information, more than I ever expected. Minute details became apparent to me. It was almost frightening that I could recall so much information.

Following coronary bypass surgery, I developed a phenomenon called pump brain. This resulted in the memory loss of a period in my life. Although some of the events have now been recovered, I think there remain some problems remembering certain things. Recalling people's names remains an irritating problem. Although this deficit is common among people of my age, I feel that I am affected more than the average person of my generation.

I started writing this memoir in 2009. I didn't think I would ever stop writing as the years passed. I have not included all the topics that I wanted to cover, but at some point, it was necessary to stop writing and to start editing these pages.

There are many people who contributed to this memoir in one way or another. My parents John and Patricia and my in-laws Hedy and Walter were such an influence on me and are frequently mentioned in these writings. My beautiful wife Janice continues to be a significant influence in all that I've done in the past 50+ years. My children were and still are a tremendous part of my life. Although I was busy in my practice, I tried to be available to them as much as possible. My grandchildren are now the stars of the family. They bring unlimited delight to my life.

The staff at the Old Colony Historical Society was very helpful in researching topics for me. They helped me confirm dates for some sections of this book. Andrew Boisvert, an archivist, and Liz Bernier, assistant to the director, handled the request for information that I needed.

My youngest son John spent countless hours transcribing and editing my handwritten notes onto the computer. Microsoft Word was not cooperative at times. It seemed that it did not want to be involved with me - its stubbornness was irritating. John had to listen to my complaints about the computer and my seemingly endless problems with it. Despite all these difficulties, I persisted in editing, deleting and adding new text. Without John's hard work in rewriting and editing, working with the publisher, and his patience and persistence, this book would have never been printed.

You can assume from these writings that my involvement in American History has been a lifetime adventure. Because of this interest, readers may note several historical events intertwined with my life story.

I have done considerable research on these historical events. It is my hope that the majority of this information is accurate. The 20th century was replete with celebrations, and I was present with my camera to photograph them. I almost never went anywhere without my camera. The camera virtually became part of me and having those pictures to review made writing this book easier.

History is not something of the past. History is a part of everyday life. Every day we live is history.

I hope that this collection of thoughts and events will continue to be of interest to my descendants for many years after I have passed on to my reward.

David F. Gouveia

GROWING UP

Some Thoughts on my Early Childhood

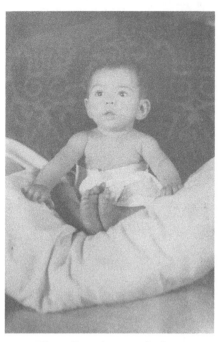

The earliest photograph of me

I was born on May 15, 1931, at my godmother's house on Baker Road in Taunton, Massachusetts, in the house owned by Joe Fresta's parents. My birth occurred in the second-floor bedroom and was attended by Joseph E. Nunes, M.D. My parents were Joao Figueiredo Gouveia, who eventually became known as John F. Gouveia and Patrocina Alvaro Netto, who eventually became known as Patricia Netto Gouveia. My parents had four children. Their first son, Julio, died at about six months of age. The birth of their older daughter, Chris, was followed two years later by a second daughter, Virginia. I was number four, the baby.

Growing up in an immigrant society had many good, and some not so good features. My earliest memory is of a day when I was home alone and decided to cross the street to our store on Lawton Street. Apparently, I was almost hit by a car! My mother had already lost one son and was not willing to lose a second one. As a result, she became very protective of me and limited my activities. I was not allowed to do anything which she considered dangerous, like bike riding. My godmother, Josephine Lawrence, broke the protective barrier by giving me a Flexible Flyer sled for Christmas one year. It got a lot of use on Baker Road hill, sledding with the Gallagher boys. I never did get a bike. I did a lot of ice skating on Carlos' Pond and at Memorial Park. Winters were colder in those days, so outdoor skating was possible for most of the winter. Other vivid memories include The Hurricane of 1938. My mother and grandmother had gone to Villa Franca da Serra in Portugal for the summer, leaving my father to take care of us. The 1938 hurricane was the first such storm in the memory of the people in the Northeast. You must understand that there was very little communication about the weather at that time. Obviously, there was no TV. Most people had a radio,

Posing on a pony circa 1934

but no one was prepared for the consequences of that violent storm. Chris, Virginia and I had a great time out in the storm. I was actually lifted by the wind for a few feet over the road. That was fun! There was one tree in our front yard that we did not like. It was about ten feet tall, and in the right corner of the grassy triangle in front of the house. Trees were falling everywhere you looked. Of course our unloved tree, even with our pushing it, did not go down.

It was several days before all of the streets in Taunton were open because of the fallen trees. Taunton had many tall elm trees that were uprooted. This was prior to the Dutch elm disease destroying this species, which has been practically eliminated in the Northeast because of the infection. Most electrical wires and phone wires were snapped by the falling trees. We, therefore, had no electricity or phone service for many days. Much flooding occurred especially along the Taunton River between Taunton and Dighton. The Taunton River is a tidal river. At normal high tide, there is no problem with flooding, but with the hurricane surge and heavy downpours, the river rose many feet above normal. Low-lying areas along the river were flooded especially along Rte. 44 near Church Green. Along the River in Dighton, many homes were destroyed and washed away. Our home was on a hill, so we were not affected by the flooding. The hurricane of 1938 was the first that most people had seen, but hurricanes now seem to be almost a normal weather phenomenon.

Saturdays and Sundays
on the Farm

Life was quite simple in the 30s and 40s. We had a radio to listen to, no television. One of our favorite radio shows was "The Shadow Knows." At the end of the show, the Shadow would say "who knows what secrets lie in the hearts of men? Only the Shadow knows, ha, ha, ha." Another show, the name of which I don't remember offered a glow-in-the-dark ring. I ordered one, and could not wait to get it. I wore it at night, and it glowed in the dark. When not listening to the radio, we learned to talk to each other and play simple games. Reading was an option, but I really don't remember spending a lot of my free time reading. School took up Monday through Friday. We didn't have as many days off as kids do now. There was an occasional "teacher's day" but not often. Saturdays and Sundays were free days for me most of the time until I became old enough to help with the grocery deliveries on Saturdays. Grocery business was quite different from what it is now. A few small chains and grocery stores were in Taunton, including the Great Atlantic and Pacific Tea Company, otherwise known as the A&P. First National Stores also had a presence in Taunton. These chain stores were no larger than today's convenience stores. Few people had automobiles. We took orders by phone for those customers who were able to afford a phone. Talking about phones, do you know what a party line is? We certainly don't have them now.

A party line was a phone line that connected to two or three households at the same time. What was fun about the party line is that you could pick up the phone and listen to other peoples' conversations. We knew when the phone call was for us, because of the number of rings. One ring for one, two for another, and three for the third household. At our store, we had a pay phone mounted near the front door. It was not a party line. It served as the phone for the store, as well as for use by the public. For five cents, customers were able to make local calls. These calls were timed. When you reached the three-minute limit, a live operator would come on the phone and say "your time is up." You could put another nickel to extend the call, or just hang up. A long distance call would be exorbitantly expensive and was to be avoided. For those customers without a phone, especially in North Dighton, we made house visits to take the orders for Saturday delivery. Sometimes my father hired John Fitta on Saturdays to help with deliveries. I frequently helped John Fitta in our 1929 Chevrolet truck with a covered top and oil cloth curtains that could be rolled down and snapped into place. I learned to drive in the 1929 Chevy with John Fitta and with my father instructing me. It had a shift with four gears on the floor. I remember first gear was on the right; second gear was on the left, unfortunately, if you didn't have your clutch down, which I didn't a few times, resulting in stripping of the gears.

Grocery deliveries were easy, but fertilizer deliveries were not. The bags weighed at least fifty pounds. My father took orders in winter for spring fertilizer deliveries. By springtime, farmers were usually out of money, so my father did not expect payment until harvest time. Some years, the farms were not productive because of weather problems, so we were not necessarily paid on time. I must say the farmers were honest and eventually paid for the fertilizer. I want to remind you we were at the height of the great depression from 1929 till the late 1930s. The economy did not pick up until after WWII started. There is nothing like a war to stimulate business.

Sundays were different; grocery stores were not legally open. Blue Laws allowed only convenience stores to open at noon time. Sales of certain foods like meat were not allowed on Sunday in Massachusetts. These laws were strictly enforced. Occasionally we would get a panic call from a customer who needed more meat than she had bought. We sneaked it to the customer at noon time. Since the store could not open until noon, my father was able to go to the 7 am mass at Our Lady of Lourdes (OLOL) Church. He sat in the same pew at the right of the altar, two or three rows from the front, near the supporting column.

I often felt that he thought that the pew was his property since he discouraged others from sitting near him. Also on Sunday, dad would go for a ride around the area in his 1938 black Buick sedan. He drove very slowly and did not care if it bothered others behind him.

After I attended the 8:30 am children's mass at OLOL, I was free to go to the Costa's farm to play with Horace, Danny, Eddie, and Albert. The Costa boys worked on the farm, when not in school. They had cows to be milked, the barn to clean. They also had a horse which was used to pull the plows and other farm equipment. Sunday afternoon they were allowed to enjoy themselves with outdoor activities like baseball and touch football. The farm had many acres and went from Dighton Avenue to the brook on what is now Warner Blvd running from Rte. 44 to North Dighton.

There was one large open field of grass that was half way down the farm. This was our private playing field. Some Sundays, Joe Lawrence would join us, giving us a total of six players. On inclement weather days, we played indoors. I will write more about these days in another chapter.

My uncle, Manuel Costa, made trips to Faneuil Hall Marketplace to sell his vegetables to wholesalers. No super highways had been constructed; you had to go up Rte. 138 to Boston, a two-hour trip in a large truck. 138 went through Mattapan, an area that is now somewhat of a combat zone. At that time, Mattapan was very different in that it was an active Jewish community, with kosher businesses and wonderful bakeries. My mother loved a particular cookie, a sugared flaky, crusty cookie similar to "cavacas," which the Portuguese also made. We would make an occasional trip to Mattapan just to buy these cookies (gas was cheap).

Back to the farm…My grandparent's original cape style house had many acres both to the left and to the right, and as previously mentioned down to what is now Warner Blvd. The house was eventually purchased by the Costas, and over the years, parcels of land were sold on which many houses were built. My cousin, Horace Costa, kept a portion of the land and used it to grow flowers and plants. He also grew plants in two or three large hot houses. He followed in his father's footsteps selling his plants in Boston. He was helped by his brother Albert and occasionally his sister Evelyn.

My paternal aunt, Mary Almeida, owned a large amount of land on the other side of Dighton Avenue. Adeline, their daughter, built a house on part of their land. A little further down Dighton Avenue, Adeline's son, Jimmy, built another house. The remaining land was sold and split into many house lots, and eventually became a major housing development which extended from Dighton Avenue to Somerset Ave. Incidentally, my father owned a small strip of land adjacent to the Almeida property. He sold this strip of land and received enough money to buy a TV set in the 1950s.

In my younger years, prior to helping out at the store, I would go to my grandparent's farm on some Saturdays. My maternal grandfather, Joaquim Netto, was a little man with a mustache. He and my grandmother spoke little to no English. Since I was bilingual, I was able to converse with them. What I remember most was helping my grandfather roll his cigarettes (the legal kind). He had a little cigarette-making machine which was manually operated to roll cigarettes. Sometimes, he would just roll them by hand, but they did not look as good as the machine-rolled. If my aunt Esther were home, she would ask me to crank the Victrola so that she could play music on the RCA "His Master's Voice." I think you have seen these Victrolas in museums; they have a large horn from which the sound was heard. The records were made of wax and were a 78 rpm. They required needles that had to be frequently changed because they broke easily. There was no automatic arm for the needles. I had to lift the arm by hand and carefully place the needle on the record, so as not to damage the needle or the record.

The Pig Stabbing

I grew up in a family environment that was not uncommon among people of my age in the United States. My parents were immigrants from Portugal, who were hard working people and who brought with them some of the customs of their native land. The pig stabbing was one of our annual events. A pig was raised over a period of months and was doomed to die. This late fall ceremony was attended by many relatives, neighbors, and friends. It was a virtual celebration. I am not sure if the pig was shaved or not. I don't remember anyone shaving the pig, but a 90 plus-year-old distant relative, Lucy Fonseca, told me that the pig was shaved. The idea was to kill the pig and get every edible piece of it into a state of preservation. In the 30s and 40s, freezers were not common as a household appliance, nor were refrigerators of the size we have now. Whatever freezer compartments we had in refrigerators were used only for ice cubes or ice cream.

The scenario was as follows: several healthy men would hold onto the pig. One person would make the incision on the neck, from which the pig would bleed out. Since nothing was wasted, the blood was collected in a large metal tub. As the blood would clot quickly, it was necessary to stir the blood at a consistent pace to prevent clotting. I can still see my mother with her apron, and a kerchief covering her hair, as she did the stirring. The blood was then combined with bread, and a sausage called morcella was made. Fresh, clean intestines (casings) were used for the sausage. There was also a sausage called farinheira that was made with bread and pork products. I did not like farinheiras! I said nothing was wasted. My grandfather, Joaquim Netto, was the person who got to eat the brain. Pork fat was rendered into lard; the skin was fried and made into tasty snacks, pork rinds, still available in stores. The meat was cut into small pieces and made into linguica or chourico (a more spicy sausage). Some of the inner organs were used for food, but I don't remember eating kidneys! The sausages were hung in the cellar to dry. Following the pig stabbing, everyone stayed for a celebration. Beer and wine were consumed, and some of the fruits of the harvest were eaten. This custom may seem primitive to you, but remember these families were working long hours for virtually nothing. Neither money nor food was wasted. Many good meals were to come from this one pig.

And don't forget the tasty, chewy, pig's feet!

Memories of 986 Somerset Avenue

Gouveia family home after 1938 renovation

The property at 986 Somerset Avenue was purchased in 1927 from my Grandmother's Sister, Maria Pereira, and her husband, Joaquim. The property was divided when Lawton Street was built, sometime in the early 1930s. We ended up with most of our property (including our cesspool which was piped under the road) on the other side of Lawton Street. As a result, my family home ended up on a very small parcel of land, with a triangle of grass in front of it. Old Somerset Avenue, Lawton Street, and my family's driveway formed the three sides of the triangle. The point of the triangle facing the south, towards the town of Somerset, was owned by the City of Taunton. It eventually became known as Medeiros Square, named after Antone Medeiros of Baker Road who was a casualty in WWII. He was the son of Mary Medeiros and Tony Medeiros. One of their daughters moved to California in the 1940s. She bought land in California, enough so that the last I heard of her, she was quite well-to-do and had more than one spacious home. Other members of the family remained in Taunton, except for Sonny who moved to Cleveland, Ohio. He was famous for being a local championship lightweight class boxer. I have seen him once only since he moved. Antoinette, their second daughter, remained in the Taunton area and is friendly with my brother-in-law Dan Rapoza and my sister Chris. One other son, Frankie, lived in the family home on Baker Road. He did catering from the house.

Mrs. Medeiros made the best Portuguese sweet bread in the world. I wish I had the recipe. I asked her daughter, Antoinette, to see if she had it, but she did not.

My mother and grandmother took a trip to Villa Franca da Serra in 1938 in Portugal and remained there for a few weeks. During that time the Hurricane of 1938 hit New England with devastating force. More information of the hurricane is in another section of this memoir. My mother returned from Portugal in the late summer of 1938 with a very severe medical condition. She contracted typhoid fever during her vacation. In pre-antibiotic days this was very serious. My father was allowed to stay in the house, but my sisters and I were forced to move in with other family members. There was a big red sign on the door of 986 Somerset Avenue "QUARANTINED – NO VISITORS ALLOWED." She remained ill for several weeks or more; I can't remember how long, but for a 7-year-old it seemed like an eternity. How much of her later medical problems were related to typhoid fever? I don't know. She had aortic stenosis and congestive heart failure in her later years. In her younger years, she required the removal of her gall bladder. She also underwent an appendectomy by Dr. Nunes. In those days patients were given the surgically removed organs to be proudly displayed, for all to see. There was a gallbladder in a glass jar in alcohol, as well as an appendix sitting in a jar on a shelf in the kitchen.

Prior to 1938, our house was enlarged and the second floor made into four bedrooms and a bath. A multi-windowed covered porch was added on the right side of the house (Lawton Street side). With the addition, the roof line became a Dutch colonial home. Before the renovations, there was a spooky floor panel in the room on the right side of the kitchen on the first floor. It led to the cellar. In order to get to the cellar, you had to lift the large panel and go down a ladder to a very dark cellar. A central heating system was installed during the renovation. Prior to that, the house was heated by a kerosene stove in the kitchen area. Our new heating system was coal-fired. It required adding coal with a shovel and "poking," the partially spent coal twice a day. My father had to go down cellar every night to poke the coal before going to bed. We had radiators in every room after the renovation. We also had a door in the kitchen leading to the cellar stairs. A ladder was no longer necessary to access the cellar. Some of the basement remained a dirt floor, some of it was cement.

My Dad had his barrel of homemade wine a few steps from the basement stairs, for easy access. Some of the grapes for his wine came from our small vineyard behind the store, but the majority of his grapes were purchased from a Providence wholesale grocery. His wine was similar to Chianti, red and not sweet. I did not like it.

My father opened Gouveia's Market at around 7 am. He did not usually have breakfast. Lunch was his big meal of the day. It included a large, twenty ounce or so glass, of red wine and ginger ale or 7 Up. I don't know how much of each. He never showed signs of the wine affecting him. After lunch, he went back to the store, or to the rather large farm located to the side and rear of the store. At the farm, he worked without mechanical or power machinery. I can still see him

Birthday celebration in our kitchen – L-R: Daniel Rapoza, Sister Chris, Sister Virginia, and my Mother

pushing the harrow ahead of him by hand. We grew a lot of strawberries, potatoes, green beans, corn, and squash. He was known for his Chinese peas and had a regular customer from a Fall River Chinese restaurant who bought as many peas as my father was willing to sell.

In 1949, the store was extended backward, adding selling space, storage space, and a walk-in cooler. We even advertised on the local radio station for the grand opening. The station was WPEP, 1570 AM on the dial. In later years on my return to Taunton, I was a guest several times on call-in talk shows on WPEP. Sadly, WPEP is no longer broadcasting. It featured a folksy type broadcast with local news, some music, and employed well-respected announcers, who knew everything that was happening in Taunton.

My mother loved to cook and bake. A good day for her would be one in which she made several pies. Her pies were fabulous. The custard pie was amazing (Joan Mello still makes the pie today). Did I tell you the apple pie was to kill for? Other pies included peach, made only with fresh peaches. I still salivate when I think about my mother's chocolate cream pie, banana cream pie, or lemon meringue pie. It is no wonder that my arteries clogged up in later life!!!

She used Fluffo, a yellow colored shortening. Golden Fluffo was a canned shortening made by Procter and Gamble from the early 1950s through the mid-1960s. She swore by that product, Fluffo. Another favorite dessert of mine is "crème com alfaropias," an egg cream with floating islands. When this was made by my mother, it required twelve egg yolks for the custard part. The alfaropias were made with whipped egg whites. There is a modified recipe for this dessert in my collection in the Mary Marques' cookbook. I should add that the meringue (alfaropias) was cooked in hot milk and became the floating islands...

Olive oil was the standard at 986; the brand she used was Saloio. I recently found that it is available in the international aisle at Shaw's Supermarkets. Southern Europeans tend to use olive oil instead of butter when cooking, or as a flavoring after cooking. Jan was not familiar with the Mediterranean diet, having been brought up in a household of Polish descent. She was shocked one day in my family's dining area. We were there for Sunday dinner, my mother had made a big bowl of green beans from our garden, and they looked delicious. She showed us the bowl of beans and then poured the olive oil over the beans. Jan silently gagged at the idea but ate the beans anyway. Sunday was family dinner day with Chris, Dan, Arthur, Virginia and their children enjoying an overwhelming amount of food. When we moved back to Taunton, we were included in the dinner. For many years there was a large dining table in the second living room area. I remember that my folks bought it second-hand from a neighboring household. It came with a wide buffet and at least eight chairs. There was also a matching hutch in the dining room. The room was later changed into a second parlor.

These renovations required the removal of the French doors between the two rooms and establishing an archway between the rooms. Each parlor had two windows on the Lawton Street side that looked onto our enclosed porch with the front entrance. No one used the front entrance. Everyone entered the house through the driveway entrance. My mother's cooking area was a small pantry with a sink, a small counter, a four-burner gas stove, and oven. It also had a small area with shelves for small boxes and cans of food. Since we owned a grocery store, we didn't need much storage for food. A small room to the left of the pantry became the TV room when we finally got a TV. Originally, only a few channels were available from the rabbit ears on the set. During the summer when I worked the second shift at Taunton State Hospital, I would come home and watch the Late Show. I distinctly remember seeing the comedian, Dagmar, who was a tall woman with big breasts. Morey Amsterdam was also a very good comedian on the show. This was prior to the late show with Johnny Carson. The small TV room eventually became my mother's bedroom, when she could no longer climb stairs. A half bath was added to the room at that time.

I want to remind you that the house had four bedrooms, and only one full bath with a tub on the second floor, prior to the addition of the half bath downstairs. A shower surround was later installed in the upstairs bathroom. My bedroom was on the left facing Lawton Street; there was an armoire but no closet. There were closets in the two bedrooms to the right of the stairs. The fourth upstairs room was used for a sewing machine and storage. I don't think it was ever used as a bedroom. My father kept an unloaded shotgun in his bedroom closet, in case he had to use it if someone was breaking into the store, which was right across the street. I think he used it only once to scare away potential thieves. I have mentioned the kerosene stove used for heat and cooking. When gas was installed in the house, cooking was done in the pantry leaving space for a large refrigerator. I think I forgot to mention the ice delivery prior to installing our refrigerator…certain days a week ice was delivered in a large block which was put in the ice box. There was a card which was left in the window with various numbers on it from 5 cents to 25 cents. The delivery man would check the top of the card, and deliver the amount of ice requested. We also had a milkman who delivered milk a few times a week during the night. Milk came in glass bottles with caps that could pop off. Homogenization of milk was not common, so the top three inches was cream. Frequently in the winter, the milk would freeze outside, and the cream would be popping over and sticking out the bottle.

Talking about cream, we frequently made our own butter, by taking the cream off the top of the bottle. We did not have a butter churn, so we made butter by shaking a covered bottle until the butter was formed. Making your own butter was necessary during WWII when rationing was in effect. Each family was given ration coupons for certain types of food and gas purchases. Rationing coupons had to be used for certain items. Margarine was available as a replacement for butter. This was sold in a thick, clear plastic bag. It was pure white and came with a ball of food coloring in the bag. To make it look like butter (I don't think it tasted like butter), we had to squeeze the ball of food coloring and spread the yellow coloring into the margarine.

My father was the air-raid warden for our neighborhood. During World War Two, there was a restriction against light shining through windows at night - so all windows had to be covered with shades or drapes. There were horns on buildings which were blown as air-raid warnings. We never had a real air-raid, but there were several air-raid practices. When the alarm horns were blown, my father had to walk around the neighborhood and see if any light was coming through cracks in the window coverings.

Gas rationing began nationwide on Dec 1, 1942, as ordered by President Franklin Delano Roosevelt. Some facts about rationing during the war – gas rationing was paramount, people were given vouchers depending on where they lived, where they worked, and what they did for a living. I remember pumping gas at this time. Before pumping the gas, vouchers were handed to me, so I knew how much gas to put in the tank. Many people during the conflict did not own a car, so rationing was not a huge problem for them. Public transportation by bus was used primarily.

Our house was on Rte. 138 which was not a busy road. During the Christmas season, however, we had a line of cars from our house to Taunton Green on weekends. We lived at least a mile and a half from the Green. Taunton was called the "Christmas City" and has decorated the Green every year since when 1914. Three years during the war, 1942 to 1944, there was no lighting of the Green, it was blacked-out. The Green continues to be decorated for Christmas. Each year is a spectacular presentation.

Back to the kitchen at 986...there was a built-in ironing board hidden inside the wall. In order to use it you needed to open the door on the wall, and then fold down the ironing board. This setup was considered unique, as we were the only house in the area that had one. There was no excuse not to iron clothes at any time. My mother also had an electric oven on a rolling stand in the kitchen. It served as an extra oven during holiday seasons. The kitchen table was big enough to seat ten people. Many good times of eating, drinking, and talking occurred around the table.

Eventually, Gouveia's Market became more than my father could handle, even though my sister, Virginia, worked there many hours a week. The store was purchased by my sister, Chris, and husband, Dan Rapoza, in 1965. Chris continued working as the payroll clerk at Eureka Manufacturing in Norton. Eureka Manufacturing made silver chests with tarnish- proof linings. The business was owned by Mr. Gebelein of Longmeadow Road and subsequently was sold to Reed and Barton. Because of the success of stainless flatware, the demand for these chests slowed down. The task of polishing sterling became unnecessary. At this time (2011) silver is so expensive that few can afford it. When Jan and I were married, sterling was the vogue and a great wedding gift! All of the brides would receive sterling place settings. We received at least twelve place settings of Gorham's Melrose design. A place setting at the time cost about $36 and included a knife, two forks, a soup spoon and a teaspoon. I don't think you can get one piece of silver at this time for $36, with silver being at the highest price in history.

Back to 986 Somerset Ave. My mother passed away on Easter 1971 at the age of 72. My father had a major stroke one week later, from which he remained disabled. He spent the rest of his life in hospitals and nursing homes unable to speak, and with considerable trouble swallowing. He died on Pearl Harbor Day 12/7/1972, about 18 months later at age 84 (1888-1972). Virginia and Arthur inherited the house at 986. Dan and Chris inherited the store. I inherited one-half of the house across from 986 Somerset Ave. Land owned by my parents was to be divided between the three siblings.

My parents' Will was an "I love you truly" will. So when my father had a stroke, he was in no condition to write a new Will. My sisters and I got together with Talbot Tweedy, the family lawyer, and agreed on a disposition of the properties. There was essentially no money left in Dad's account. Most of his estate was used in nursing home care, so there was no problem in settling the estate. Dad put his "X" on the Will making it legal without any complications. My sisters and I wrote the Will. There was no hassle over the estate since all of the children were in agreement. Unfortunately, in many families, a great deal of in-fighting is known to occur as some siblings feel left out, or don't inherit what they feel they are entitled to. I was pleased that my family avoided any problems with the Will.

Vicks VapoRub

Vicks VapoRub is a formula that contains menthol, camphor, eucalyptus, and Vaseline. It continues to be available at local pharmacies. In the 1930s and 1940s, it was an extremely popular treatment for chest colds, sore throat, flu symptoms, etc... I can't tell you how many times it was used on me. It was almost magical in some peoples' eyes. Vicks could be applied directly on the chest and neck, and the area was then wrapped with warm flannel cloth to keep the ointment in place. Many times it was applied to the cloth itself, and then the cloth was tied around the neck. The menthol vapors were soothing and helped to clear congestion in the nose and chest. I remember also breathing in the VapoRub, which was put in a pot of boiling water, allowing the menthol to escape, thus helping clear the chest and nasal passages. I must remind you that the period in which I am talking about existed before antibiotics and other effective respiratory medications were available.

Some people that I knew actual took tablespoons of the VapoRub by mouth. I don't remember doing that, but maybe I did. The use of this product has continued through to the present day, but not with the popularity it had during my childhood. As better and more scientific treatments were developed, the use of VapoRub declined. I actually feel a little sentimental about Vicks VapoRub. In my mind, I can still smell the vapors coming from the Vicks.

Growing Up Catholic in an Old "Yankee" Town

Our Lady of Lourdes Church (OLOL) was established in 1905 on First Street in Taunton. My parents John and Patricia Gouveia were married there in 1919 and celebrated their 50th wedding anniversary there as well. They were life-long parishioners of OLOL. My sisters Chris and Virginia were also married there. The church served the Portuguese-speaking Catholic population of the Weir Village and the South end of Taunton for more than 80 years.

The Diocese of Fall River decided to consolidate OLOL with Sacred Heart Church, also on First Street. OLOL was eventually closed. The consolidated church was named the Annunciation of the Lord. OLOL was torn down in the late 1990s or early 2000. It served well as the religious center for the Portuguese immigrants from mainland Portugal, the Azorean Islands, Madeira, and the Cape Verde Islands. My Catholic upbringing from baptism to confirmation was at OLOL. I was a weekly member of the congregation until I went off to Tufts College in 1949.

At Tufts, I joined the Newman Club. Monsignor E. Sousa de Mello was the pastor at OLOL for more than four decades. He was a stern disciplinarian, at a time when the church was very rigid in its interpretation of church law. He was not easy to get along with. One day, I was sitting in the front pew with other catechism students. Unfortunately, I dropped the prayer book. Monsignor de Mello was not happy with me. He came up to the pew and slapped me on the face. So much for "love your neighbor." We used the Baltimore Catechism in our religion classes. Many of you, who are of that period, may remember the questions in the booklet.

Question – Who is God?

The Answer – "God is the creator of heaven and earth and all things visible and invisible." What an impression it made in my mind! It is more than 75 years since a catechism class, and I can still remember many of the questions and answers.

Another question to think about: What are the chief sources of sin?

The answer – The chief sources of sin are 7 – Pride, Covetousness, Lust, Anger, Gluttony, Envy, and Sloth.

It is difficult for me to explain how anyone would remain a Catholic under the conditions in the church. At the time, few people questioned the doctrines. They just acted like sheep and got in line with the faith, by accepting the pronouncements from the pulpit. Staying out of hell was made very difficult since almost any action could be interpreted as a major sin. There was little ability for divergence in thought or action.

Over the years, several assistant priests helped run an active parish. In my teen years, Father Edward Oliveira was assigned to OLOL in 1947 as the assistant. He made the religion come alive, by involving the young people in parish activities. We had frequent meetings of the Catholic Action Club for Teenagers. Excursions and trips were planned and were very successful. We even went to Martha's Vineyard for a day trip. That doesn't sound like much now, but in the 1940s travel was not as easy as it is now. The routes to the Cape were two lane highways (Rte. 44 and 28), going through several towns along the way. There were no superhighways to the Cape. Route 495 is relatively new. It took almost 2 hours to get to the Bourne Bridge from Taunton. We took the ferry to the island, where we rented bikes and rode around the island. It was a long, pleasant day, and a tiring excursion.

Father Oliveira remained at OLOL for many years. He celebrated the 25th anniversary of his ordination at OLOL. A short time later, he announced that he had asked the Bishop to relieve him of his priestly duties so that he could marry. Permission was granted, and he was married in a Catholic service.

We had several priests at OLOL after him including Fr. John Gomes, Fr. George Almeida, Fr. Resendes, Father Arnold Medeiros, Fr. Lagoa and many others. My favorite priest remains Father Oliveira.

Here are some facts about Catholicism that you may not be aware of. It was a common belief that unless you were a Catholic, you would not be going to heaven. You know the alternative – remain a Catholic or else – Hell, Fire, Brimstone!

Other beliefs: As a Catholic, you were not expected to go into a Protestant church. In fact, Janice was not allowed to be a bridesmaid for her closest friend, Judy Pilblad, because Judy was a non-Catholic, and the service was in a Protestant church.

One of our neighbors married a non-Catholic. The major proviso to be followed as a condition for marriage - All children must be raised Catholic. She was married by our pastor, but the ceremony was in the rectory, not the sanctuary. A point of interest in this couple's life was that the groom eventually converted to Catholicism. Even more interesting, he became one of the first Catholic deacons in the Diocese of Fall River. Deacon John Schondek served in that position for many years.

In my Taunton High School classes, I was exposed to people of different religious denominations. By the mid-1940s, Catholics numerically were probably the largest religious group in Taunton. My friend. Jim Frates belonged to the Seventh Day Adventist Church. Jim Borra was a Roman Catholic. Many of the students in the advanced studies group attended services at St. Thomas Episcopal Church.

I never felt that there was a prejudice against me for my beliefs, but I understand that prejudice was a common problem with many members of the community, who were from foreign countries. As one of the "brains" in high school, I felt on an equal level with all of the members of the class of 1949. I even took Marjorie Hall to the Senior Prom. Marjorie was a descendant of the East Taunton Halls, (early arrivals in Taunton), and not one of the followers of the Vatican. (And I was not struck down by a bolt of lightning for taking her!)

The only time that I felt that there was prejudice against people of non-Yankee background occurred as follows: On returning to Taunton in 1964, I needed a mortgage for my home/office construction on Winthrop Street. I went into the Bristol County Trust on Taunton Green, where I discussed my situation with an older officer of the bank. He apparently felt that my prospects were not favorable. His attitude was almost abrasive. It was quite obvious to me that he had very little intent on granting me a loan. He gave me an application to fill out at home. As I was leaving the bank, I made certain that he saw me throw the application in the wastebasket at the door. Needless to say, I never did business with Bristol County Trust.

The next day I went next door to the Taunton Cooperative Bank, where Charles Galligan (a Catholic) was president. His family owned J.P. Galligan and Son Wholesale Grocery Company on Tremont Street. My Father was a regular customer of J.P. Galligan. James Galligan, Charles' brother, called on our store weekly to take orders and set up delivery times. What a difference in attitude! Charles Galligan simply asked one question – "How much money do you need?" The loan was approved in a very short time. By the way, my payment was $224.70 monthly.

My mind wanders from the original topic of this section. Let's return to my pre-teen and teen years, and talk about Portuguese Feasts. The Holy Ghost Feast is an Azorean tradition and generally held on Pentecost weekend. I will not go into detail of the religious aspects of this feast. For more information on "Festas," I recommend reading a master thesis presented by Shirley Ann Rebello entitled "The Portuguese Life in Taunton, Massachusetts 1860 to 1930." Copies of this thesis are available at the Old Colony Historical Society Library, and possibly at the Taunton Public Library.

At the Feasts, on Saturday and Sunday, bands played, people danced, and food and wine were abundant. People could cook their own steak or linguica over burning logs. The steak was put on a wooden stick and barbecued – it is called "carne de espeto." Linguica was delicious when eaten with freshly baked Portuguese rolls. Booths were available with a variety of home cooked foods including morcellas (blood sausage), malasadas, fava bean casserole, chicken casseroles, etc.

One of my "Yankee" friends liked a fava bean casserole made by my Aunt, Mary Almeida, which we served at a party at our home. I was generous to give him a large platter of fava beans left over after one of our house parties. He ate quite a lot of the favas over the next few days, unaware of the effects of the beans on the lower bowel. One might say he was "jet-propelled."

Auctions of homemade Portuguese sweet bread and other donated foods were held Saturdays and Sundays at the "Festas." As a teenager, I could not understand why anyone would pay ten or more dollars for a sweetbread when bread was available for much less than a dollar. This sweet bread was made specifically for the auction, and with love. I now understand the reason behind these inflated prices. Men and women in the parish would frequently make promises to the Virgin Mary and other Saints in the hope of a positive result for their requests. To be specific, if a serious illness or major problem occurred in the family, the women would pray for a cure or solution to the problem. In response to the positive result, a gift to the church would be promised. Women would bake pastries, sweet bread, regular breads, Portuguese rolls, malasadas, and other foods as a thank you. These foods were either auctioned off or sold at food stalls. Paying inflated prices during the auctions gave the donors a great satisfaction in supporting their church.

The Holy Ghost feast included a Sunday parade or procession on the local streets. Religious organizations, such as St. Vincent de Paul Society, the Legion of Mary Sodality, and the Holy Ghost Society marched in the parade. The Taunton City Band and other musical groups were part of the celebration. After the procession, everyone was invited to a free meal of soup in the church basement. The soup consisted of meat, potatoes, bread and a sprig of peppermint. Following the lunch, the previously mentioned auctions were held. Band concerts and a battle of the bands were held on the grounds. Dancing was enjoyed, especially, the "Chamarita" a traditional Azorean dance which was very popular.

I attended many of these Festas during my pre-college years. They were a great place to meet friends, have conversations, and mostly eat! Let's not forget that socially, feasts were a great place to meet people of the opposite sex. I think many romances were the result of going to the feasts.

Today is May 19th, 2013. The Holy Ghost Society of Falmouth is having a feast today – Pentecost Sunday. Major feasts are still held in many cities and towns where there are people of Portuguese descent. Very large, successful celebrations occur in cities like New Bedford, Fall River and Taunton in Southeastern MA. Other areas – Rhode Island and New Jersey continue these celebrations on an annual basis.

Dr. Stephen Cabral is quoted in a newspaper article saying – "The Feasts are an opportunity for Portuguese Americans to remember the generations that preceded them, to express their religion, devotion, and to reaffirm their social identity."

I hope you have enjoyed these reminiscences of my Catholic upbringing.

Going to the Movies

Movies were a major form of entertainment in the years in which I grew up. Attendance was at least once a week, and many weeks, a second movie was viewed. Again, I remind you that entertainment at home in the 1930s and 1940s was mostly listening to the radio. Some families had record players as well, but owning a record player was too expensive for the lower income families.

A full day at the movies could cost only twenty-five cents. In my teen years, I went to the movies frequently. The cost for a days' entertainment was five cents for the bus to town, ten cents for the movie ticket, and five cents for candy or popcorn. If I splurged and spent ten cents on goodies, it meant I had to walk home.

A day at the movies was different from current day standards. Each major film was preceded by a series of short films, some previews, and then the ever-present news film which ran ten to fifteen minutes. Its slogan was the "Eyes and Ears of the World." The first movie of the day (double feature) and was called a B-movie. It was not usually of great quality and was about an hour in length. The feature film was then shown.

Unlike present day movie schedules, the theater was not cleared of viewers at the end of the main movie. It was possible to sit through a second showing of the films. If I liked the films, I frequently stayed to see them again. Most feature films lasted for less than two hours.

My favorite movie house was the Park Theater on Broadway, which was originally used for live vaudeville performances. The Park had a big balcony and a magnificent crystal chandelier over the center of the first floor. The second first run theater, The Strand, was built right next to the Park Theater. It was a one-story structure which was quite long and lacked the decorative features of its neighbor. Because of its length and size, for me, it was not a great movie experience. The screen seemed too far away. It lacked intimacy.

There were at least three "second run" theaters in Taunton. They showed the films after their first run at the Park or Strand Theaters. There was the State Theatre on Court Street, the Grand Theater on Bay Street in Whittenton, and a small theater in the stone building on Cedar Street, in the previous home of the Old Colony Historical Society.

The Grand offered a special gift on Wednesday evenings. Each ticket holder was given a dish, a different dish each week. Eventually, our family would have several place settings at no cost. We used those plates for many years at our house.

At age eight or nine, I sat on a wooden folding chair in the aisle of the State Theater to view a sold-out presentation of "Gone with the Wind," after its run was over at the Park. "Gone with the Wind" is the longest of all movies to win the Best Picture award at the Academy Awards. It opened in 1939. It was the first color film to win the coveted best picture award. Hattie McDaniel was the first African-American to win an Academy Award. The movie is ranked as the eighth greatest film of all time. "Gone with the Wind" is still shown frequently on television. Its quality has held up well over the years.

My all-time favorite movie is the 1952 "The Greatest Show on Earth." It is a film about circus life. Produced by Cecil B. DeMille, and featured Charlton Heston, Betty Hutton, James Stewart, and many other famous performers. It also had Emmett Kelly in the cast. Emmett remains the greatest circus clown of all time. The film was a massive production with extras numbering in the hundreds, or perhaps thousands. I saw this film several times, but never got bitten by the bug to run off and join the circus!

Gouveia's Cash Market

My parents bought the store from relatives named Pereira (AKA Perry) in 1927. The kitchen area of the house at 986 Somerset Avenue was the original space for the grocery store. The rest of the house was living quarters. On reviewing Taunton City directories, I found a "variety store" listed at 986 Somerset Avenue attributed to John F. Gouveia in 1927 and 1928. Sometime after that year, Lawton Avenue was built. Lawton Avenue divided my parent's land into a small parcel on the Somerset Avenue side, and a multi-acre parcel on Lawton Avenue. No further listings were found until 1933 when a store run by John F. Gouveia was recorded on Lawton Avenue.

Gouveia's Cash Market 1934

As far as I know, my parents ran a store all the years since 1927. In a 1934 photo of the store and gas station, there is a large shingled garage on the property. My father is standing near four gas pumps. The Tydol gas was .16$ a gallon. In addition, we sold Richfield and Sinclair gas. Kerosene was also pumped. Many customers heated their houses and cooked with kerosene. Not until the 1938 renovation did we have central heat in our home. The photo mentioned above also shows Gouveia's delivery truck, a 1929 Chevrolet. It had a roof and open sides with roll-down curtains probably made of oil cloth. I learned to drive on the truck. I also stripped the gears more than once. The tricky part of learning to drive was shifting gears – first, second, third, reverse. Releasing the clutch at the right time was what I was not good at. Both my father and an employee, Johnny Fitta, taught me to drive. I don't think the idea of driving schools had been conceived yet.

The Chevy truck was used for deliveries of food. We also sold fertilizer, mostly to Dighton farmers. I have memories of delivering fertilizer in the truck and carrying the bags into barns. The bags were heavy and probably weighed more than fifty pounds. No attempt was made to have payment on delivery. Payments for the fertilizer were expected at harvest. These farmers were very honest. Some years, the crop was not good. As a result, payment could be deferred until the following year.

My Father at the counter

My father carried a lot of credit on his books. The farmers eventually paid their bills, so the fertilizer credit books were not a problem. I am talking about the 30s and early 40s. In the 30s, the Great American Depression was in full force. Roosevelt's socialist programs were being instituted. The WPA (Works Project Administration) hired eight million men, who were generally unskilled and learned on the job. A smaller number of artists, actors, musicians, and writers were employed as well by the WPA. You can still see the many murals painted during the depression in public buildings, especially in post offices. These murals gave exposure to art to the average citizen. Almost every town in America had a new park, a new bridge, or a school constructed by the WPA. One of the WPA projects was the Merritt Parkway with its architecturally unique bridges.

So many people were unemployed during the depression. Hunger was commonplace. My father recalled that many times he was asked for free food. He frequently made sandwiches for customers at no charge.

My father farmed acres of his property. In season, he sold fruits and vegetables from his farm. At this time, most people had small vegetable gardens of their own. Many people also raised chickens for eggs and meat. Some had rabbits. Others raised pigs. People had to be resourceful. Many women, including my mother, canned fruits, and vegetables in Ball Jars to be used for winter meals.

Gouveia's Cash Market circa 1950

There were many small grocery stores like Gouveia's Cash Market. The Weir Cash Market was very busy. Most every neighborhood had a small store. Even chain stores like First National and the Great Atlantic and Pacific Company (A&P) were just small stores, about the twice the size of ours. The biggest grocer in Taunton was Cobb, Bates, and Yerxa, Known as "Cobb Bates." They had a downtown address, and it was considered the place to buy food for the more prosperous members of the community. It was in business for more than six decades, first on the south side of Main Street, and later at the corner of Taunton Green and School Streets. Like the original Gouveia's Cash Market, Cobb Bates had no self-service, no pushing grocery carts up and down long aisles. Clerks were given lists of needed items, and they carried baskets around to fill items. Like Cobb Bates, prior to everyone having a phone, Gouveia's Market made house calls to take customer's orders.

As the national stores expanded, competition increased for the "mom and pop" stores, making it more difficult for the small stores to stay in business. One method of keeping customers by the smaller stores was offering S&H Green Stamps. The Sperry and Hutchinson Company had been in business since the late 19th Century. Their green stamps programs predated the current loyalty marketing programs, now seen in most chain grocery stores. The system worked like this: a green stamp was given out for each purchase of a dollar. The stamps were then pasted into a book which when filled was worth a certain amount of money to be used to choose from a catalog of gifts. The more books the customer filled, the larger the choice (small appliances, etc…). S&H green stamps were popular from the late 1930s through the 1980s. The books could also be redeemed for cash. I kept a partially filled book of S&H green stamps in my bedroom dresser for many years, but never redeemed it.

Much of our business was done on a charge basis. We kept a book for each family. On payday, the customer would pay what he could. Unfortunately many were never able to pay off their total charges. When my father died, we found dozens of charge books with significant amounts of money owed to the store, which were never collected. I think you might say that this was John F. Gouveia's gift to his customers and the community.

Interior of market post renovation

With the new addition in 1949, the store was doubled in size. A walk-in cooler was installed in the back of the store, which allowed for offering a larger variety of meats. Talking about meats, the chopping block was a very wide tree trunk, around thirty inches in diameter. It was on that chopping block that I learned how to cut meat. Little did I know at the time, how much more cutting (in a different environment) would be a significant part of my life.

We also had a penny candy rack at the check-out counter. I was a frequent "free" customer of the penny candy rack. Needless to say, I had my fill of candy as a child. I rarely eat candy now!

In 1965, my parents sold the store, the gas station, and the garage to my sister, Chris, and my brother-in-law, Danny. With the help of my sister, Virginia, they ran the store until 1973, when they sold it to Cumberland Farms. The original properties were demolished. A new gas station and store were built. I have to admit that I could not go into that Cumberland Farms for many years.

The South End Portuguese Club

The entity called Gouveia's Cash Market included the store, a gas station with several pumps, and a large wooden garage built along Baker Road. The wooden garage was destroyed by a fire in 1938. A larger cement-block building replaced it. The garage was used mainly for small repairs, but also served as a storage area. Oil was changed in a pit on the Baker Road side. For an oil change, the driver would carefully drive his car over the pit's opening. My Father would then climb down a ladder and drain the old oil into a container. The hood was then lifted, and new clean oil was put in. As a teenager, I occasionally changed oil, but not often.

In 1942, the back half of the garage was renovated and became the South End Portuguese Club. Mr. Lawrence, also affectionately known as "Pork Chops," was a part-time chef. Parties and dances were held there. A folkloric group was also formed of which my sisters and my Aunt Esther were members. The Club was open evenings, for food and drink. The only significant problem was that the club did not have a liquor license. An occasional raid by the police required the closure of activities for a short period of time. Despite this problem, the club survived.

South End Portuguese Club – now called Taunton Sports Club

Eventually, my father and a man called Albuquerque gave a mortgage to the club to build a larger facility on a few acres of property, across the street, at the corner of Baker Road and Somerset Avenue. For many years, banquets and wedding receptions were held there. Bridal showers were also a thriving business. When Jan and I were to be married, my family held a large bridal shower at the club. The dance floor was well maintained, it was very smooth to dance on.

Saturday night dances were frequently held. Dancing was a major event at that time. The era of Saturday night dancing has ended. Ballroom dancing is also now, mostly, a thing of the past. Live bands would play both American and Portuguese music. The club was also used for an occasional "spectacular" (the word in Portuguese used to advertise a concert by an important Portuguese performer or a popular music group.) My Godfather, Joe Fresta was a booking agent, and a host for many of these "spectaculars."

The new club was of cement block construction. It had a restaurant in the basement and a liquor license! Finally! The kitchen was open certain nights a week. Comfortable seating was available in booths. A good, reasonably priced menu was available. The typical Portuguese foods were offered on the menu. Portuguese style fried steak topped with a fried egg, and cod fish casserole (bacalhau) were favorites. Other specialties included linguica sandwiches, pork chops, fava bean casseroles, and the ever-present kale soup.

For upstairs functions like weddings, the food was supplied by caterers. For many of the smaller functions, it was common for food to be prepared in several homes and brought to the club. As you can see by the facts above, the South End Club was the social center for the residents of the South End.

After a successful run for many years, the club ran into financial problems. Unable to pay the mortgage, the club closed. It became the property of my father and his business partner who held the mortgage. The location is now owned by the Taunton Eagles Soccer Club. Semi-pro soccer is now played there in their large soccer field.

New Year's Eve on Dighton Avenue

I have several black and white photos showing how many people crowded into the antique cape house (the Netto-Costa House) at the intersection of Baker Road and Dighton Avenue. It is amazing that I could capture so many people with a simple Sylvania blue cube flash bulb. I am sorry that I did not take a photo of the kitchen table which was covered with so much food. There was linguica for sandwiches, linguica bread, cod fish cakes, Portuguese homemade egg bread, fried dough (filhoses), an assortment of pies - apple, custard, etc. There were multiple kinds of cheese, including a soft white homemade cheese, made of milk and rennin. I have a recipe for this cheese from my aunt, Mary Marques. One of my photos photo shows more than thirty revelers smiling and happy to celebrate the holiday. In it are members of the immediate family, the extended family, and friends. Wine and beer were consumed with gusto.

New Year's Eve party with family and friends, circa 1948a

We would eat a lot; sing songs in English and Portuguese. We talked a lot. This is the period in the 40s and 50s that I am writing about. There was radio available. Much later we had limited TV reception (with rabbit ears). People actually talked to each other, not just during commercials, as we do now. The "couch potato" had not been thought of yet.

Think about how different life is now. Electronics are everywhere. There were no electronic games, no cell phones, or Hi-Def. TV. Mobile phones were invented in 1971. Phones are now capable of sending messages, photos, and text to anywhere in the world instantaneously. Who would have believed that Skype can send live video via a modem and computer with no fees attached?! I think that if you predicted all these inventions in the 40s and 50s, that you would be considered to be kooky, crazy, a dreamer, or just plain "nuts."

The Netto-Costa home on Dighton Avenue was a very old antique cape with an enclosed entryway that opened into the family eating area. To the right was a small bedroom. Two equal-sized living rooms were in the front. To the far left was a small four by eight-foot cooking area with a stove, sink, and cupboards. The bathroom was to the right of the cooking area.

A short note on the bathroom. I vividly remember the celebration that was held when Grandma installed an indoor toilet. Before this, we had a "two holer" outhouse which was not wonderful in the winter. I know this sounds like the 19th century, prior to Dr. Thomas Crapper's invention of the flush toilet, ("Crapper's Valveless Water Waste Preventer"), but, remember that I am writing about the late 40s and 50s.

My aunt and uncle Costa were farmers, which was a difficult occupation, as it still can be if the weather does not cooperate. I am talking about immigrants who came to America in the early 20th Century with little or no money but were willing to work long and hard. I know that when my mother came to this country, she shared a bed with one or two other women. She lived with Mrs. Fonseca on Dighton Avenue. I don't think my grandfather, with whom she emigrated from Portugal, stayed there also. He had a cousin a couple of doors down Dighton Avenue also named Netto. This Netto family had two children, a son Arthur, and a daughter Lucy Netto Fonseca. Their mother was afflicted with Joseph's Disease as was their grandmother. This genetic problem was unfortunately passed on to Arthur, but fortunately not to Lucy, who is still living with her grandson. She is in her nineties. Lucy and another grandson were recently featured in an article in the Cape Cod Times Food section. He is a chef at the Four Seasons Hotel in Boston.

The Dighton Avenue house had a central room with a chimney in which was a baking oven, but I don't think they ever used it as an oven. The chimney was five or six feet in diameter. This room was a favorite place to hide when my cousins played hide and seek. Hide and seek was a lot of fun, there were many hiding places in the house, but we were always found.

On New Year's Eve, before midnight, Uncle Joe Marques would round some of us to go out and serenade friends. A guitar or a ukulele was our accompaniment. We mostly sang familiar songs in English and Portuguese. We were welcomed into the houses with smiles, even though some of the hosts were already in bed. Food and drinks were offered at every location. I don't know if the Times Square celebration had started. We had our own celebration.

It's amazing that we were able to do all these things without electronics. We made our own fun! I think the current generation of children is missing out on interpersonal relationships because of electronics. To me, there is nothing personal about email or texting. I am not even thinking what life would be like without video games.

I hope that you get the idea from these comments that life was simpler in my adolescence, and that the family was the source of much satisfaction, love, and unity.

10,000 Units of Penicillin and Portuguese Customs of Mourning

My Grandfather Joaquim Netto, photo by Santos, 3 Summer Street, Taunton MA, the early 1920s

In 1928, at St. Mary's Hospital in London, the Scottish scientist, Alexander Flemming discovered the germ-killing antibiotic, Penicillin. The discovery occurred apparently by accident, as do many important scientific discoveries. When first made available to the public, it was difficult to get penicillin, and it cost a fair amount of money. The reason I bring up this topic is that of an injury suffered by my maternal grandfather (I never met my paternal grandparents, since they never came to the U.S.A.). Incidentally, my father never returned to Portugal, so he never saw his parents after he left Portugal. My grandfather was thin and small in stature, but he was very strong. One day he was helping my godfather, Manuel Lawrence, tear down a structure on his land on Lawton Avenue. Unfortunately, a wall of the structure collapsed and hit my grandfather causing significant injuries. I was quite young, so I don't know all of the details, but an infection occurred resulting in the death of my grandfather, Joaquim Netto (aka Neto). The whole neighborhood was abuzz because of the use of the new miracle drug, Penicillin, in this case. A massive dose for the times was given – 10,000 units! Everyone was talking about the dosage. Currently, penicillin is still in use, but much more effective drugs are available. When penicillin is given now, a million units are a normal dose, and usually more than once a day.

My grandfather was the first to die in my immediate family, and the first dead person I had ever seen. As was the customs of the time, he was waked at his home, in the front parlor at Dighton Avenue. A 24 hour a day vigil was observed for two days. Some sort of symbol was placed on the front door, using black crepe, indicating that a wake was being held at the home. You may not have heard the term "hanging of the crepe." Sometimes elaborate crepe hangings and other symbols of black material were used to indicate that a wake was in progress. People would come to pay their respects at any time during the day or night. Some close relatives stayed awake 24 hours at a time. The large Portuguese community in the area would spend hours at the wake in mourning. Food was brought in by visitors and placed on the large dining table in the kitchen, resulting in a continuous 24hr buffet with all of the favorite foods of the culture. There were soups, homemade breads, chicken, pork, codfish balls, linguica and chourico, fried dough (filhos or malasadas), rice pudding, cakes, pies, an endless variety of other food choices. No one left the house with an empty stomach.

Some of the mourners were very theatric in their methods of mourning. It was not uncommon to hear loud wailing in the room. My grandmother's niece, Olive, was a perfect example of this behavior. She was known to start wailing prior to entering a wake and continued to wail for a short time while kneeling at the coffin. It was said that no period of mourning was complete until Olive arrived from Danbury. She was our "official family mourner" who attended almost every family wake and funeral until her passing. We anticipated her arrival, and her show of emotion, more than she realized.

Gradually home wakes were replaced by wakes held at funeral homes for one to two days. Usually, the visiting hours were 2 pm to 4 pm and 7 pm to 9 pm. The day after the wakes, a Roman Catholic burial mass was attended by immediate family, extended family, neighbors, and friends. The funeral corteges were quite long. Burials were at St. Joseph's cemetery in various family plots. Again major changes have occurred in the burial ceremony. When I was young I saw the following – the casket was placed on an apparatus which allowed the lowering of the casket. At funerals now, the casket stays at ground level until the mourners leave. In older days, family members put a trowel of sand on the casket. As we stood there, the casket was lowered into its final resting place. This was a very dramatic happening and resulted in a lot of wailing, and some fainting.

Along the lines of Portuguese customs is the wearing of black by the spouse of the departed. In Portugal, a widow wore black for the rest of her life. Wearing lighter colored clothing was considered inappropriate, and some would question the morality of the widow. Even the underwear had to be black! Over the years we gave Grandma Netto white or pink underwear. It was never worn. On her death, we found a drawer full of light colored underwear. Grandma Netto died a few years after my return to Taunton in 1964. She was bedridden for quite some time and "old age" was probably her cause of death. I pronounced her and made out her death certificate. There was a problem in creating it. No one knew how old she was, and certainly not her date of birth. We made up some dates, and the certificate was signed. Grandma was a very small lady. I was one of her pallbearers, along with several of my cousins, and we were surprised when we carried the casket down the stairs at Silva's Funeral Home. We felt the body shift in the casket; I don't think that is a good start for a restful peace.

All members of our family were buried from Silva's Funeral Home in Taunton. I was involved in choosing caskets for some of them. Most of the females in the family were buried in a casket that had light purple violets as its inner décor, although different designs were available. I must mention floral arrangements, although most of the family was not prosperous, no expense was spared for funeral flowers. "Please omit flowers" was not in vogue at the time. Mourners would spend time looking at the flowers and remarking at their beauty. The most popular arrangement that I remember was at my mother's wake. It was called "gateway to heaven" with flowers on the sides and the bottom. In the middle of the arrangement was a gate entering heaven - a path that our family was certain that our mother went through.

As you may have deduced by now, photography was a big part of my life, since grammar school. The following lines may make you squirm a little. For many of the deaths in the family, I was asked to photograph my relatives lying in state. This required staying after visiting hours to perform a photo shoot. It also meant I had to stand on a stool to get better angles. There were some requests for pictures of the floral arrangements. At that time, slides were the preferred method of making images. I recently destroyed 10,000 slides that were of no further interest to me. That left more than 25,000 slides which I still have hanging in acid-free containers, holding twenty slides each. In addition, there are many more in their original Kodak or Fuji Film boxes. The photos taken at wakes remain in these boxes. Never has anyone ever asked to see them! You frequently hear these words at wakes "doesn't he (or she) look good?" I have proof that this is not true. The slides show a different story. I think the flash penetrates cosmetics, resulting in a somewhat unflattering photo. Talking about doesn't "he look good," I have had conversations with Bill Silva of Silva Funeral Home about an idea I had. I asked if it was possible to have my voice recorded and then activated when the mourner knelt to pray. They would hear me say "thank you for coming, and don't I look good!" Bill is not a person of comedic nature. He was appalled at that request. I thought it was a great idea.

I am reminded of the time that I went to Silva's and was on call at the hospital. I arrived with thirty to forty-five minutes left of the visiting hours. Unfortunately, as I was kneeling at the casket, my beeper went off. Most of the people at the wake heard the beeper and took it for a signal that it was time to leave. There was a virtual evacuation. The family was in disbelief as most everyone had left. They had no idea what caused the sudden exit of so many people.

A few times in my life, I requested that some of the floral arrangement be used to decorate the altar at church or be taken to nursing homes. I was met with a glare and a quick refusal. I was told that these flowers were "dirty" and should not be used elsewhere. What a waste of natural beauty! I will be a client of Silva's Funeral Home in the future. Unfortunately, the "red room" has been redecorated, and I will not be lying in state in the room with the flocked red wallpaper of which my remaining family is quite familiar. Bill Silva has shown me a beautiful casket with carvings of the Last Supper. The price of the casket was thousands of dollars twenty years ago. I cannot see putting a casket, costing that amount of money, into a cement liner for eternity. I trust that my heirs feel the same.

A further comment on funeral customs…I have recently seen an article describing a funeral home with a drive through window. Imagine that! You don't need to get out of your car to express condolences. To me, it sounds like a Saturday Night Live skit with relatives inside the funeral home waving and smiling to occupants in the car and, saying "thank you for coming." I also notice in the obituary columns in the Cape Cod Times that at the end of the death notices are a short paragraph "for online condolences and directions, please visit wakes.com and funerals.com." The world has changed, customs have changed. I think the changes are something to think about. There is a need for the family to accept that a relative has passed on. There is considerable comfort in a short waking period, although being in a receiving line at a wake can be exhausting. There is a good feeling that the grieving family receives from the presence of family and friends expressing their sorrow on the loss of a close relative.

For an in-depth study of this topic I recommend the book "The American Way of Death Revisited" by Jessica Mitford.

Joseph E. Nunes, M.D.

Joseph E. Nunes, M.D. with his favorite plant – birds of paradise

Joseph E. Nunes, M.D. opened his medical office in July 1928. He is thought to be the first Taunton-born Portuguese speaking physician in the city. Until I started my medical practice in Taunton, he was the only doctor who spoke fluent Portuguese. (For a short while, there was a doctor in Taunton, Dr. Camoeses, who was trained in Portugal and practiced there for some years. Because he opposed the Portuguese dictator, Salazar, his life was in danger. He was fortunate to escape the country, and moved to the United States.)

Dr. Nunes was a graduate of the Tufts Medical School; and had postgraduate training at Mercy Hospital in Springfield, at Lying in Hospital in New York City, and Cook County Graduate School in Chicago. He had to leave his office to serve in the US Navy. On December 7th, 1941, he was a Senior Lieutenant stationed at Pearl Harbor. Fortunately, he survived the Japanese bombardment during the "Day of Infamy." On discharge from the Navy, he held the rank of Lieutenant Commander.

He was a prominent member of many medical organizations including the American Medical Association and the Massachusetts Medical Society. He was a founding fellow of the American College of Obstetrics and Gynecology, and a member of the International College of Surgeons. This amount of training came in handy on May 15, 1931, when he delivered me. Besides having a very busy practice, he also served as Associate Medical Examiner for North Bristol County.

The Portuguese-American community benefitted from his charity and generosity, which he preferred to keep anonymous. I was told that he was the major donor to the fund to build the current St. Anthony's Church on School Street. St. Anthony's was founded in 1903 to serve the Portuguese immigrants who had settled in the Taunton area in the early 20th century. The original building was a basement church built in 1906. In the mid-20th century, an above-ground church was built next to the basement church. The first church was converted into a primary school. Parishioners totaled 8000, belonging to 1500 families. I doubt that many of these communicants were aware of Dr. Nunes' generosity.

Other Catholic churches were built in the early 20th century to serve Portuguese speaking immigrants – Holy Family Church in East Taunton, and Our Lady of Lourdes Church in the Weir Village.

My Mother had a chronic cardiac condition which required house calls by Dr. Nunes. I noticed that these house visits seemed to be tied around the lunch hour. I can still see him lifting the lids on the pots on the stove, to make sure he wanted to sit down for a meal, which he did on many occasions.

I have a problem discussing his personality, which, at times, he was easy to get along with, and at other times he could be a very difficult person. Although he was always cordial and supportive of me as a consulting surgeon, he made me wonder what was going on in his mind. One Sunday evening, I received a call from him with a brief message – "tomorrow, 730 am, be there." He hung up the phone before I could answer. Since two can play this game, I decided to call back with my message – "I won't be there," and I hung up. A few seconds later my phone rang again; he was on the line saying "What do you mean you won't be there?" I answered him saying I just wanted to get his reaction to my call. At other times he would pick up the phone and say "it's your nickel, talk." Incidentally, pay phone calls were five cents for three minutes at that time.

Andrew Boisvert, the Archivist of the Old Colony Historical Society, found an interesting article in the Taunton Daily Gazette entitled "Old Indian Skull comes back to Haunt Medical Examiner." The article said that a human skull was discovered at the Taunton Dump. Apparently, the skull was originally discovered in Berkley several years earlier. As the medical examiner, Dr. Nunes was given possession of the skull. To rule out foul play, he consulted with a Harvard Medical School lab, and their examination resulted in the conclusion that it was a female American Indian who died more than 200 years earlier.

On arriving at the scene at the dump, he looked at the skull, held it in the air and proclaimed the famous words from Hamlet – "Alas, poor Yorick, I knew him well." The skull had remained in his possession until a neighborhood student borrowed it for a science project. Apparently, the student discarded it, and it ended up in the trash collection. Dr. Nunes decided to bury the skull – thus it would not return to haunt him.

The following letter sums up my thoughts of Joseph E. Nunes M.D. - It was printed in a local paper from an admirer of his:

A Complex Man –

No man is easy to understand, and Dr. Joseph E. Nunes might have been one of the most difficult. One minute you loved him, and often you wondered if he was playing a game with you. Chances are he was. You never really found out what he was like underneath.

One writer, however, probably said it better in this note to us.

"In losing Dr. Nunes, I've lost a friend, a second father, and that someone special who will heal my children's cuts, and bruises and skinned knees. Oh, how I will miss that gruff voice answering the phone with, 'Yah go ahead,' and then with a sympathetic tone, 'Bring her down, I'll be ready.' During a recent illness in my family, when several lengthy operations were needed, I thanked him for his special attention. With a serious thought, he said: 'don't thank me, thank the guy upstairs.' Will I ever find a doctor who will come to my house at 7 am, stay by my child's side for 5 hours, and then leave saying 'Pay me next time.' But, the next time would never come."

It's funny how you do not realize what people mean to you until it's too late. But I can truly say that I have always had faith and trust in Dr. Nunes, as I have in God. After all, they worked together.

And when St. Peter meets Dr. Nunes at the Golden Gate, I hope Dr. Nunes doesn't greet him with "Well, whaddya you want?"

The Enigma of Figueiredo or Gouveia

A few words about my father's family - I did not meet my father's side of the family except for my aunt Mary Almeida, and once or twice I saw an uncle who later moved to Brazil. My Aunt Almeida lived on the corner of Baker Road and Dighton Ave, kitty-corner from my maternal grandparents. Many times she reminded me that my last name was Figueiredo, not Gouveia. A few days before her passing, I visited her, and she repeated her opinion to me that Gouveia was not my last name. My father's immigration papers do not use the name Gouveia except to show the district of northern Portugal from which he came. Talking about people's names, my sister, Chris, was unable to get a government-related job because she was told that she did not have a legal name. Apparently, her birth certificate had one name "Conceicao." She used the name Chris mostly but was also called Chrissie, Connie, and Constance. Because of the obvious problems with exactly what our family names were, it was necessary for the entire family to go to court and legalize our first, middle and last names. The legal notice was humorous enough to make the New Yorker magazine. Our family doctor, Joseph E. Nunes, was in Hawaii in the Navy in 1941 (Pearl Harbor). He saw the legal notice in the magazine and sent us a copy of it. In that notice, the court requested that anyone who objected to these changes could do so at the time of the court hearing. The New Yorker editor's comment was, "we are the last to object." A copy of this legal notice is paraphrased below.

Commonwealth of Massachusetts Bristol County

Probate court:

I, James P Kelly Junior, register of the probate court for said county of Bristol, having by law the custody of the seal and all the records, books, documents, and papers of or appertaining to said Court, hereby certify the paper here to annexed to be a true copy of a paper appertaining to said Court, and on the file and of record in the office of said Court to with the certificate of change of names:

Joao Figueiredo otherwise called

John Gouveia otherwise called

John Figueiredo Gouveia

To Be: John Figueiredo Gouveia

Patrocinia Netto Figueiredo

Otherwise called Patrocinia Gouveia

Otherwise called Patricia Gouveia

To Be: Patricia Gouveia

Conceicao Netto Figueiredo

Otherwise called Crissy Figueiredo Gouveia

Otherwise called Constance Figueiredo Gouveia

To Be: Constance Figueiredo Gouveia

Virginia Dorothy Figueiredo

Otherwise called Virginia Dorothy Gouveia

Otherwise called Dorothy Figueiredo Gouveia

To Be: Virginia Figueiredo Gouveia

David Figueiredo

Otherwise called David Figueiredo Gouveia

To Be: David Figueiredo Gouveia

In witness whereof, I have hereunto set my hand and the seal of said court, this twenty-first day of May, in the year of our Lord, one thousand nine hundred and forty-six.

Signed James B. Kelley, Register

The Honeymoon

The Bride and Groom before leaving for their honeymoon

On April 18th, 1959, Jan and I were married in Pawtucket, R.I., at St. Theresa's Church. After the reception at Lindsay's Lodge, we went on a brief honeymoon. Jan's wedding gown had a large hoop on the bottom, because of this she could not easily get into the stalls in the ladies room. Our honeymoon started with a stop at a gas station. What a way to start a life together! Our next stop was at the Hartford Sheraton. As I think about it now, why did we go that far out of the way from the direct route to Williamsburg, V.A.? Jan was wearing a corsage when we left the reception. Upon arriving at the Sheraton, she threw the flowers into the backseat. She didn't want people to think that we were honeymooners. The valet noticed the corsage and when he came in with our bags said "I think you forgot your corsage" to Jan.

We got up early and went to the 6:30 am Mass, which was attended by a few people dressed in work clothes. We, of course, were dressed like honeymooners in 1959. Jacket and tie for me, a pretty dress for Jan, no corsage of course. The trip to Williamsburg was very long. We arrived at our room late in the evening and stayed at a small guesthouse along one of the major streets in Williamsburg. The room had a canopy bed. When I called for the reservation, I requested the canopy bed as I had seen in the advertising brochures. It was a pleasant room, just a few steps from the various historical locations in the village. As I remember, we stayed there for two nights.

From Williamsburg, we went to Washington D.C. for two nights. Washington is such a great tourist destination, and we thoroughly enjoyed the sights. On our way to the Astor Hotel in Times Square, we spent a night in a motel off of the New Jersey Turnpike. The motel looked like it specialized in couples having one night stands, but it was clean and comfortable. We frequently joke about the "no tell motel" when we are traveling. Fortunately, things are better now. We now choose the Hilton's, the Marriott's and Hampton Inns. The beautiful old

Astor Hotel, where we stayed, has since been demolished, and on the site in Times Square is the very luxurious high rise, Marriott Marquis.

On Saturday we attended both a matinee and an evening theater performance: "The Music Man" with Robert Preston, and "My Fair Lady" at the evening performance. "The Music Man" was so invigorating and exciting that "My Fair Lady" seemed a little lame in comparison. Sunday was spent getting back to the reality of my surgical residency at St Elizabeth's Hospital. Jan returned to her R.N. position. As you can assume from our frenetic honeymoon, we are not a couple that goes to a resort and bask in the sun. All of our vacations, with and without the children, have been very active. We are interested in the history, culture and the foods of the locations we visit. Every town has its story to tell, and we have made it our goal to absorb the histories and cultures of other areas of the world as we travel.

Living with My Parents – 1964–1965

When my family and I arrived in Taunton in July 1964, we expected to move into our new home and office at 252 Winthrop Street. Unfortunately, the building would not be completed for several months.

My mother and father were very generous to offer us the use of their home until construction was finished.

I don't think they realized what it was like to have another family with two children ages 3 and 4. We arrived with a very large, very active Dalmatian who was Georgian – born and had always been allowed to run free at Fort Stewart. Unfortunately, 986 Somerset Avenue had no yard to run or play in.

The house had three bedrooms, and one full bath – somewhat tight quarters for four adults, two children, and a dog. Somehow, we all adapted to major changes in lifestyles.

Initially, in my practice, I used 824-4498 (the house phone at 968 Somerset Avenue) as my business phone. My mother was a built-in answering service. I had no pager until much later, so I had to let my mother know my whereabouts at all times. As anticipated, my practice was slow at first. Calls were few.

Jan and I had a Blue Rambler station wagon which I needed for my practice. That left her without transportation. My father allowed Jan to use his pride and joy (a 1938 Buick sedan) to do things around town. He used the Buick every Sunday morning to go to church, and then drove around Taunton and Dighton at slow speeds – a typical "Sunday Driver!" He could take this time for pleasure because the store could not open until noon.

Jan and the children went to Hedy and Walter's house on weekends. I joined them when not on call. Meals were happily prepared by Patricia Gouveia, from John Gouveia's farm, and of course, from our store. In addition, my mother had some home-canned food in the basement. It was still common to do home canning in Ball Jars which we got from Gouveia's Cash Market. I know I have mentioned my mother's great cooking. We had big meals every night. Some nights my sisters and their family joined us. Large amounts of delicious food appeared on the table, and all of it was made in that little pantry with a stove and four burners, a gas oven, and very little counter space. No stainless appliances, no granite counter tops, which are now "di rigueur" on TV shows like "House Hunters." Watching these shows now on HGTV, it seems that unless stainless steel and granite counters are in the kitchen, the home is undesirable, and will certainly require immediate renovations if purchased.

"Make do" does not seem to be the attitude of the current generation of couples.

Personal privacy was difficult for Jan and me, as well as for my parents. The house was not big. There was no place to hide, neither for my parents nor us. Both couples were accustomed to being able to find a time and place for the private conversations that married people must have. That activity was pushed aside temporarily.

A major positive benefit for my parents was that they could spend time with their grandchildren, and really get to know them, as well as to reacquaint themselves with Jan and me. It had been many years since I last lived with them.

Living with my parents also gave them the opportunity to better know Jan and me as grownups with a family. There was also an opportunity for us to get reacquainted with my parents – an opportunity most married couples do not have.

Despite the major disparity in ages, we got along well.

I am really quite happy that circumstances were such that we were forced to alter our lifestyles for an interim. Those 7 to 8 months made us appreciate my parents even more than I thought possible. They have passed on to their reward, but we still miss them after all of these years that have gone by.

Oh, Those Hot Portuguese Rolls

Our family routine on Sunday mornings in Taunton started with either the 8:15 am or the 9:30 am Mass at Our Lady of Lourdes Church on First Street at the Weir. In the late 60s and early 70s, people dressed well for church. Our children were no exception – no baggie jeans, no t-shirts. The girls usually wore skirts or dresses. After Mass, a short ride down First Street took us to what our children felt was the best part of any Sunday morning – a visit to the Ideal Bakery in the Staples Block opposite the Weir Bridge.

On the left side of the Staples building, at the corner of West Water and Staples streets, was this wonderful old bakery run by August Fonseca. He was an older Portuguese immigrant. He baked the best Portuguese rolls I have ever eaten. The taste of the rolls was enhanced by the aroma of bread baking in the antique ovens. The crust on the rolls was crunchy, and biting into the rolls filled our mouths with the wonderful taste of perfectly baked bread. What a delight!

Every week we bought a dozen or more of the freshly baked rolls, sold in paper bags. We rushed out of the bakery with our bags to our Rambler station wagon, and we all quickly grabbed a roll and devoured it. Often, there was little left in the bag by the time we arrived home to Winthrop Street. The bakery sold out of rolls every Sunday. If we went to the 9:30 mass, sometimes the rolls were sold out by the time we arrived at the bakery.

Mr. Fonseca stopped making these rolls in the late 70s or early 80s when the building was converted into an apartment complex. Our children have many fond memories of the bakery. My daughter, Lisa, recently asked me if I remembered going for rolls on Sundays. You can presume "YES" was my answer. I remember them well. The simple things in life are sometimes the most unforgettable.

248 Winthrop Street a.k.a. The Perry White House

248 Winthrop Street was a dream home. Before I write about ownership of the house, I will give you a brief history of the property. The information of the early history of the house was relayed to me by Christine White who was a daughter of Peregrine White, a descendant named after the first child born on the Mayflower to Pilgrim parents. Christine's mother was Sara L. White.

Sketch of 248 Winthrop Street by K. Divino

The original house on the property was a small Cape-style home which was moved a few houses to the west around 1870 to make way for a larger house on the property. That Cape house is now used as an office for a used car business.

An exquisite Victorian home was built at 248 Winthrop Street by William L White, Senior who later built a house for his son, William L. White, Junior at 242 Winthrop Street.

The William White, Sr. house was a two-story elaborate Victorian with a mansard roof, making it a three-story house (the mansard roof was popular because it allowed a house to have a third floor while being taxed only as a two-story property). It had an elaborate Victorian-style fence around the property.

Sometime around the turn of the 20th century, Peregrine White purchased 248 Winthrop St. from William L. White, Senior. According to Christine White, the property included a large wide meadow going several hundred feet to a little pond. At

Lois King and her sister Catherine Cambell, previous owners

the pond was a slaughterhouse (abattoir) which Mr. White Sr. had operated. The pond was used as a runoff for materials from the slaughterhouse.

The meadow, big enough to build at least ten houses, was later developed and was named Davenport Terrace. It is now a quiet residential street with a cul-de-sac at its dead end. This cul-de-sac served as a playground for my children and other children of the same age from the neighborhood.

One day I lifted a loose floorboard in the attic and found a log detailing sales of meat by Mr. White Sr. It had the names of many old Yankee families who bought meat from him. The log listed the name of the customer, the type of meat ordered, and the price of the transaction. I donated the log to the Old Colony Historical Society archives, as an example of a late nineteenth business log.

Peregrine White also became involved in the meat industry by investing in a startup company headed by a man from Cape Cod whose last name was Swift. The new business was known as Swift And Company and became a major wholesaler of meat in Chicago. It also became a source of considerable income for Peregrine White.

The intersection of Highland and Winthrop Street became known as "White's Four Corners" with the two William L White houses on one side of the street. Opposite these were the Davol house and the Lawrence house. Both families in those houses were related to the Whites. Peregrine White came from Worcester and was not related to the Taunton Whites.

Christine White told me that her mother, Sara, gave an ultimatum to her husband, Peregrine, that by the time of their 20th anniversary, she wanted a total renovation of 248 Winthrop St., or else! The ultimatum was effective. A prominent Fall River architect, Joseph F Darling, was contracted. He proposed a beautiful plan for the renovation project. I was given the original plans by the previous owners, Catherine Cambell and Lois King. These plans show the extensive architectural details evident throughout the interior of the structure.

Christine related that it was decided to build a new third floor under the mansard roof, and then remove the original roof. Christine was the only child to live in the house until our children moved in. Christine went off to college and had a successful career in college athletics. Her final position was at Wheaton College in Norton Massachusetts, where she worked for several years before retiring. On her return to Taunton, she became a driving force in many municipal committees and organizations. Her involvement in the First Parish Church included being the chairperson of the 350th-anniversary convocation honoring the founders of the church in 1637.

It is now time to write about our ownership of the Perry White House. On a weekend stay at the Plaza Hotel in New York for $25 a night; our room had a crystal chandelier over the bed. We liked the idea of having a chandelier in our bedroom. We had been given a beautiful Irish crystal chandelier by Lois King and Catherine Cambell when we purchased the house from them. The chandelier originally hung in the formal dining room but was removed when we converted the dining room into our family room.

Having moved from a much smaller dwelling at 252 Winthrop St., our furnishings were inadequate for the large rooms at 248. For example, the living room measured 33' x 14'. One could not sit at one end of the room and carry on a conversation with someone at the other end. The living room had many great features. A fireplace with a hand carved mantle was the centerpiece of the room. There were two large bay windows, one of which had a small door opening onto a covered porch. The porch had a cement floor and was supported by several rounded wood columns. A large double French door at the front of the room led to the full- length central hallway.

View of 248 Winthrop Street living room at Christmas

Let me return to the original dining room. At the front of the room, looking onto Winthrop Street were two long windows. On the opposite wall was a fireplace. The room also had double French doors opening into the central corridor, and a very wide door leading to the "plant room" which later became a children's playroom. The third set of doors went into the pantry and kitchen areas.

Prior to removing the crystal chandelier, we installed a ping-pong table. It was humorous watching aggressive games of table tennis on the table lighted by a crystal chandelier. The ping-pong table also took on other uses. It became a large dining table when we had company. I have many slides showing anniversary parties, birthdays, and other celebrations on the table. For these more formal occasions, the table was covered with fine Portuguese linen tablecloths. We eventually furnished the room with comfortable sofas and chairs. Goodbye to the ping-pong table. Incidentally, we had to remove the floor buzzer which the Whites used to call the maid from the kitchen, or from the third floor maids quarters. We had no maid!

There are many tales to tell about our magnificent home that was called by many as "the most beautiful house in Taunton." Time and space prevent me from writing all the good memories of the Perry White House. Over the following years, we renovated all five bedrooms. The living room became a combination living room/dining room, with a sofa separating the two areas. A large rosewood table with eight chairs was placed at the front of the room. The other half of the room held multiple chairs, couches and cocktail tables.

Our house was the site of many other parties and celebrations. We met a few times a year with our "potluck" dinner group which included the D'Andrea's, the Hellides, the LaRocque's, the LaFrance's, the Peotrowski's, and the Farrell's. We met for many years. My favorite potluck gathering was the Halloween party to whom everyone wore a costume.

Our potluck group met at our house for an annual pre-Christmas party. Carols were sung in the spirit of the season, with Dolores Laroque at a small keyboard. Each year some of the guests would not sing-along, even though we had books of carols for them. I don't understand some people's hesitance to join in with others celebrating the birth of Jesus. I guess not everyone is as outgoing as I am. I have always enjoyed singing.

Perhaps the best party was for my 50th birthday ("Hawaii 50"), to which guests were encouraged to wear luau outfits. The house was a little crowded with 80 guests, but a good time was had by all.

Other memorable events included a cocktail and hors d'oeuvres party for the benefit of the Star Players theater group in Taunton which was directed by Yale School of Music graduate, Joel Thayer.

Our home was on a tour of homes in celebration of the 350th anniversary of the city of Taunton. We had a brief foray into the political arena when we were asked by Dr. Jordan Fiore to hold a reception to benefit the campaign of Congresswoman Margaret Heckler. About 30 people attended and hopefully supported Mrs. Heckler. Bringing in the New Year was always a mildly wild occasion with many friends and neighbors eating, drinking and socializing.

We started the Christmas season in October or November when we dressed our children in nice clothes and posed for the annual Gouveia Family Christmas Picture. Uncle Jim was the photographer. We posed for the picture mainly on the stairs in the foyer, or on the front steps of the house. Apparently, people looked forward to receiving the Christmas card. Feedback was positive. Those photos were sent out annually for more than a decade.

Santa made it to our home every Christmas Eve. He brought many presents in response to our children's request to him in the mail, in person, or on his lap at the mall. After placing gifts around the tree, Jan and I welcomed quiet time together, as we opened our gifts to each other. We knew the Christmas Day would be very busy in the morning as our children tried on their gifts of clothing, and played with their new toys and games with much enthusiasm. When our in-laws, Hedy and Walter arrived with their presents, the wrapping paper was excitingly opened by the children and scattered all over the room.

Whatever presents Santa had forgotten, magically showed up with Walter and Hedy's arrival. Early afternoon, the activities were followed by Christmas dinner at which we stuffed ourselves enjoying all the food prepared by Jan and Hedy.

By late afternoon, and into the late hours of the evening, we held an open house for our family, extended family, and friends. 248 Winthrop was perfect for large group parties with the French doors of the den and living room open into the central hall. There was plenty of room for nieces, nephews, in-laws, cousins, friends and any members of our extended family.

Our large dining room table was covered with plates, bowls, and large platters of food. It was a beautiful array of delicious items including cold cuts, cheeses, roasted turkey and chicken, Polish and Portuguese delicacies - various pasta salads and green salads and plenty of breads.

The buffet table held many special desserts brought by our guests or made by us. Many cakes, pies, and Portuguese rice pudding were among the choices which tempted the palate and eventually enlarged out waists.

My parents passed away within two years of our buying the house. My father was able to attend only one Christmas party after his stroke. Hedy and Walter were there every year. Friends of theirs, especially Frank, Wanda, and Kay attended many of our family parties.

I cannot complete the section without mentioning the annual Christmas night family slideshow. Many people were bored with slideshows, but these shows were different. Family members and guests asked for them each year. Every year, I tried to include at least one photo of every member of the family. With my extensive collection of slides, I was able to show people in various stages of growing up and growing old. Many baby pictures were projected followed by more recent images. There were many laughs and chuckles over the way people looked as they matured and aged. Some years, I used different themes – photos of weddings, christenings, and birthdays. I made a point of showing how people changed. Hairstyles changed so much over the years. Clothing styles varied. Elaborate Easter hats were fashionable. It did not matter how many carousels of 140 slides were shown, and there never seemed to be enough for my audience.

After we had sold the Perry White House, I did a few slideshows at Joan Mello's house, but it was not the same. When digital photography emerged, it was time to discontinue the annual Christmas slideshow.

For so many years, my life was brightened by my ability to share photography with my family and friends. The joy of photography remains with me now in the digital world.

Before I finish this topic, I have to tell you a humorous tale. Hedy Such was often in the audience at my shows. The presentations were held in the evening, with most of the room lights out. In the darkness, Hedy was known to doze off (especially in movie theaters). As soon as the lights were back on, Hedy would say "that was such a nice slideshow, David." I knew she had not seen the whole show, but I thanked her anyway for expressing her enjoyment of it.

A Pot Holder Christmas

We celebrated Christmas as a family at 252 and 248 Winthrop Street, in the same way, each year. We gathered into the living room to exchange gifts on Christmas morning. Jan and I would exchange gifts on Christmas Eve every year after the children went to bed, before Santa's arrival. I feel that a husband and wife should have a quiet time together, after all the activity that comes in preparing for the Christmas holiday.

One Christmas was a little different. I suggested to our children that each of them buy pot holders for Jan. My idea was that each first gift from the children should be pot holders, beautifully packaged and wrapped. By the time Jan opened the second set of pot holders, it was obvious that this gift giving was a setup.

Including the set from me, Jan received five sets of pot holders, enough to last for many years in the kitchen. We had a lot of laughs during the gift opening. In addition, we had a silly story to tell our grandchildren. You can never have enough potholders.

EDUCATION STORIES

Herbert E. Barney School, Taunton High School, and Tufts College

Herbert E. Barney School, circa 1970

My sisters and I attended Herbert E. Barney School for eight years. It was located on South Street, near the North Dighton line. I started school there in 1937. My teacher was Miss Smith, the same Miss Smith who taught my aunts in the earlier decades of the 20th Century. The school was named in memory of the first Taunton-area fatality in World War One. The school had four large, equal-sized rooms with two grades in each room, so it was a four room, eight grade school. The rooms were separated by a central hall and a coat closet. The toilets were in the basement; I vividly remember having to raise my hand for permission to go to the "basement."

Grades three and four were taught by Miss Alice B. McKechnie who lived at 250 Winthrop Street, at the home later owned by Sol E. Berk. Miss Costa was the grade five and six teacher. She lived on Dighton Avenue and was a former nun, who had left the convent. She was a strict and severe disciplinarian. I will give her a little more time in this section of the book because of my contact with her at Gouveia's Cash Market. In the early 40s, the store did not have an adding machine. We would use a pencil and write the charges on a brown paper bag. We then added the figures for payment. Each time I waited on her, I was shaking in my boots. What would happen if I overcharged her by adding incorrectly? It's a good thing I performed well in math; I never had a problem with Ms. Costa at the store.

7th and 8th grade stick in my brain because one of our classmates transferred to an out of town prep school. This was a very unusual happening for our school which did not have students from affluent families. I think he went to medical school eventually. Alice C. Winslow was a long time principal of Herbert E. Barney. She taught 7th and 8th grade. I assume she was a descendant of the Winslow family of Mayflower heritage. She retired from teaching in 1945. My graduating class of 1945 was the last year for eight grades at Herbert E. Barney School.

My Grammar school graduation with Principal Alice C. Winslow, far left

I had the occasion to visit with Miss Winslow's father who reminisced about the Civil War with me. I don't think he was old enough to have fought in the war. In later years as her physician, I made house calls at her Orchard Street family home. By this time, she was approaching 100 years of age. Unfortunately, she had lost her eyesight. She lived alone, and the radio was her companion. Boston Red Sox were her passion. She listened to every ball game. Fortunately, she had a family living next door to check in on her. She was well taken care of by them. Their adult son did everything for her that she needed. He ended up inheriting the house, deservedly.

A comment about the Winslow house…it was untouched, inside, probably from the time it was built. The original soapstone sink remained in the kitchen, and minimal modern conveniences were evident. Miss Winslow's physical condition gradually degenerated requiring her to become a patient at Wedgemere Nursing Home. She celebrated her 100th birthday at the nursing home. One of her neighbors, Senator John Parker, his wife Mae, and I attended the celebration. One hundred candles were blown out, mostly by the Senator and me, although

Miss Winslow tried her best to extinguish them. I took photos of the party and donated them to the Old Colony Historical Society for their archives.

Let's go back to schooling and my youth. Children now are quite pampered. Very few walk to school, some go by bus, others in family cars. I frequently would kid with my children that I walked through rain, mud, sleet, and snow uphill, both ways to get to school. I did walk a mile each way daily, even sometimes going home for lunch. My lunch bag at school usually contained a Genoa salami sandwich on white bread. Little wonder that in 1999 my coronary arteries were 95% obstructed requiring a quadruple bypass.

My grades were good; I still have some of my report cards. I have donated some of them to Old Colony Historical Society as examples of grading systems. Miss Winslow recommended me for the Advanced Programs at Taunton High School. I was in the classroom with many students who became my friends again, on my return to Taunton in 1964. Among these were Pat Slade Marston, Audrey Parker Pollard, Nancy Doyle and Linda Brabrook Pratt. My close friends in high school were Jim Borra, and James Frates. Jim Borra became a Washington, D.C .lawyer, and James Frates taught at Dighton-Rehoboth High School. The Borras lived in an old Victorian on Somerset Avenue, across from Memorial Park. His mother was a fabulous chef who specialized in Italian food. She was involved in starting one of the first Italian restaurants in Taunton. After school, Jim and I frequently went to her kitchen to eat lasagna, spaghetti, and other Italian delicacies.

Latin was a requirement for the advanced group. I took Latin for four years and French for three years. We read the Iliad and Odyssey in Latin. We conversed in Latin and were members of the Latin Club. I guess you could call us "nerds." Those days we were called "brains." Herbie Vieira was the smartest kid in our class and graduated Summa Cum Laude, a giant step from my Magna Cum Laude. As a freshman in Mr. Edward Kennedy's class, I was sitting in the front row, but could not read the board. I have worn glasses ever since. They are a feature of my appearance.

Miss Elsie Salthouse was our French teacher. She conducted the entire class in French, a novel approach for the time. She was trained at the Sorbonne in Paris. Our first class was started by her saying "j'ontra dans la salle de classe, je regard au tour de moi. Je dis bonjour a la classe." Translation: "I enter the classroom, I look around the room, and I say good morning to the class." We were all required to stand up and recite these words individually. She was a real task master. We frequently had one-on-one sessions with Miss Salthouse in which we conversed in French.

Mr. Lawrence B. Norton was our history teacher. He was an excellent teacher, an inspiration to his students. On his suggestion, we wrote and presented a history of the "49ers" and the Gold Rush. The title of the play was "The 49ers." Members of the club did research at the historical society and used the names of Tauntonians who went to California during the 1849 Gold Rush. We then wrote a play based on those characters. It was a lot of fun; we dressed in clothing of the period for our performance at the high school, and for a presentation at Old Colony Historical Society. Incidentally, I had what might be called my "debut," i.e., my first public singing performance as a soloist. I sang two songs of the period, "Oh Sussana" and "My Darling Clementine," with the other students singing the chorus. Tony Martin played the accordion for us. The Old Colony has a copy of the photo of the cast that I took on the steps of Taunton High School. The best line of the play was delivered by Faye Louison, sister of Attorney Leonard Louison. She proclaimed, as she departed for California "FAREWELL TO TAUNTON, HOME OF SWAYING ELM TREES AND TAUNTON HIGH SCHOOL." (There wasn't an actual building called Taunton High School in 1849). Another activity I was involved in was the high school glee club. The club had concerts a couple of times a year in the auditorium. My involvement with singing continued when I went to Tufts College.

I applied to three schools for college – Harvard, Tufts and Boston University. I was accepted at Tufts and BU; BU also offered me a scholarship of $50. Per semester. $50 doesn't sound like much, but with tuition at $250 per semester, that is the equivalent of a $10,000 scholarship. Tufts was my first choice, but no scholarship was available from it. In the post-WWII period, colleges were overwhelmed by students who were veterans of World War II. They were eligible for tuition dollars based on their military service. This made it very difficult to get into any college. By the way, at Taunton High School, an arrangement was in effect with Massachusetts Institute of Technology, that any Taunton High student recommended by the principal for admission to MIT, was automatically accepted.

About 250 to 300 students were admitted to Tufts College annually, and approximately 100 of these were pre-med students. A small number of these actually stayed with the pre-med program for four years. The one course that made or broke all of us as a pre-med was organic chemistry. If you didn't do well in organic, you were not getting into medical school. I did well grade wise, I got an A in organic chemistry, but I had a problem in the lab. I erroneously mixed chlorosulfonic acid with something; I don't know what. The combination caused an explosion that went right to the ceiling. The ceiling was at least 20 feet high. It also hit me in my arms and legs, and I still have small spots of burned skin that I can show you.

Jim Connell was in the pre-med program but changed his major after a year. Chris Salvo was also in the program and finished it. We became fraternity brothers and friends for life. Tufts limited dorm rooms to students who lived more than 50 miles from the campus, so I was ineligible to be assigned to a dorm room. Rooms in private homes off campus were listed. I ended up freshman year at a home on the Medford-Somerville line. My private room on the 2nd floor was $5 per week. To take a shower, I had to ask the landlady to heat up the water. With this arrangement, I showered at the gym most of the time. I roomed in another private home my sophomore year. Housemates were Gildo J. Sevardio from Connecticut and Jorge from Peru. They were juniors. The other occupant of the house was a high caste Indian boy who was not friendly and stayed in his room. The only thing we saw of him was the "ring around the bathtub." He was too superior to clean the tub after bathing. Little wonder that we nicknamed him "Shithead."

My third year I had a teeny, tiny room off Hillside Avenue in Medford. Senior year I lived at Alpha Sigma Phi. John Kurkjian and I shared the first floor rear room. John was of Armenian background. We were the only room with an oversized, real oriental rug in it. Alpha Sigma Phi was known as the drunkest and worst fraternity on the campus. Why? I don't know! Maybe it was because we had a Rathskeller (German beer hall) in the basement. Everyone knew our house as the "Kippie House." I joined the fraternity in my sophomore year, even though I could not get a room in the building until my senior year. The pledge period was not easy. We were made to do ridiculous things to become brothers. The worst thing that was done to me was a "mystery ride." I was blindfolded and taken for a long ride, ending up in Ayer, Mass., home of Ft. Devens. I was left there, near a farmhouse with no shoes and no money. I was picked up by the Ayer police who were very nice. They let me sleep overnight on a wooden slab in the jail. The police officer gave me enough money to take the train back to Medford, and I returned to the fraternity house unscathed. It is my only night in jail. You might say there were a few nasty people in the Kippie house.

Kippie House (Alpha Sigma Phi)

One fun thing that we did was a trip to Boston, where Chris Salvo and I were required to camp out on the Tremont Street sidewalk. This was during "hell week" We had a little tent, a Bunsen burner, dirty clothes and a clothesline. Chris and I did our laundry, hung it on the line and cooked eggs!!! It caused quite a commotion because of the number of people who stopped to watch "two crazy college kids" in action. Traffic slowed down to see what was happening. Eventually, we were asked to move by the police.

Another great event was the scavenger hunt in Boston. We found most of the items, but could not get a g-string from the strippers at the Old Howard or The Casino Theatre. Both strip joints were in the "combat zone." The area is now the Federal Government Center. A finer event was our weekend away at Manchester by the Sea, a somewhat run-down hotel at a beach on the North Shore. We had a formal dance and dinner, with an overnight stay at Manchester by the Sea. A not so classy event was Kippie night at the Old Howard. We were required to take a date to this. Remember this was in the early 50s when morals were considerably higher than in the past thirty years or so. Going to a strip joint with a date was considered taboo and disgusting. I finally found someone to take to the show ("a townie"). As soon as the performance began, my date said: "oh crap I have already seen this show." Well, at least she wasn't shocked by what we saw. A lot is said about that sort of entertainment, but not much flesh was exposed.

There were poorly danced numbers. In one of them, a dancer in the back row was in the late stages of pregnancy – not very sexy! Lilly St. Cyr was an exception; she was magnificent with her large hand-held fans, hiding all the interesting anatomy. As the show progressed, the dancers shed some of their clothes. The lighting became progressively dimmer and even blue. So, if the dancers did take all their clothes off, you couldn't see anything anyway. It was not the "Follies Bergere" in Paris. We had many parties in the Rathskeller, where I learned some German songs from Max Klitski. Max was a Pennsylvania Dutch who spoke German. We learned several drinking songs from him.

Parker Green was our chef. He was a retired black chef, who had worked at several high-class Boston restaurants. He came in early in the morning and prepared breakfast Monday thru Friday. Our main meal was dinner which he made and was always delicious. We were on our own for lunch. We could eat anything that was in the kitchen. Peanut Butter and Jelly was a main staple at lunch. Parker Green was one reason I joined the fraternity. After eating in the college cafeteria run by the Crotty Brothers (their name should have been Cruddy Brothers because the food was awful!) During freshman year of college, for a week or two, most of the students went on strike against the cafeteria. We would take the food, but in defiance, we would not eat it. They must have paid someone off to keep the cafeteria contracts. They were there year after year, despite complaints to administration.

My graduation from Tufts College

Although Alpha Sigma Phi was supposed to be the worst fraternity on campus, some good things can be said about it. I was the conductor of the Kippie house group for the Christmas Sing competition. Our group sang "Go Tell It on the Mountain," and we won honorable mention. This was the first time in memory that our fraternity house competed and actually won something. The other good thing about the kippie house was the graduating class of 1953. Several classmates were accepted at medical school including Chris Salvo, Jack Saglio, Bob McCarthy, John Kurkjian, and myself.

This is quite impressive for a fraternity with the reputation of "animal house" on campus. It makes you think that a good party on Saturday nights is what is necessary for medical school acceptance.

Graduation for all schools from Tufts was held outdoors on the lawn in front of Ballou Hall. It was a lovely day. I can't tell you who gave the commencement speech. Can you tell me who gave yours? I graduated Magna Cum Laude, in the top ten of my class, with the degree of Bachelor of Science in Chemistry-Biology. Not bad for the son of a shepherd from Portugal. But wait till you see what it was like in medical school where everyone accepted was a top student.

The 4x6 Card

I may have previously mentioned that Dr. Joseph E. Nunes delivered me in 1931 and continued to be my physician until I left for college in 1949. During those years, he treated me for multiple problems including a perforated eardrum, a tonsillectomy, a hernia repair, and an evaluation for abdominal pain and vomiting which frequently occurred, resulting in my being sent to the Truesdale Clinic in Fall River for evaluation. The eminent surgeon Dr. Truesdale admitted me for observation. Tests obtained showed no specific cause for my symptoms, I was discharged without requiring surgery.

Other involvements with Dr. Nunes included a repair of my left thumb flexor tendon, which I cut on a broken soda bottle at the store. He did the repair in his office under local anesthesia. The anesthetic was not very effective; the pain was severe, in fact, so severe, that I fainted during the procedure. He warned me that I might have problems moving the thumb if healing wasn't perfect. Fortunately, I regained full use of the thumb. I seemed to have a problem with soda bottles. Another time, at the store, I was arranging bottles of soda in the front window, to my surprise, a bottle exploded, and glass hit me between the eyes on the bridge of the nose. "Calling Dr. Nunes…stitches needed." The scar is still evident. Apparently, soda bottles shouldn't be stored in the windows, where sunlight can hit them.

One day I was on a see-saw with Lily Lopes, we were going up and down fast. I panicked when I thought I was too high and jumped off at the highest point. I broke my right wrist. Dr. Nunes manipulated it and applied a plaster cast. The healing was perfect. No x-rays were necessary.

A side note about Dr. Nunes. At that time, considerable dispensing of medications was done at the office instead of at a pharmacy. Dr. Nunes was well known as a dispenser of "pink pills" for pain. In fact, our relatives from Danbury would make an appointment to meet with him, and leave with a little bag of "pink pills." As I progressed in my medical career, I think I figured out what the pink pills were, most likely a combination of aspirin, phenacetin, and caffeine. In medical parlance, they were called "APC." Years later this combination was discontinued because of the side effects of the phenacetin.

Some of the more interesting characteristics about Dr. Nunes were his stubbornness and his sometimes bizarre sense of humor. One day, I was visiting him at his office, socially, after returning to Taunton to join the medical staff at Morton Hospital. It was a short time after St. Patrick's Day. He showed me a stack of letters on his desk, pointing out that he had received a similar letter each year after St. Patrick's Day. These letters were sent to him by the hospital administrator because of his actions every March 17th. On that day, he wore an orange necktie with a sketch of a naked woman on it. The letters said he was doing a disrespectful act, as well as being vulgar by wearing the tie to Morton Hospital. He chuckled over the reprimands and did not appear bothered by the comments. He was his own man, an interesting character, and one not necessarily swayed by others' opinions.

The reason I bring up the topic of the tie may surprise you. But if you know me well enough, it might not. After his death at age 66, I was offered the use of his orange tie by one of his daughters. I readily accepted the offer and proudly wore the tie on March 17th every year after that. I never received a letter of condemnation for these acts. In fact, some nurses even checked around for my whereabouts, so that they could view my beautiful orange tie with a naked woman on it. It still sits in my collection of ties but has not seen much use in many years.

I can't finish this topic without thanking Dr. Nunes for his letter from Honolulu (he was there on Dec 7th, 1941). He read the New Yorker magazine regularly. One day while reading The New Yorker he saw a copy of a legal notice of Bristol County, M.A. court proceedings. In it was a legal notice of an upcoming hearing in the court to approve changes to the Gouveia family names. These changes were necessary because of a question of the legality of my sister Chris' name. In the legal notice is a request for objections against the changes. The editor of the New Yorker added: "we are the last to object." (Additional information on this subject is in the section "Enigma of Gouveia or Figueiredo")

I want to go back to discuss the title of this chapter "The 4x6 card." At my pre-college physical, I noticed my medical record; it was a 4x6 card with entries in the main portion and small notations around the edges. Imagine that, 18 years of medical history on one 4x6 card! Compare that to the multiple pages and even multiple volumes of medical records now required for physicians and their practices. In the 21st century, medical records are changing again – now they will be electronically preserved, hopefully with added backup in case of computer failure. No more need for 4x6 cards.

Three Summers at
Taunton State Hospital

Taunton State Hospital was one of the first progressive mental institutions in the country. Built in 1852 to 1853, it was recognized for being in the forefront of the care of the mentally ill. The history of Taunton State Hospital has been appended at the end of this topic. I worked there during the summers of 1951, 1952 and 1953. Most tranquilizers and psychotropic drugs with which we are so familiar with had not yet been developed. Paraldehyde was commonly used to sedate alcoholics with delirium tremens (DTs).

Librium had not been developed yet. I am not certain what medications were administered by the nursing staff. The hospital hired college students for the summers. This made it easier to give vacations to the regular employees. Political maneuvering was necessary to get the summer job. My job was a result of my parent's conversation with State Senator John Parker. "It's not what you know, but who you know" stood then as a statement, as it does now.

There were two other college students working in the same position - one was Bill McCaffrey, who is Matt McCaffrey's father. Matt is a policeman in Taunton. The other was Tommy O'Dea. Tom entered the priesthood in the Fall River Diocese.

My first summer, I was assigned to ward B, a floor with ambulatory patients who were usually calm and easy to work with. We played a lot of cribbage and card games every day. There was no television in the main room, so patients had to find things to keep their minds busy. I had little to do except to entertain the patients. One of my most memorable patients was an engineer, a graduate of MIT, who was paranoid (paranoid schizophrenic). He was certain that there would be a violent attack on ward B, and it would be necessary for all of us to leave the ward before an explosion of an atomic bomb hit us.

Most of the time, I was able to talk him out of being violent. One day, he was very agitated, frightened and convinced that an attack on the building was imminent. He could not be convinced otherwise and was trying to get out of a locked window in the front of the building. In my attempt to stop him, he punched me in the mouth and chipped one of my front teeth. My dentist, Dr. Henry Alves, was able to smooth the damage despite the fact that current cosmetic materials were not available.

I just had to learn to duck when someone was punching me. The patient did not get out the window. My supervisor, an angry red-headed man, not my favorite person, made light of my injuries, and nothing was ever done about it.

At lunch time we were sometimes required to go to the violent ward (ward 7) to supervise the meal. We were warned to always have our back against the wall. We also had metal dining trays to use as protection, should something be thrown at us. Fortunately, I was rarely sent to the violent ward, so I escaped potential injury.

Another memorable patient on ward B, a man from Nantucket who was not violent, but was quite a smooth talker; he could now be called a "con artist." He was a "frequent customer" of Taunton State Hospital and would voluntarily commit himself to dry out from alcohol. Part of the ward routine was that each night at about 9 pm, we did a bed check. Unfortunately, one night on my shift, he was nowhere to be found. I was unaware that he had left the building until bed check. The question was how did he get out? All of the doors were locked, and my keys were secured to a chain on my belt. The supervisor was not happy with me. He thought I let the patient out. A few hours later, the patient appeared at the door. As a "frequent traveler" he was in possession of copies of the door keys. He let himself out. After going to a barroom for a few pops, he came back on his own. At least they couldn't accuse me of allowing him to get out. Interestingly, a few years later I saw him in Nantucket, and he saw me. There were no obvious signs of recognition on either side, but I knew it was him, and I was sure by the look on his face that he recognized me. No words were spoken, and life went on without any embarrassment for him or any of his acquaintances. That's my Nantucket story.

My second summer, I was assigned to one of the infirmary wards; in these wards were some bedridden patients and some ambulatory patients. The habits that some of these patients had cannot be described here unless this tome is rated an "R" or "X." My job was to wash bed patients, change linens and occasionally wash the floor. On this ward, there was a patient who I will call "ain't that umm." He would sit at a window looking out at the pastoral scene. Anytime anyone spoke to him; his answer was "ain't that umm." I don't recall him saying anything else – no other words at any time. He was content to sit and only say – "ain't that umm." I have used this phrase in the past resulting in strange looks from the person I was addressing.

Keep the phrase in mind; you might find it useful sometime in the future – ain't that umm?

In the summer of 1952, I dated Trudy Zawaki who was the daughter of the Assistant Superintendent of the State Hospital. She was a lovely young lady, and fun to be with. She eventually married Joseph Califano, who later was appointed as head of U.S. Health and Human Services (HHS). I understand that they eventually divorced, other than that I have not heard anything about her.

One summer, I was approached by a full-time orderly at the hospital. He offered to show me his collection of etchings. I was not interested in his etchings or whatever activities he had in mind. I declined the invitation. After summers of working at the hospital, it was my impression that some of the full-time employees were a little "strange," to say the least. Working with the mentally ill is very challenging on a regular basis. I complement those who can do it. I have great respect for how people react to unusual situations with patients who are disoriented, confused, anxious, violent and needing understanding and compassion. Those who voluntarily enter for care, or are placed in a mental institution by court orders, are stripped of all of their freedoms.

In the 1950s, electric shock treatments were a common mode of therapy. In some states, shock treatments are banned by law at this time. The current method of treatments is as follows: the patient is given an intravenous muscle relaxant – these medications prevent the terrible muscle contractions (convulsions) caused by the electric shocks. In contrast, in the 1950s, these treatments required a few people holding down the patient as firmly as possible during the electric shock, which produced convulsive states. Immobilization was necessary to prevent fractures from occurring. I worked in the shock room many times. I did feel some possible bone fractures occurring during the treatments. My wife Janice was involved with shock treatments known as "insulin shock" during her nurse's training rotation at Waltham State Hospital in the late 1950s. She does not have good memories of these treatments, nor do I of electric shock therapy. During my practice in Taunton, I had some patients who required shock treatments for severe depression, with excellent results lasting for many months. It would be a great mistake to ban shock treatments altogether. Those three summers at Taunton State resulted in my being more accepting of those inflicted with mental illness.

"A Brief History of Taunton State Hospital" - A significant contribution to health care reform was made in 1851 when the Massachusetts legislature chose Taunton as the site for its second State Mental Asylum augmenting an existing facility in Worcester. Governor Marcus Morton and Samuel Crocker lobbied for the hospital's advantageous placement on a secluded knoll overlooking Whittenton and fronted by a majestic grove of trees. Elbridge Boyden, a Worcester architect, famed regionally for his many public buildings and institutional designs, was commissioned to produce a grand building. Completed in 1853, the asylum housed offices, reception rooms, superintendents' quarters and wards for patients. Both this building and the entire hospital facility were enlarged in the late 19th and early 20th centuries by the addition of many ancillary buildings, housing, nursing school, residence quarters, infirmaries, and other hospital support services.

In addition to its superior architectural quality, the hospital deserves recognition for its role in bettering the treatment of the mentally ill. Subjected to primitive and unenlightened moral concepts, the insane were traditionally treated like criminals, incarcerated in cells, and cut off from human contact. Particularly the Irish, who flooded Massachusetts' cities in the 1850s and 1860s, were subjected to severe prejudice, accused of speaking a "bewitched" language, practicing sorcery, and behaving in a wild, sexually unbridled manner. The Taunton Asylum's administration had some impact on reversing inhumane treatment of mental health patients when it instituted an experimental "dormitory plan," a series of isolated, but unlocked, rooms united by a central corridor – that set a precedent in hospital ward design.

*Statements taken from the book "Taunton Architecture" published 1981, written by Christine White and Phillip R. LaFrance.

Tufts Medical School – 1953 to 1957

What a surprise, everyone in the Tufts Medical Class of 1957 was at the top of their college class – intelligent and aggressive. Our classes were held in a renovated textile factory donated by a generous Jewish industrialist. It was on Harrison Avenue in what was called the "combat zone." In other words, drugs, alcohol, loose women, and crime. It was quite a change from the pastoral setting of Tufts College in Medford. A group of four of us from Tufts, Chris Salvo, Charlie Vassalo, Ken Foster and I rented a fourth-floor walk-up apartment on the lower end of Beacon Hill, one block from Cambridge Street and its notorious tenants – The Old Howard and The Casino. In addition to these, there were numerous liquor stores and bar rooms. Imagine that? We were only a few blocks away from the Mass General Hospital - the number one hospital in the country, according to anyone who worked there. I think the Harvard Medical School relationship with Mass General resulted in considerable braggadocio, overstated egos and swollen heads. You can tell by these comments that Mass General was the place for the "Gods of Medicine" to work. The peons worked at the inferior institutions. But I wander away from my topic.

Our four-room apartment had two bedrooms with bunk beds, a living room, a kitchen and a bath. It didn't take too long for us to realize that Charlie Vassalo could not cook. The three others in the group did the cooking, and Charlie was relegated to cleaning up. The kitchen was small but adequate for four medical students. My mother sent food and pastries for us so we would not go hungry. Her brownies were famous and delicious. Once I made the mistake of baking a pie, using the pie crust that I made myself. The contents of the pie were good, but the crust could be compared to cement. It brought back memories of my Aunt Lucy's pound cake – a tooth breaking dessert.

The first year of medical school was very difficult for me. In fact, at one point of the year, I questioned if I had made a correct choice of a career. I certainly would not want to repeat the year again.

Occasionally on weekends, our lab assignment was to collect urine for 24 hours. It was strange to be carrying jugs of urine up Beacon Hill, across the Boston Common to Harrison Avenue to perform laboratory tests on it. We put the jugs in bags, but you could hear the liquid slosh as we walked down the street. The cadaver lab was set up where we shared a cadaver with three other students, who were not our roommates. My cadaver was named Mortimer by our group. We named him so that in polite society the word cadaver was not used. One of our lab instructors suffered from what is now called "OCD" (obsessive compulsive disorder). It was very strange to watch him wash his hands any time he touched anything. If you have ever watched the TV series, "Monk," you know what I am talking about.

Our Beacon Hill apartment was rented until September 1st, so I decided to stay in Boston for the summer. Positions were open for medical students at the Beth Israel Hospital. I don't remember the exact title, but basically, we were available to comfort patients, and sit and talk with them – I guess we would be called "Ambassadors." In the 50s, patients remained in hospitals for extended periods of time. It was normal to be admitted to a hospital days before surgery for a "prep." Postoperative days could be one to two weeks in length for a gallbladder operation or similar procedures. If a patient didn't feel like going home, he could stay as long as he wanted in the hospital. My most memorable patient at the Beth Israel was an elderly gentleman (perhaps sixty years old) who had a horrendous case of psoriasis, a skin disorder that caused large red patches of inflamed skin that was itchy and caused the patient to scratch almost continuously. As a resulting of frequent scratching, flakes of dry skin would fall onto the floor. This patient was a very pleasant, very wealthy Jewish man who assumed that I, too, was Jewish. I looked the part, and he called me by my Jewish name, "Duvid." Later in my life in Taunton, many of my Jewish friends called me "Rabbi" because of my looks, and later because of my beard. The patient and I spent many hours discussing life, politics, business, etc... we did not discuss religion, and I don't think he was ever aware of the fact that I was not Jewish. A million dollars in the 1950s was probably the equivalent of five million dollars in 2010. The patient repeatedly said that he would give one million dollars to anyone who could relieve him of his terrible skin disorder. Even today, there is no specific cure for psoriasis, but there are many treatments to relieve the symptoms and partially or completely clear the skin for a period of time.

I failed to tell you about the patient's room; it was constantly covered with skin flakes, looking similar to the floors in western restaurants that use sawdust as a décor. The use of sawdust was not uncommon, in fact, Jacob Wirth Restaurant on Stuart Street, a fine German restaurant with great weinerschnitzel, used sawdust on the floor in the 1950s until it was determined that sawdust was a fire danger, and was banned. Jacob Wirth restaurant had been in business for 150 years without any negative effects from sawdust. The Massachusetts government knows what is best for us whether or not it makes sense. I liked the sawdust effect at the restaurant.

The first year of medical school was difficult. I took solace and comfort in eating. Of course, we were not good cooks and perhaps ate too much junk food. In any case, I went from 155 pounds to 200 pounds by the end of the first year. I am now around 185 pounds, but as we age, we tend to be less active, so we tend to be just a few pounds heavier. I am 86 years old now, so based on that premise, I should probably weigh 250 to 300 pounds!

My supervisor, Ms. B, at Beth Israel Hospital was worried about my weight. We talked about it, and she suggested that I have the dietician at the hospital order my meals from the cafeteria. When I showed up in line, I was handed my meal for lunch and dinner Monday through Friday. An example of a meal consisted of a salad with a low-calorie dressing, a protein, a piece of fruit and a low-calorie drink. To encourage me, Ms. B offered to take me out to dinner at Café Amalfi which was one of the finer Italian restaurants in Boston, next to Symphony Hall. In order to go there, I had to lose 45 lbs. in the three months. To help lose that much weight, I walked from Beacon Hill to the Beth Israel, some days back and forth, other days just one way. On Friday evenings, I was allowed to go to the Brigham's ice cream shop for a mocha ice cream soda. Psychologically, the weekly reward of ice cream worked. I lost 45 lbs. and had a beautiful Italian dinner with my Ms. B.!

My second year at TCMS (Tufts College Med School), a new dormitory was opened named Posner Hall. Chris Salvo and I decided to room together at Posner. The room was nice, but not The Ritz. 2nd year was not as traumatic as year number one. The food at the cafeteria was not good, so I frequently ate at a Lebanese-owned diner, down the road on Harrison Avenue. The woman who ran the place always seemed to pile the food onto my plate. I appreciated that. I guess after losing 45 lbs. in 3 months, I must have looked pathetic to her. Life was very different in the dormitory, but the location was good. We frequently went out for a glass of beer after studying. Beer was available in ten cent glasses, so our budget was not damaged. It couldn't be. We had little money to spend anyway.

I dated Ann Lenehan, from Dorchester. She was a student nurse at Boston City Hospital (BCH). My roommate, Chris Salvo, asked me if I was serious about her. I really wasn't, at that stage of our relationship. He asked if I minded if he went out with her. I said sure, ok. Their romance blossomed, and they were married prior to Chris finishing medical school. We remain close friends with Chris and Ann who now live in Mashpee in the summer and Naples, Florida in the winter. They have been married more than 50 years, so basically I guess, I was like

Yenta, the matchmaker from "Fiddler on the Roof." 2nd year at TCMS was better than the first; I was heard to say that if all four years were like year one, I would probably be running a chain of grocery stores, based on my knowledge and experience at Gouveia's Cash Market. Why not? Joe Fernandez started out the same as I did, and he ran a chain of at least 20 supermarkets. But seriously, there is no way that would have happened. As far as I was concerned, I was told that since age three or four, I would consistently say to others that I wanted to be a doctor.

Year three was a better year, we needed a car to get to some of our assignments, and my parents bought me a used blue Ford sedan for $500 cash. You won't believe the "door story," the car ran well, but soon after I got it, I think it was too early to say "Houston we have a problem." The problem was that the driver side door would get loose about every 50 miles. It had to be screwed back in after that. I remember picking Janice up at Waltham State Hospital, where she was taking mental health training. That day the door almost fell off when I opened it. What a way to impress a girl with my mechanical capability!? That wasn't the only problem I had with the car. One day driving back to Cambridge City Hospital from a clerkship, I was on Rte. 2, and all of the sudden there was a loud cracking noise, the car came to an abrupt stop. I got out of the car and saw that my front wheels were crooked, my front axle had broken. I finally got the front door and axle fixed and got safe transportation.

4th year of medical school was entirely clinical. We were assigned to services in various Boston hospitals, Tufts Med was in the complex of the New England Medical Center, but I was never assigned a clerkship there. In those 4th year clerkships, we became part of a team of doctors of various specialties for periods of one to two months. My worst clerkship was one month on the obstetrical service at the old Boston City Hospital. The way the staff treated pregnant women was deplorable. They were treated like animals. New patients were placed on a cement bathing table and hosed down with water before going to their rooms, or to the delivery room. Statements like "you had fun making it, now have fun delivering it" were commonly heard. Boston City was the hospital for indigent patients, but they are like everyone else and deserved to be treated with dignity.

As a medical student, I was treated not much better than the patients at Boston City. I became the scut boy. Most of my time was spent drawing blood samples or doing lab tests. I witnessed a few deliveries; I don't remember assisting on any deliveries myself. Living conditions for medical students at BCH were disgusting. The whole place was old, dirty and not in good condition. There was a tunnel under the buildings used for walking between buildings. At night sewer rats were running around, as I walked through the corridors to patients rooms to draw blood tests. At the end of this rotation, I complained to the Dean of the medical school. I was not happy with the arrangement at BCH. I certainly wasn't paying tuition to be used as a lab technician.

My rotation in psychiatry was at a state-run facility outside of Boston. The one thing I remember vividly was an accusation made about me to the hospital staff. I was accused of having sex with a female patient in the day room filled with other female patients. When this was brought to my attention, I didn't know whether to laugh or to cry. I was innocent of any alleged illegal behavior and was upset that the administration would believe such an accusation. It was a mental hospital with many young women whose fantasies are a reality to them.

My most enjoyable clerkship was in surgery at St. Elizabeth Hospital. It was enjoyable enough for me to want to take up a surgical residency there. The residents in surgery were easy to get along with. They taught well and were a welcome help to the medical students. "St E's" was a community hospital with a contract to teach Tufts Medical students in their 3rd and 4th years. Teach they did. The atmosphere at the hospital was friendly, doctors and nurses were eager to help. Although it was a major teaching hospital, there was no snobbish attitude that many people receive at some academic centers. It was more like a place, accepting of new ideas, without being elite. They were regular people treating regular people, with an attitude I liked. It was greatly different from BCH.

For a while, during my 4th year, I shared an apartment with a roommate, Bill Cook. It was in Brookline and had one bedroom and a living room. Bill and I were on opposite nights, so we only needed one bedroom. The kitchen was shared by several other renters. It would not have passed a health inspection. I invited Jan to come over to see my mini apartment, and to have appetizers there. Being the proper woman that she was, she insisted on having a chaperone. We invited Ollie and Wally Dunn to accompany Jan to my apartment. This was more than 50 years ago, and the world's morals have changed in that period of time. Most people that age now have never even heard of a chaperone.

Some of the clerkships gave us room and board, but others did not. One two or three month period, I had no place to stay so I called Jim Connell's mother in Winchester to ask if I could stay at her place. Jim was in the service then and she was very happy to have someone stay there with her. May 1957 finally came.

Graduation was held on the Medford campus. I was a Doctor of Medicine. It was very difficult to have to be away from Jan for a long time, but I got into my blue Ford which was checked out thoroughly by a mechanic and drove to Columbus Ohio. For what happened there, please read the chapter "A Year at Ohio State."

A summer on Marion Harbor

Between my 3rd and 4th year of Medical School, I answered an ad on a bulletin board for a summer job in Marion, MA. The job consisted of taking care of Francis C. Gray of Marlborough Street, Boston. Mr. Gray had been employed as a vice president of a major Boston bank. He was under 60 years of age, but he suffered from early senility. He required around-the-clock attendants. I was interviewed for the position by his wife, whose maiden name was Joy, for which Joy Street on Beacon Hill was named. She was a Catholic convert and become a member of the 3rd order of St. Francis which required her to wear a hair shirt under her clothes. She attended Catholic mass daily. Other than that I never became aware of her religious activities. By the way, the ad on the bulletin board was posted by the Catholic medical students association.

The house in Marion was partially in the harbor. The building had been severely damaged by a hurricane the previous summer. The Grays were able to restore it to its original condition. They even replaced several Currier and Ives originals which had been damaged by the high waters of the storm. The Currier and Ives prints were in the living room on the water side of the house. This room had a second-floor balcony which led to my bedroom allowing me to sleep over the water above Marion Harbor. Our next-door neighbors were the Taylor family, who owned the Boston Globe for several generations. They had a larger more elaborate house on the harbor. The Gray house was not elaborate, but very comfortable.

Mrs. Gray employed three people at the Marion house; an excellent chef named Rico, who also worked full-time at their Marlborough Street apartment. The apartment in Boston, on a corner of Marlborough Street, occupied the entire floor of a fairly large complex. Rico's food was simple but very well made and very tasty. She also employed a teenager as a general worker in the house, doing dishes, cleaning up, and serving meals. It became apparent that he was not reliable, and not a good worker. By mid-summer he was gone; therefore my assignments increased.

My job was basically to keep Mr. Gray out of trouble, i.e., not allowing him to fall off the porch, and into the harbor, and also not allowing him to wander off. I helped to get him dressed and to keep him clean up. My one "boo-boo" was losing him one day. Somehow he got out of my sight long enough to walk away. I found him wandering a short distance away. He told me that some pretty girls walked by the house, so he followed them. One day he and I were standing on the balcony looking down into the living room. He said to me "who is that beautiful girl down there?" It was his daughter. His brain may have been weak, but apparently, his male hormones remained strong.

After the teenager had been dismissed, I had an occasion to wait on tables. My most memorable time as a servant was serving Mrs. Gray's friend, Mrs. Saltonstall of the Boston Saltonstalls. Before this meal, Mrs. Gray instructed me in great detail as to which side to serve from, which side to take away the dishes from, etc. This was not quite "Upstairs, Downstairs" but along the same lines. There I was serving two women who were Brahmins of Boston (An article in a recent New England Journal described a Boston Brahman as tall and trim, kindly, bow-tied, seer suckered, and thoroughly Harvard). As I may have said before: "not bad for a child of a former shepherd from Portugal."

I worked six days a week at Marion harbor. On my day off, I drove to Cambridge City Hospital where I worked 7 pm to 7 am in the emergency room as an orderly. I have written a separate chapter of my experiences at Cambridge City – the place I met, fell in love, and eventually married Janice Anne Such, R.N. of Pawtucket RI.

Marion Harbor was filled with boats of various sizes. The boats were close enough that on my daily time off, while Mr. Gray slept, I would swim around the harbor going from boat to boat by myself. Mr. Gray and I would take many walks around town. It got me out of the house and got his circulation going. One of the best things I did for Mrs. Gray was picking up ice cream at the local shop that made its own ice cream. The ice cream was sold in returnable stainless steel containers, probably a quart in size. My job was to pick up the containers and put them in the freezer. The ice cream was great.

My blue Ford was very handy and drove well back and forth to Cambridge. On the way back, I would stop in Taunton to visit my parents once a week. The Gray's and their cook Rico returned to Marlborough Street for the winter. Mr. Gray was hale and physically healthy. He had not drowned under my care. I had no further contact with the Grays. Fourth-year medical school took up my entire life, after my interesting summer on Marion Harbor.

A Year at The Ohio State University Hospital

The Ohio State University Hospital, 1958

Buckeye Stadium

I got into my trusty blue Ford sedan, with a driver's side door that had been repaired and did not loosen or unscrew, and headed for Columbus Ohio, in June 1957. OSU Hospital was not my first choice in the Interns Matching Program, but I left Taunton with high hopes. I knew that both Dr. Zollinger (Dr. Z.) and Dr. Ellison were on the teaching staff at OSU. They made a name for themselves for describing the Zollinger-Ellison Syndrome, a disease involving the pancreas. I was privileged to work with both of them. University Hospital was a receiving center for referrals of complicated cases from many local hospitals in Ohio and West Virginia. We treated many people from the hills of Ohio and West Virginia – "hills people" were poor people with little education. I treated a patient who had no shoes and came to the hospital in stocking feet.

Our rotation as interns included a month in pediatrics, emergency medicine, hematology, cardiology, obstetrics, and general medicine. I also had a few months in surgical specialties and one month on Dr. Z's team. Dr. Z called me "broccoli." I don't think he ever learned my real name. My "broccoli" name came from the time Zollinger was working at Harvard Medical School. He told me that when he was working in Boston, he frequently drove to the Taunton area to buy fresh vegetables from farm stands. Apparently, he was a broccoli lover, so I became "broccoli" in his mind since I was from Taunton where he would buy fresh vegetables. Zollinger was one of the best-known surgeons in the world. His textbooks in surgery were used universally by residents and staff. The early editions were co-edited by Dr. Cutler. Two of my medical school classmates were from the Cutler family. They also went to OSU for their internships.

The later edition of the textbook was edited by Dr. Zollinger and his son and was called Zollinger and Zollinger. I had the privilege of working with his son during the summer. At that time he was a medical school student, and fortunately, he was very different from his father in personality. He was a nice person. His father was difficult to work with in my opinion.

His surgical ability was fabulous. He could operate on any organ with no difficulty. I certainly would have trusted him to operate on me. In fact, I became a patient of his. One day I wasn't feeling well and was in an elevator when he entered. He looked at me and said: "Broccoli, you look sick - I am admitting you to the hospital." I was running a high fever and a high white blood count due to an unknown infection which cleared well in a few days on antibiotics. I don't think we ever found the source of the problem. My question is: can physical and mental exhaustion cause this much illness? I was admitted to my own floor, and some of the people working there thought that I should do the history and physical paperwork, necessary to be admitted to the hospital!

Some memorable events with Dr. Zollinger come to mind. One day I was in an abdominal procedure, Zollinger asked me the name of a small, insignificant artery. I did not know the answer. His crazy response was to have me sit on a stool in the corner of the operating room, and recite nursery rhymes, like hickory, dickery, dock. On Zollinger's service, I was teamed-up with an intern from New York City, who was of Italian background and probably had a touch of a violent personality. On rounds with Dr. Z one morning, he was particularly insulting to Tony from New York. You have heard about Irish temper; Tony had an Italian temper. He was so upset that he was ready to attack Dr. Z, and choke him. I got between them and Tony relented. Does anyone have an extra horse's head? Remember the movie "The Godfather?"

Each night on Dr. Z's service, the intern on call had to phone him, precisely at 9 pm, and give him a report of all his patients on the floor. This had to be from memory, no shuffling of paper was allowed. One fateful night, I reported to Dr. Z. at 9 pm giving him lab results, patient's conditions, etc. I informed him that his patients were doing well, and our conversation ended peacefully. Within a minute or two after hanging up the phone, we heard a loud cry from one of Dr. Z's patients and found him dead in bed. 1958 was prior to CPR with chest compressions and mouth-to-mouth breathing, so no attempt at resuscitation was performed. He probably threw a blood clot to his lungs. Shaking in my boots, I called Dr. Z. back to inform him of the incident, He was not pleased, to say the least.

Let us change the subject; I am tired of Dr. Z. and his shenanigans. The first few months of internship, I lived in hospital housing. I had a small bedroom with bath, conveniently located on the hospital property. There was no air conditioning, but the previous occupant was nice enough to leave a great Vornado fan, an item absolutely necessary in the humid Ohio summer. Later in the year, I rented a small apartment with a fellow intern, Dr. Stan Stern. We were on opposite shifts, so essentially we had the place to ourselves. The apartment had a small living room and another room with twin beds on either side of the room. There was a tiny kitchen and a stairway going up to nowhere. The toilet and shower facility were in the basement, wide open with no privacy. The rent was quite cheap, and it was apparent we were not in luxurious surroundings. We had a couple of parties there with other interns. The most popular area in the apartment was the bizarre open bathroom in the basement. The house was on Chittenden Street in the middle of the OSU campus. It was comfortable and in a convenient location, just minutes from the hospital.

Since the hospital had not filled its internship program through the Interns' Matching Plan, at times, we were required to work to the point of not being able to function. Every other night call became two nights on and one night off, starting at 5 pm on certain rotations. There was just enough down time to eat supper and go to bed for some sorely needed sleep. I was on that ridiculous schedule during my obstetrics rotation. Obstetrics was very busy, so we got little rest on two consecutive nights on duty. In this state of exhaustion one night, I delivered a baby without any problem, but a problem arose because I had no recollection of the delivery. When one of the nurses asked if I had dictated the operative delivery notes, I was befuddled. Another faux pas of mine was that I sent a patient home, telling her that she was not in active labor. By the time she got to the elevator, it was obvious that she was close to delivering. The delivery was unremarkable. Would you say that "all work and no play" wasn't good for the intern or the patient?

I worked one month at the Columbus Children's Hospital which was a major referral center for hydrocephalic babies (babies who have excessive spinal fluid, surrounding their brain). We had about ten children with this condition. It was very depressing to see them all in one room. It should be noted that their heads were so big they could not lift them. This was during a period prior to the development of the shunt which takes spinal fluid from the head and puts it in the abdomen, where it is absorbed. One of our assignments for treating these children was to aspirate the fluid, using large syringes, therefore reducing the pressure on the brain. Unfortunately, no definitive treatments were available for this condition. These children eventually succumbed to the problem. Children born now with congenital hydrocephalus, and adults who develop it, can live relatively normal lives with a shunt. Children with congenital hydrocephalus continue to have larger heads than those without it, even after shunting.

My most interesting case at Children's Hospital came in the Emergency Room. One Saturday, when I was on call, I received a radio message from an ambulance driver who said he was en route with a child with a head injury. No specifics were given over the radio. On the patient's arrival, I saw a young boy, probably about six years old, lying on the stretcher conscious and alert, with a curtain rod sticking out of his forehead. Again, we are talking about 1957-1958, at that time there were no CT scans or MRIs. With these scans, we could have found out exactly where the curtain rod was situated in the brain. The scans could also clarify the condition of the brain. By the way, the accident happened while the boy was watching his father mow the lawn with a rotary mower. The mower picked up the curtain rod, which became a missile and embedded itself into the middle of his forehead, and into his brain. It was very scary to watch him move his head and to see the curtain rod move as well. The case was turned over to a neurosurgeon that cut the rod off at the skin level until additional testing could be done. Several years later the case was reported in a surgical journal. The rod was in the sagittal sinus (a fluid filled cavity). It did not involve any blood vessels or brain tissue and was eventually removed with no obvious damage to the boy's brain.

Let's move on to lighter topics, football, and basketball at OSU. As interns, we were on the Medical School faculty and as such could buy season tickets for $35.00 for OSU football and basketball. Unless you have lived in Columbus, Ohio, you may not be able to understand the hysteria that goes along with football in the city. My seats were at the 35-yard line about twelve rows up, a fantastic location to watch the game. The seats were so good that I sat about fifteen feet away from Richard M. Nixon when he visited Columbus. Every seat in the horseshoe-shaped stadium was filled. Local radio stations, on Saturdays, did public relations announcements stating the availability of seats from a ticket holder who was unable to attend the game. All they had to do was call the holder of the ticket to buy it from them at regular prices.

The city was virtually shut down for OSU football games. Little to no movement was evident except at the stadium. I attended all but one home game. For that game, I was part of the skeleton crew on duty. Just as in the city, little activity occurred in the hospital. This was before the availability of cell phones and pagers. We developed a communication system as follows – certain windows facing the open ended stadium were designated to be used if additional medical help was needed at the hospital. The hanging of a white sheet out of a specific window was "SOS at OSU" on football day. Interns and residents knew which window to use as a call for help. I did not have to hang a sheet on my day on call, thank God.

Basketball was also a big deal at OSU. The arena had no obstructing columns. Compare that to the old Boston Garden which had many partial view seats. I attended only a few games of basketball during that season.

There was a splendid event that occurred in September of 1957, Janice Such visited me! It was a very proper visit with arrangements made for Jan to stay with Jack and Naomi Gold. Jack was one of my medical school classmates. Pre-marital dalliances were not the norm. Jan and I had a wonderful time, we visited the Columbus Rose Garden, had meals with the Gold's, and I showed her the muddy Scioto river, the closest body of water we had to the Atlantic Ocean. Jan's visit was short but was just what I needed. It also helped solidify our future together.

Columbus, was not like Boston, with its many attractions, theaters, music, and great restaurants. Talking about restaurants, a group of us went to the Jewish deli with a visiting Jewish family. The food was very good and generous, but you know me, I have to have dessert. I was the only one to have the cheesecake; everyone else was too full. What a mistake! I got severe GI symptoms - abdominal pain, vomiting, and diarrhea. There I was on the cement floor of the cellar bathroom, not knowing which end would erupt. Symptoms were bad enough that I was disabled for a couple of days.

I did visit the Ohio State Fair which was one of the biggest things in Columbus aside from OSU football. It was a lot of fun - as the movie song says "My State Fair is the Best State Fair." We went to occasional movies. We saw Victor Borge with free tickets. They were unable to sell out the house for Victor Borge, so they came to OSU and distributed tickets to anyone who would attend the program. I also got free tickets to a ballet program. It was the first time I attended a ballet without a live orchestra. It was performed to pre-recorded music.

One of our orderlies was a middle-aged black man who was very friendly. A group of us were talking with him one day, and he invited us to go to some of the small jazz clubs in Columbus that catered mostly to blacks. We took him up on the offer and went to two different clubs in rather shady locations. Neither club would serve us – we ended up returning home with a feeling of reverse discrimination. A couple of times, we went to dinner in downtown Columbus restaurants which were mostly empty but had "reserved" signs at every table. These signs were placed there to keep blacks out of the restaurant.

One of the highlights of the year was when Joe, one of our interns, was married in Cincinnati Ohio. He was a Jewish boy from N.Y. City who married a Christian in a Christian service. The wedding was held without the knowledge of Joe's family. We had a great time in Cincinnati and were glad for Joe and his wife. At the end of the internship, Joe and his wife planned to go back to N.Y. City and have a proper Jewish wedding.

A group of interns got together to form the IBC, the "Intern's Bitching Committee," and not the root beer IBC. As you may have probably figured out, our intern class was not happy with OSU hospital. As a result of this dissatisfaction, the interns got together to bitch about the conditions of their employment. We bitched about the hours we worked, about our salaries of $125 per month, the lack of cafeteria vouchers, and the way we were treated in general. The administration appeared to get the message, so perhaps some good came from our unhappiness. We hoped that future internship classes were treated more fairly. No changes occurred in any OSU policy based on the IBC during my time in Columbus.

Ollie Roth was a fourth-year student at the medical school. He was in his thirties, was married, and had two children. He was one of my medical students for a month, and we got along very well, to the point that he started inviting me to the Friday night Jewish supper at his home. Typically, chicken was served for dinner on Friday night. Obviously, the Roth's had very little money with two children, only his wife working, and medical school tuition to pay. Despite that, they bought fish for me every Friday, in order to not insult my Catholic customs. At that time it was a sin to eat meat on Friday; this rule has since been eliminated from Catholic doctrine. By inviting me, you might say that the Roth's were acting the way Christians should act. I certainly enjoyed a home cooked meal once in a while.

Talking about food, who knew one could survive eating mostly brownies? My mother's brownies were not world famous, but they were famous at OSU Hospital. My family had a neighbor, John Schondek, who was the Taunton Postmaster. He was very helpful in getting brownies to me at OSU. He would pick up the box of six dozen or so large brownies on his way to work. Somehow he facilitated delivery to Columbus Ohio within a two day period. The brownies arrived fresh and delicious. Brownie day at OSU was a treat for all of the house staff to glory in. Deliveries were at least once a month. For people who were making $125 per month, and who had to pay for room and board on that salary, the brownies were a great boost for their morale.

One of our interns was Jack Collins from Collinsville GA. I got the impression that Jack's family was very prominent in that town and maybe owned most of it. Jack was a real gentleman, with no airs of importance about him. I think it was safe to say he was a "southern gentleman." He was as unhappy at the OSU program as I was. He and I left Columbus June 29th, 1958, never to return. Jack went to the Brigham for a residency in surgery, and I went to St. Elizabeth's Hospital, Boston for mine. He became one of the most prominent surgeons in Boston, on the forefront of many improvements in cardiac surgical techniques. He was appointed Chief of Cardiovascular Surgery and was considered one of the best heart surgeons in the country. I spoke to several Boston surgeons who said he was a great surgeon, a great person, and a real gentleman.

Next, you will be exposed to my training at St. Elizabeth's, a much more receptive environment to work in, compared to Ohio State University Hospital.

Surgical Residency at St. Elizabeth's Hospital of Boston

I returned to Boston after a year at Ohio State University Hospital to start a residency at St. Elizabeth's Hospital. I had done clerkships there during medical school and liked the feeling of working in a smaller, friendlier, and more comfortable environment. In the next chapter, I have written "Heart Stories in the 50s and 60s," specifically about mitral valve surgery, and about "cracking open" chests in patients suffering from cardiac arrest. This chapter is about the daily workings of a resident at the hospital.

Dr. John Spellman was Chief of Surgery during my first three years, and Dr. Richard Stanton became Chief for my fourth year of residency. As residents, we were members of the faculty at Tufts Medical School, teaching students who made morning rounds with us and were allowed to view some operations. About one-third of Tufts' third-year medical students rotated through our service annually. During my first year of residency, I assisted on many operative procedures. I was also allowed to perform some less complicated operations at the discretion of an attending surgeon.

My first surgical case was a 100-year-old woman. Unfortunately, she had developed gangrene of her lower leg that required a below-the-knee amputation. The procedure was explained to her in detail, and she was in agreement with it. She seemed to understand what would be done. However, her attitude changed when she was fully recovered from anesthesia. She became aware of the amputation and decided she did not want to live anymore, without the use of both of her legs. She stopped eating and passed away quietly in the weeks that followed. Thankfully, my future operative results were better than this troubling first operation.

Senior residents, especially Dr. Sam Gargano and his sidekick, Frank DeLuca, were both very helpful to me. As my exposure to the variety of operations performed at St. E's increased, I was allowed to do many procedures on patients, while assisted and supervised by attending physicians in private practice. Our rotations were in all fields of surgery – general surgery, thoracic, orthopedic, vascular, urology, thyroid, head and neck, and gynecologic surgery made up the gamut of what was considered surgical training in that era. The chief resident assigned cases and was usually fair with his choice of assistants. For six months in my second year of residency, Dr. Spellman assigned me to the pathology service. Dr. Spellman felt that surgeons should know the differences between healthy tissue and diseased tissue. To learn this, one had to work in an anatomic laboratory to see, feel, and examine specimens submitted for diagnosis. During this six month period, I examined thousands of specimens, describing them in detail. The first exam was the evaluation called "the gross specimen." A portion of the specimen was then placed in a machine for complex processing of the tissue, resulting in it being placed in paraffin and dyes applied to the tissue, which was then sliced very thinly. This thin specimen was then studied under a microscope. The final diagnosis was made by microscopically evaluating the cells. Was it cancer? Was it inflammation? Scarring? All reports were transcribed from taped recordings. The final diagnosis was made by the two pathologists on staff. As I became more experienced, my diagnosis was rarely questioned by the pathologists.

There is a humorous story about one of the pathologists who was of French heritage. Each summer while in school, he accompanied his mother to France, staying with relatives. Each year, he looked forward to a special meal in his favorite restaurant. He relished ordering the same entrée repeatedly. However, in his teen years, he was made aware of the ingredients in the meal. It was calves testicles! On finding that out, he stopped eating his favorite French meal.

During the pathology rotation, I performed more than ten autopsies. I remember taking Jan with me one night, to help with the procedure. One or two autopsies were enough for her! I found that examining the brain was the most unpleasant part of the autopsy. This required making forehead flaps and scalp flaps to allow for a portion of the skull to be removed in order to access and remove the brain. These procedures had to be performed in a way that no evidence of an autopsy would be visible on viewing the body, at an open-casket wake.

Eli Thomas and I were the two residents at our level. Eli and I were sent as senior residents to the Quigley Memorial Hospital at the Chelsea Soldier's Home for one year. In my third year I was Senior Resident in Surgery at St. E's – a position usually held for a fourth-year resident. The spot was given to me because there was no fourth-year resident in the program. I was fortunate to have some very good interns and residents under my guidance. They included Phil McCarthy, Dick McCarthy, Arthur Veno and Bob Oishi, all of whom did a superb job assisting the doctors on staff and me.

My fourth year of training was at Quigley Memorial Hospital, an institution operated by the Commonwealth of Massachusetts. It housed, free of charge in dormitory rooms, any service veteran. There was also a section of the hospital to assist veterans who required medical care. It was the Massachusetts' version of a Veteran's Administration Hospital. Surgery at Quigley Memorial was free for military veterans from Massachusetts. We also treated many patients who were not indigent. They were business owners, politicians, lawyers, etc. This surprised me since many of these people had private insurance.

At the hospital, we ran clinics for evaluating and treating non-surgical patients as well. We did a variety of major and minor surgeries in the operating rooms. Considering the age of some of the patients (men in their seventies to nineties), our results were highly satisfactory. Postoperative complications and deaths were consistent with general hospital statistics. Our anesthesiologist had vast experience in surgery of the elderly. We also had a very competent visiting, attending staff, and nursing staff.

I want to tell you a story and let's call it "where did he get the alcohol?" There was a middle-aged patient on the ward who became intoxicated frequently. He baffled us because there was no way he could have left the hospital to buy alcohol. This was a clever alcoholic, who perplexed the nursing staff. A close watch was put on the patient to try and determine the source of the spirits. He frequently received baskets of fruit with many oranges, and he ate a lot of oranges. Further investigation revealed the culprit – the oranges were injected with vodka. His many friends, who often visited the hospital, pulled the wool over our eyes! Very clever!

In the operating room, we were often revolted by a strong garlic odor. The culprit was one of our junior residents, from another teaching hospital. He was of Indian background, and his diet was rich in garlic. Apparently, some people, more than others, exude the odor of garlic through their skin pores. When questioned he always said: "I eat garlic at every meal, every night!" Another mystery solved.

At Quigley Memorial, there was a slower pace of activity, compared to the hustle and bustle of a large metropolitan hospital like St. Elizabeth's. The year at Quigley was very productive and resulted in a considerable increase in my surgical abilities and my confidence when performing surgery.

I have a few short stories about St. E's that I would like to share with you.

At 7:30 am weekdays, Cardinal Cushing was on the radio reciting the rosary. At that time, patients were being prepared for surgery. The rosary was piped into the entire hospital and was even broadcast in the operating room. Some of the patients were waiting to be put under anesthesia during the radio broadcast. I still can't figure out whether these prayers were helpful for the patients, or resulted in unnecessary anxiety. The Cardinal had a gravel voice due to many medical problems with his throat. He was often hospitalized and stayed in the "Cardinal's Suite." My Chief of Surgery, Dr. Spellman, brother of Cardinal Spellman of New York, made a courtesy visit to Cardinal Cushing every day that he was an inpatient. It is a Catholic custom to greet a Cardinal by bowing and kissing his ring. Each time we tried to kiss his ring, he would wave away our attempt to do it.

Some humorous things occurred at St. E's that made working there even more interesting. I was sharing a room with Gene Sweeney (OB/GYN) in the intern's quarters. Since we were on alternate nights, we did not see much of each other. There seemed to be a problem with the heat in our room. On further investigation, there was a definite problem. One of the house staff had lost his pet. When the maintenance man removed the radiator cover, he found the solution to the problem. There was a live boa constrictor a few feet long in the radiator – it was not a danger to Gene Sweeney or me, but caused me some apprehension after I found about it. With the boa removed and the heating system checked, I felt more relaxed. My "on call" nights were easier to deal with.

I must tell you about Sister Catherine's closet. It was a closet that was felt to have a magical ability to repair surgical instrument. Sister Catherine was the nun in charge of the supplies for the operating room, and for instruments in need of repair. When instruments were given to her for repairs, some were placed in the closet, and many never left the closet for repairs. Instruments from the closet reappeared on the operating room table, allegedly repaired! At Falmouth Hospital, when an instrument is not working correctly, I jokingly suggest it be placed in Sr. Catherine's closet! My comments result in questioning stares. Since many surgical instruments we now use are disposable - there is little need for magical repairs.

One of our nuns was a very good salesperson. She walked around the hospital selling green scapulars (a green cloth badge bearing a religious icon which is worn under clothing). She would approach me on a frequent basis with the same question, with her lovely Irish brogue – "surely doctor do you have a green scapular?" I had many green scapulars because I had a problem refusing this wonderful lady. There should be more nuns like her!

One story that I must relate involves a gift that I gave to my future wife, Janice, for Christmas in 1958. I was trying to find a good joke gift for her. I knew she would be getting many nice things in preparation for our marriage in April 1959. A light bulb went off above my head - what about a diamond ring? Taunton still had an F.W. Woolworth Store. I went to the jewelry section of the

Five and Dime, walked up to the counter and asked to see their largest diamond rings. I think the female clerk thought that she was dealing with some loony bird. She brought out a tray of "diamonds" for my approval. I chose the one that was at least 3 1/2 carats; the finger size was not important since all the rings were adjustable. I placed the ring in a beautiful ring box and gave it to Jan on Christmas Eve. With the Christmas lights reflecting on it, it could have been real! For a second she looked at it, realizing that I could not afford anything that colossal, we both burst into laughter. I promised her that by our 10th wedding anniversary she would choose a real, good-size diamond. I kept my promise.

We had a Christmas dance in the interns' quarters. Jan wore the ring proudly. It looked real with all the colored tree lights reflecting on it. Several people noticed the ring. Necks almost snapped to get a good look at it. No one actually said anything about it that night. The next day, comments were heard like "I didn't know Gouveia had money!" "Did you see the rock on Jan's finger!" It was the best three dollars I've ever spent!

I returned to St. Elizabeth's from Chelsea Soldier's Home for the last two months of my residency. Eli Thomas and I shared the chief residency position for that period. I was honored to be an assistant on a procedure by Joseph E. Murray, a medical doctor and plastic surgeon. Dr. Murray received the Nobel Prize in Physiology or Medicine in 1990 for his contribution in the field of human organ transplantation. His team completed the first-ever human organ transplantation on December 23rd, 1954. This kidney transplant was between identical twins. Five years later, the first fraternal twin kidney transplant was performed. There now seems to be no end to what can be transplanted, even a human face has been successfully transplanted. Dr. Murray pioneered a revolution in surgery.

A few days before leaving Boston, Jan and I went to Anthony's Pier 4 Restaurant to celebrate the completion of my residency. At the next table to us was a young couple, whose conversation we could easily overhear. We found it quite humorous that the young man had graduated from medical school and would be starting his internship shortly. Their conversation was about his starting at the hospital. He was worried that he would be given assignments that he was not capable of doing. His companion continually tried to calm him by making statements that Jan and I found humorous – "they won't have you working right away, they won't give you complicated patients at first, and they will go easy on you for a few weeks." In my opinion, all these statements, although encouraging were far from the truth.

July 1, any year, is not a good day to need hospital or emergency room care. Studies have shown that medical care administered in early July tends to be of lesser quality compared to that given the rest of the year. The poor boy at the next table did not know what he was getting into. I silently wished him success in whatever field he chose to pursue. After four years of surgical studies and training, I was ready to leave Boston, on June 30, 1962, with the confidence to assume the position of Chief of Surgery US Army Hospital, Fort Stewart Georgia.

Heart Stories from the 1950s and 1960s

I saw a male patient, aged about 50, with some nonspecific symptoms at my office. These symptoms seemed serious enough that I felt an evaluation of them was in order. I arranged for a battery of blood tests, an x-ray and electrocardiogram. The next day while on the ground floor of the hospital, I said hello to the patient. He looked very sick, so I suggested that he go immediately to the emergency room, which was just a few yards away. It was fortuitous that I should see him in the corridor. On arrival in the emergency room, he collapsed and was in ventricular fibrillation (heart beats so rapid and irregular that the blood pumping mechanisms of the heart cannot function).

Morton Hospital had recently purchased a new device designed by Dr. Zoll of Beth Israel Hospital in Boston. This device, called a defibrillator, could shock the heart electrically, and hopefully, return the heart rhythm to normal. The hospital staff and I diagnosed ventricular fibrillation on the electrocardiogram. We prepared to defibrillate the patient. The defibrillator had never been used at Morton. The paddles carrying the shock were placed on the chest, and the mechanism was activated. To our surprise, the machine blew up and was actually in flames.

Fortunately, the one shock to the heart worked, and the patient's heart rhythm converted to a regular rate. No doubt you have seen numerous uses of the defibrillator on medical TV shows. It is often necessary to shock the heart more than once before normal rhythm occurs. In this case, a repeat shock would not have been possible, since our only defibrillator blew up.

I assume that we got a "lemon" for a defibrillator. I certainly don't think that this was a common problem. Many changes have been incorporated in defibrillators since then. They are now compact and portable and are common in all airports, malls, schools, churches and other public places. The revised software in them makes them more efficient and easier to use.

The whole history of the treatment of cardiac disease has changed dramatically since the episode above. We now have implantable pacemakers with the ability to shock the heart as necessary, without any patient involvement. These implantable devices are powered by batteries with a very long lifespan, rarely needing replacement. The development of pumps to replace heart functions has been dramatic. The original pumps were the size of rooms, and the patient was unable to leave the room. The pumps now available are portable. The bionic man is now a possibility.

In an unrelated story, one of our older neighbors was out driving with his wife. A cardiac problem occurred causing him to lose consciousness. His car went off the road and hit a tree (this was before the invention of airbags). He hit his chest on the steering wheel with enough force to get his heart beating normally again. He was very happy to tell people that he was dead, but was revived by his steering wheel, which brought him back to life, with a forceful bang. In the hospital, it is common to bang the chest forcefully to try and get the heart beating normally, before doing electric defibrillation.

Let us talk about sudden cardiac death at St. Elizabeth's Hospital in the 50s and 60s. Hospitals were equipped with what was called a "code cart" which was rushed to the patient's room in response to "Code Red." "Code Red" was announced over the public announcement system and was answered by doctors from all specialties. The crash cart or code cart was equipped with IV fluids, IV adrenaline, atropine, and other cardiac drugs. Also on the cart was a surgical kit that included instruments to open the chest, allowing a responder to open the chest, and manually massage the heart in an attempt to restore cardiac function.

I made a few attempts to resume heart function. They were gory, to say the least. The procedure was as follows: we made an incision in the left anterior chest, the ribs were spread open and held in place by a self-retaining retractor. The hand and forearm were inserted into the chest cavity, and the heart was squeezed in a way to resemble a normal heartbeat. Unfortunately, most of the patients who underwent this procedure did not fare well. Some resumed a heartbeat for a short time but, none of the cases I reviewed left the hospital alive.

A new technique was being studied which appeared to be a better solution. It was obvious that opening the chest was not the answer to the problem. CPR – cardio pulmonary resuscitation quickly became the standard method of attempting to revive the patient. CPR has been very successful and is practiced throughout the world.

One other heart story that is worth telling – In the days prior to the availability of extracorporeal pumps, (pumps that replace the heart function) some heart surgery was performed on the beating heart, mostly for narrowing or thickening of the mitral valve (mitral stenosis). If the leaves of the mitral valve have fused or have calcified, the heart cannot pump blood efficiently.

On the two patients I operated on for mitral stenosis, the procedure was as follows: The chest was opened under general anesthesia. The lining of the heart (pericardium) was opened. A circumferential silk suture was applied to the ventricle of the heart. An incision big enough to insert a finger was created. The insertion had to be quick, or the surgeon would be bathed in blood. On the inserted finger was a surgical blade held by a metal band. The surgeon did not wear a glove because full finger sensitivity was essential. Using the finger, the valve was identified, and an incision was made in the valve to allow for better function.

The assistant surgeon tightened the suture as the surgeon removed his finger from the heart. Although this may appear to the reader as a rather primitive approach to a heart problem, many patients did well after the procedure. In the current period, valve replacements are mostly done by chemically stopping the heart and replacing the heart function with a mechanical pump. Long-term results are excellent with this procedure. Other new treatments have been developed in valvular disease that does not require a major surgical operation. Veins or arteries of the extremities are used for access to the valve, thus eliminating an open surgical operation.

Heart surgeons can also perform minimally invasive procedures to repair or replace a valve without stopping the heart. Long-term results are generally good with whatever procedure the sergeon performs.

The Adventures of Captain Gouveia

We bought our dog, Captain, in Georgia on the same day that our friends, the Cohen's, bought their dog. Captain was a Dalmatian with beautiful markings. He was the son of Hup Two, a neighbor's dog, who was a frequent visitor to our home. Hup Two lived behind us and came over many times to be petted by me.

His admiration of me came to an abrupt halt when we purchased Captain. He became very jealous of Captain. His jealousy culminated in his lifting his leg and urinating on me. Thankfully, he stopped visiting our house after that behavior. Hup Two was far from a Southern gentleman! Both Captain, the dog, and I were called Captain Gouveia. This moniker resulted in some surprised expressions at gatherings. Captain was a popular dog in the neighborhood and was talked about at parties. The funniest thing I heard about him was when someone was discussing a problem with her bushes because of dogs urinating on them. One girl said "you must be kidding" when she heard that Captain Gouveia urinated on her roses. She thought that I was the one who did the damage!

During our two-year stay at Fort Stewart, we returned to New England a few times. On Captain's first trip north in November, it had snowed in the Virginia area. A true southern gentleman, Captain had never seen snow and did not know it existed. We stopped to refresh ourselves, and eat something. Captain got out of the car. He stepped into the snow and started jumping around, unhappy with what he found on the ground. He returned to our blue Rambler station wagon without doing any bodily functions. I guess the snow was too cold for his sensitive Georgian paws.

Captain had a problem with motion sickness but responded well to Phenergan (an oral medicine used for nausea). It was funny to listen to the children tell us that it was time for a dose of "feganin" when Captain looked like he was going to get sick. We still chuckle at the word feganin!

Our first house in Taunton was at 252 Winthrop St., and our back yard was at the dead-end turnaround at Davenport Terrace. Our children used the turnaround as a playground, as did other children of similar age in the neighborhood. Captain was with the children at all times. This was a time when dogs were allowed to roam free, without a leash. We felt comfortable because Captain was very protective of all of the children playing in the circle.

Captain was not neutered. This led to some humorous situations with neighboring dogs of the female persuasion. More than once, we received calls from neighbors whose dogs were in heat. The funniest call came from a neighbor who had columns on his porch. Captain was trying to climb the columns to get to the 2nd floor where their dog was in heat. It was said that the howling from both dogs was frightening. Why couldn't we control our dog? I guess the hormones took over.

Perhaps the best Captain story involves the Brockton Public Market which was a supermarket, a short distance down Winthrop Street. Dr. Bill Donohue's dog and our dog were very familiar with the BPM. They would go down to the grocery store, step on the automatic door opener, and proceed to the meat department begging for meat. More than once we received a call from the BPM to come down to the store to pick up Captain. I don't know which he preferred, choice or prime cuts of beef.

On July 4th, 1976, the United States celebrated its Bicentennial. Sadly, that was the day Captain died. He was around 12 years old. He was hit by a vehicle and crawled into a neighbor's barn. The neighbor heard his cries and went to the barn to find him dying of serious injuries. I still get tearful when I think of him passing away under such conditions. He was the best dog and impossible to replace. He was considered a member of our family for so many years.

The Cuban Missile Crisis

In October 1962, the world almost came to an end. If a war had started, there would be no stopping the atom bombs. I was intimately involved in the Cuban Missile Crisis.

Fifty years have passed. In commemoration of the Cuban Missile Crisis, the media has been full of stories in print and on TV. One very enlightening program was on PBS. What a revelation! Although I lived through thirteen days of the crisis, I was not aware of many of the situations that occurred. Some of the information that I learned was astonishing. The United States of America was in considerable danger, much more than I was told at Fort Stewart. Fort Stewart was the closest army base to Cuba. Atomic bombs could be deployed to our area!

My first knowledge of the crisis occurred on a telephone call from my commanding Colonel; as Chief of Surgery, I was told to expand our twenty to forty-bed hospital into a two hundred-bed hospital overnight. No explanation for the sudden expansion was given to me by my superior officers. Increasing the hospital size was possible because each building in the complex had twenty beds, so ten units were opened to accommodate the request. The individual buildings in the complex were connected by long corridors.

The next morning we were told that our small army post was expanding to 20,000 troops!!! Troops from many other areas were brought into Fort Stewart by car, truck, airplanes, and helicopters. This was probably one of the largest overnight deployment of Army personnel in history. The new troops were housed in tents and old buildings which had not been used for years.

This activity was the result of the USA finding silos with Russian missiles in spy plane photos of Cuba. The missiles were placed in Cuba with the approval of Nikita Khrushchev, who thought they would not be discovered by the USA.

I haven't mentioned that I was ordered to pack my duffle bag, and to be prepared to get on a train going to Florida. It was said that the train had so many cars that it extended from Georgia to somewhere in Florida. There was a problem with my being given orders to be ready to go to Cuba as a thoracic surgeon. I was the only trained surgeon at Fort Stewart. A phone call was made to my commanding officer, who realized that he would have a problem delivering medical care without me on the post. Within a short period, my orders were canceled.

Thus started the most dangerous 13 days in the history of our country, and maybe in the history of humanity. President John F. Kennedy was well aware of the possibility that a nuclear war was imminent.

Khrushchev thought that Kennedy did not have the "balls" to do anything about the missiles. The potency of these nuclear warheads was seventy to one hundred and forty times that of the A-Bombs dropped on Japan. Castro knew that Cuba would be decimated if war occurred, but he was willing to sacrifice Cuba if Russia would attack the USA.

Russia drew blood first by shooting down a US (U2) plane that was mistakenly flying over Russian territory. The US military power was felt to have weakened after the defeat at the Bay of Pigs, allowing Russia to think that we would not retaliate. They were wrong.

On October 24th, a naval blockade of Cuba was ordered by Pres. Kennedy. The Russian ships and submarines, armed with nuclear warheads, were blocked. The Russian ships and submarines turned around at the orders of Khrushchev.

A word about communication in 1962. Satellite communication was not available. Telegram by Western Union could take up to 12 hours to be processed and sent. Discussions between Russia and the US were very difficult. Eventually, Pres. Kennedy agreed to avoid war by secretly removing US missiles in Turkey, near the Russian border. In exchange for this removal, the missiles in Cuba were removed by Russia. Nuclear war was averted.

Now that you know the history of this problem, I can return to my activities at Fort Stewart during the crisis.

Our hospital became quite busy with the influx of thousands of potential patients. Several serious accidents kept us busy. The most horrible accident resulted in the death of a soldier. He was directing a tank while standing behind it. The tank driver was not experienced and failed to stop when signaled to do so, resulting in the soldier being crushed.

Fort Stewart adapted well to its newly arrived individuals. However, on their first day, we did not have sufficient tableware for 20,000 people. All readily available forks, spoons, and knives were purchased from wholesale distributors in Savannah to alleviate the problem.

At the end of the crisis, battalions, little by little, left us and returned home safely. Talking about safety, Sandy Cohen called Jan at the start of the crisis and asked if she was considering returning to the Northeast with the children. Our opinion was that if the attacks happened, they would occur in highly populated cities like New York, Boston, and Washington, D.C. We waited out the situation. In the PBS show, one of the upper-level personnel called his wife with a message that if he should call again, she should immediately drive their family to the Midwest, where he felt they would be safe. There was great joy at "Camp Swampy" when the news came that the crisis had been averted.

A short time later, President Kennedy visited us to thank us for the extraordinary work we did during the crisis at our base. He spoke at the tank field and was driven around the complex in an open top car. Unfortunately, I was unable to see him. By the time I finished rounds at the hospital, all activity on the roads including walking was forbidden. In the distance though, I thought a caught a glimpse of J.F.K.

On that awful day in November, President Kennedy was shot in Dallas. Everyone seems to remember what they were doing at that particular moment in time. I happened to be on the phone with a representative from Merrill Lynch, who had just received word that the President had been shot. This was a few moments before it was announced to the public as a whole. His recommendation was not to buy any securities at the time until things settled down.

As I sat there in shock at the news, my mind flashed back to the day President Kennedy visited Fort Stewart. What if he had been shot then when visiting Fort Stewart? How would our hospital handle the situation? Would I be capable of handling such a serious injury? Thankfully the President was safe that day.

A short time later I was informed by the Post Commander that I would be awarded the Army Commendation Medal for my efforts during the Cuban Missile Crisis.

Civil Rights

I recently saw the Academy Award winning movie, Lee Daniels' "The Butler" (12 Years a Slave), which is a true story of the life of Cecil Gaines who was a butler to Presidents Eisenhower, Nixon, Regan, Carter, Kennedy, Johnson, and Ford. Some of the events during the Civil Rights Movement by blacks, and the resistance by segregationists were depicted with the use of archival news clips of the period. Tim Miller, a movie critic for the Cape Cod Times, wrote: "the film provides a mini-history lesson of what was going on in America from the late 50s to the present." The couple who accompanied us to the movie was in total agreement with that statement.

An early scene in the movie depicted Cecil Gaines' mother being forced into a building where she was raped by the white land owner. The setting was in a field where blacks were picking cotton, and witnessing the event. A black man (Gaines' father?) confronted the landowner who performed the act. He was killed with a gunshot to the head immediately. White men in the South were rarely accused of an illegal act by the police, as occurred in this case.

Having lived in southeast Georgia for two years (1962-1964) during part of the civil rights movement, I was reminded of stories that I heard in conversation with local blacks about everyday experiences they were subjected to.

Negroes were poorly paid. We had a very nice cleaning woman named Velma. She was with a group of women who were driven weekly from their homes, in the back of an open truck, and dropped off at their homes of employment at Fort Stewart.

Some maids were paid $4 for a day's work. We were paying Velma $5 a day. Velma was an honest, clear-thinking person. Since we were "Yankees" from the North, she was able to speak frankly about her life, and what it was like to be raised and grow up black in the deep south. She was not a radical, but she was in agreement with civil rights movement. Jan and Velma had many discussions about social problems. I was at the hospital most of the day, so my information came from Jan.

One important comment from Velma was that if she thought her children would be subjected to the discrimination that she endured since birth, she wasn't sure if their lives would be worth living. She told the story of a Negro man who was captured and wrapped in heavy chain. He was thrown into a river to drown. His captives were heard saying "ain't that just like a nigger to steal more chain than he can carry?"

Blacks at that time went to segregated, inferior schools. They were not allowed in white restaurants. There were separate public bathrooms from whites and blacks, marked "white" or "colored." Drinking fountains were also marked that way.

The director of the laboratory at Fort Stewart was a well-educated black man. His wife had a Master's Degree from Boston University. We were very cordial to them and welcomed them to our house. One day they told us they were going on vacation to a mid-western state. That would normally be a two-day trip with an overnight stay in a motel. They, however, were driving straight through. I asked them why not stop overnight? The answer shocked me – because of the color of their skin, they could not find suitable accommodations due to the unwritten rule of "No Blacks Allowed."

During my internship at Ohio State, I occasionally had enough money to go out to a nice restaurant. Many times, only a few diners were seated in the restaurant, but all of the tables had a "reserved" sign on them. No blacks were allowed as customers, they were not accepted.

As I mentioned earlier in the chapter on OSU, I was a victim of reverse discrimination in Columbus Ohio. One of our hospital orderlies was a very likable black man. One day we were talking about some jazz clubs that catered mostly to blacks. He thought it was a good idea that a few of us join him at one of the clubs. One Saturday night, we all went out to a club, sat down, and waited to be served. Unfortunately, we were not asked what we would like to drink or eat. Our table was totally ignored by the servers at the club. Our host apologized for the inconvenience. We got up and left, now understanding what it felt like to be a black man in a white man's world.

It is now over 50 years since the March on Washington and Martin Luther King's "I Have a Dream" speech. A half century after the freedom movement overcame the Jim Crow system, prejudice still remains. Freedom is still limited by a criminal justice system that jails blacks at a higher rate than whites for similar offenses. The freedom movement has evolved into a situation in which large segments of the black community are imprisoned, or on parole. There remains a longing for the day when we can say that "All Men are Created Equal."

In 1962, my wife Janice went on a shopping trip to Savannah, one hour drive from Fort Stewart. She was accompanied by a friend who was in her 9th month of pregnancy. A pleasant day of shopping was interrupted by a civil rights demonstration. Jan, her friend, and Susan and David stopped for lunch at a very popular cafeteria named Morrison's in downtown Savannah.

After eating they were unable to leave through the front door. The exit was blocked by civil rights demonstrators who were lying on the sidewalk and obstructing the doorway. A young black employee rushed to them saying "come with me." They followed him into a kitchen and out the back door of the cafeteria. Fortunately, Jan's friend did not become too frightened in her late stages of pregnancy. The demonstrators involved were in a peaceful demonstration. Unfortunately, many other activities of the civil rights movement were not peaceful.

Morrison's Cafeteria, Savannah GA, 1962

PRIVATE PRACTICE

My First Years in Practice

We returned to Taunton in early July 1964. Arrangements had been made previously with my cousin, Joe Lawrence of Royal Builders, to construct a home/office at 252 Winthrop Street. Legal problems with zoning arose. The foundation was found to be a foot or so too close to the neighbor's property. Sol Berk was the abutter. He was a wonderful neighbor and offered to sell me two feet of land for a mere pittance. The Board of Appeals was not willing to accept this remedy for the problem. Considerable discussions were held with the city commissioners regarding this zoning issue.

Prior to getting the building problems solved, we were at a function with Dr. Curtis Kingsbury, who did not add to our confidence. He said he knew of a case in the city where the building had to be moved a foot or two in order to follow city guidelines. This was not much help. We left the party devastated! Would we have to find another location? Would we have to change our plans for home/office, or would we have to tear down the existing foundation? Without an office, I could not start a practice. No office meant no income.

I was doing a little assisting in the operating room. Dr. Burden was very generous with having me assist with his operations. He also would sign out to me and go to his Mattapoisett beach house for days at a time. Dr. Edgar Lattimer, a general surgeon, was also very helpful. He allowed me to use his office on Wednesdays when he was off. Jan served as my receptionist and nurse on those days. We saw only a few patients a week.

When we arrived in Taunton, we moved in with my parents. I used my parents' home phone number 824-4498 as my office phone. This was before cell phones, so communication was not as easy as it is today. There we were at 986 Somerset Avenue with a four-year-old daughter, a three-year-old son and a two-year-old Dalmatian named Captain! My parents were very generous by taking us in. On weekends, when I was on call, Jan, Susan, David and Captain would go to 85 Tobie Avenue, Pawtucket R.I. to stay with Hedy and Walter. Talk about uprooting two quiet households with our brood!

Transportation was also a problem. I had our Rambler station wagon. Jan was fortunate enough to be offered by my parents the use of their black 1938 Buick. In early January 1965, I finally opened an office at 252 Winthrop Street, and a short time later, our family moved into the house. My office consisted of a waiting room with chairs for 6 to 7 patients. The receptionist's desk was also in the waiting room. There were two examining rooms and a consultation room, which connected with the family living space. The first floor of the main house had a dining room, kitchen, full-length living room with a fireplace, and a downstairs half bathroom. On the second floor, there was the master bedroom with an en-suite bath, three other bedrooms, and a second full bath. The house had two basements, one under the office, and one under the house. We also had an incinerator in the basement to burn office materials and household trash.

The house was very comfortable, but soon we outgrew the office and the parking lot. When I opened my office, the published announcement said "Practice Limited to Surgery." Because I knew so many people in town, I was repeatedly asked to do adult family medicine as well. Eventually, I succumbed to these requests. In the meantime people like Mary Medeiros, a neighbor and family friend was very upset because I would not accept her as a patient, because of her multiple medical problems. Even though she was disappointed, she still sent us the best Portuguese sweet bread we have ever had.

My first office at 252 Winthrop Street, with Janice, Susan, David and Captain

Even before I opened my office, a group of Portuguese-Americans got together and arranged a welcoming party for me at Lewis Lodge on Winthrop Street. The party was quite successful. There was a full house, a good dinner, and remarks from several prominent people in town. The plaque from this event reads as follows:

Presented to

David F. Gouveia, M.D.

In recognition of his return to our community to which he has already endeared himself

Sunday, November 8, 1964

Taunton Massachusetts

At first, things were slow at the office. I even joked that I hired my elderly aunts to sit in the waiting room at the windows, to make it appear that we were busy. Things picked up rapidly, and within a year or two, it was evident that I needed to move to a larger office.

One of our friends was Ernie Helides, an aggressive, successful realtor. At one of our potluck suppers, I mentioned to him that I would like to buy property near the hospital. A short while later, Jan and I and our children were joined by my in-laws on vacation in Miami at the Eden-Roc Hotel. I got a phone call from Ernie saying that a property at 89 Washington Street was up for sale, directly across from Morton Hospital, which is located at 88 Washington Street. I trusted Ernie's judgment and told him I would buy the property regardless of its condition as soon as we returned to Taunton.

89 Washington Street was a mess. It was a former rental building, a structurally sound late Victorian, three stories high. I suspected that it was used as a place of business by "ladies of the night." Washington Street was a favorite location for that profession. What makes me say that is there was no evidence of food in any of the refrigerators. The other rooms on the first floor were furnished with only mattresses on the floor and no other furniture. The basement was still mostly a dirt floor. Some of the tenants must have had dogs. Doggie poop was very evident in the cellar. Jan's Uncle, Jim Preneta, who was a builder and carpenter, approved the purchase of the building after inspecting it. We hired architect Nelson Woodward of Norton to plan the renovation project. His plan included two offices on the first floor, one with two exam rooms, one with three exam rooms and a very spacious common waiting room.

Apartments were planned for the second and third floors, two on the second floor and one on the third floor. A small office was also planned for the basement, which included a waiting room, two treatment rooms, and toilet facilities. Part of the renovations included the removal of fireplace surrounds made mostly of marble, which are now stored in the basement of 68 Governor Bradford Lane. The kitchen on the first floor had a massive chimney and baking oven. It was necessary to take down the entire chimney brick by brick starting at the top. Uncle Jim did this by hand.

Renovations were completed in 1968, and I moved into the office. Soon the building was totally occupied, including the basement office, which was rented by a podiatrist, Dr. Gene Romano. The saga of the office buildings continues in the next chapter when we purchased 91 Washington Street.

89 & 91 Washington Street – Medical Office Buildings after renovation

The Author relaxing in the 89 Washington Street waiting room

89 & 91 Washington Street

Shortly after completing the renovation of 89 Washington Street, Jan and I were on the common driveway between 89 and 91 Washington Street. We were greeted by Gertrude Fitzpatrick, who owned 91 Washington St. She called out her window with the question "do you know anyone interested in buying my house?" The obvious answer was "of course we do!" We definitely would buy the building. Office space was needed across the street from the front entrance to Morton Hospital. If she sold to someone else, the common driveway could become a problem. We also needed more parking spaces which would come with ownership of the second building. With the addition of 91 Washington Street to Gouveia Realty Trust, we could have a total of four offices, and six apartments for rent.

After the sale of 91 Washington St., Gertrude Fitzpatrick moved into the second-floor apartment at 89 Washington St. She was thus able to look at the home that she lived in most of her life, by just looking out the window.

Nelson Woodward was again contracted to design the renovations of the building. A good sized office was planned in the front of the first floor. A handicap ramp was designed for access to the office. An efficiency-sized unit was planned for the rear of the first floor. Two small apartments were designed for the second floor.

Jan's Uncle, Jim Preneta, was having cardiac problems. He was unable to do the kind of "bull work" needed to complete the full renovation. On his suggestion, we hired the Preneta brothers from Rhode Island. They were Jim and Hedy's cousins. They did most of the reconstruction, while Jim supervised.

We were fortunate that during our ownership of both buildings, we were able to mostly rent the apartments to older, single or widowed women who were no problem to the owners. 91 Washington Street was financially rewarding for many of the years that we owned it. It also resulted in a considerable profit when it was sold.

The ownership of these two buildings got its start with a phone call from Ernie Helides to us in Miami. Some say it was "meant to be."

David F. Gouveia, M.D. – Medical Examiner

When I returned to Taunton in 1964, Dr. Bennett and Dr. Nunes were the medical examiners for North Bristol County, which included Taunton, Easton, and other surrounding towns. Dr. Nunes decided to resign from the position, which he had held for many years. Someone recommended me to Gov. John Volpe, who in March 1966 appointed me to the position. Swearing in was at the State House in Boston. Jan was very well dressed for the ceremony. She wore a large fashionable hat that day and received several compliments on it. Gov. Volpe's praised the hat. He knew his hats since his wife was a designer of them. Another compliment came from Senator Edward Brooke, a U.S. Senator, who was the third black person elected to the Senate (1966 to 1978). (Hiram Revels became the first black senator in 1870. In 1875, Blanche K. Bruce was elected to the Senate for a six-year term.)

Governor Volpe swearing me in as Medical Examiner, 1966

As the assistant medical examiner, I covered the days and nights when Dr. Bennett was not available. We were fortunate to have a pathologist from Attleboro, Dr. Shamey, who was certified in forensic medicine. At our request, he performed autopsies on deaths that seemed suspicious or could have legal ramifications. In addition, sudden deaths that occurred in patients who were not under recent medical care had to be referred for evaluation and perhaps required an autopsy. Drownings, crib deaths, and suicides were all under our jurisdiction. All bodies which were scheduled for cremation required medical examiner clearance. This meant that the medical examiner had to go to the funeral home, examine the body and certify that there was no legal reason not to cremate the body.

I know that many of you watch TV shows that include medical examiners. These programs tend to make medical examiners all-knowing, and sometimes glamorous. The job was far from glamorous. A call in the middle of the night to view a victim of a crib death was very disturbing to me. I tried my best to comfort the parents in these unfortunate cases. They had tremendous guilt feelings, although they had no responsibility in the event. Suicides were also very disturbing. My most memorable suicide was a woman who was found hanged in her basement. There was no evidence of foul play. The mind can do many strange things. This woman had set the dinner table and cooked supper before hanging herself. I doubt that the family members even thought of eating dinner in such a situation.

One hot summer day I was called by the police department to investigate a very strong foul odor in a rooming house on the second floor, over a downtown Taunton bar room. Bill Kenny, whom I knew quite well, was the policeman on the case. Bill and I started climbing the steep steps to the second floor, but the odor was so strong that we turned around, ran down the steps and out the back door. To help us to get to the source of the smell, I gave Bill some money to buy two Lysol spray disinfectants. We climbed the stairs spraying ahead of us. We went into a room where a decomposing male body was in the bed. I will not repulse you with the conditions in the room. We pulled off the sheets and did a superficial exam of the body. There was no obvious evidence of foul play. Case closed.

The body now belonged to me, since there were no known relatives. I called several funeral homes, but not one would accept the body. With a lot of begging, I got Bill Wade of O'Keefe's Funeral Home to accept the body. I am talking about a decomposed body that had probably been dead for at least a week, in the heat of summer. The odor from the decomposition and putrefaction was overwhelming. No funeral home would want to expose its clients' families to such conditions. O'Keefe's Funeral Home had a small separate building where they could keep the body until proper arrangements could be made. The city was required to pay only $150 to bury an unclaimed body. You can understand the reluctance of funeral home directors to become involved with an unclaimed body. Talking about payments, the Medical Examiner was paid $25 for each case plus ten cents per mile driven. And like all states and counties, payments were very slow.

Eventually, my practice became too busy for me to continue as Medical Examiner. I decided to leave the position. Dr. Bennett remained as M.E. into his late 80's and early 90's. He was able to do this because he had a younger female companion who was a great help to him and drove him to his viewings. One day, I bumped into Dr. Bennett in an elevator at Morton Hospital. At that point, he was approaching ninety years of age. I asked him when he thought he would retire from his office practice. His reply was amusing. He said, "I still have three patients in my practice, when they die, I will close my office!"

Things We Don't Do Now in the Hospital

I have been involved in the field of surgery since 1957 - starting with a one-year rotating internship at Ohio State University Hospital in Columbus OH. There, I had several months of surgical training, some of it with a world-renowned surgeon, Dr. Robert M. Zollinger. During my rotation with him, I had the occasion to observe and assist him in the operating room, doing complicated open surgical procedures. The reason why I say "open procedures" is that much general surgery is now performed endoscopically. Endoscopic surgery is done through tiny incisions. The endoscope contains a light and small camera that allows the surgeon to view anatomy on a large digital monitor clearly. The endoscope for abdominal surgery is called a laparoscope. The endoscope for joint surgery is called an arthroscope. Several small incisions are made which allow surgeons to repair tissues in joints using the arthroscope. In abdominal and gynecologic surgery, besides the incision for camera and light, two or three smaller incisions are made – the surgeon is then able to manipulate organs, remove tissue or organs, and cauterize bleeding and to staple or apply clips to tissue using small instruments. This type of surgery is called laparoscopic surgery.

Surgeons today rarely do an open gallbladder removal. Gallbladder removal remains one of the most often performed abdominal surgical procedure. When laparoscopic procedures became available, I began to educate myself on how to perform them by taking courses. By that time, I was approximately sixty years old and made the decision not to start an entirely new armamentarium. I, therefore, started to refer patients whose procedures could be performed with minimal laparoscopic surgery to my fellow surgeons. To me, this type of surgery required video game skills that I felt uncomfortable performing. Currently (2013) I assist in all sorts of operations including gallbladder surgery done laparoscopically. This procedure makes up more than half of the cases in which I assist.

Open appendectomy is also rare. Again, the laparoscope has replaced the surgical knife. Many other procedures are now done with scopes including bowel, vaginal and stomach surgery, etc. In my younger days at Morton Hospital, I assisted Dr. C. Nason Burden, an orthopedic surgeon in many open knee surgeries, such as torn cartilage removal, and repair of torn ligaments. These procedures are now done with an arthroscope in most cases. The replacement of hips, knees, and shoulders is now routine but was science fiction in my surgical infancy. These replacements are still done with an open procedure.

Abdominal explorations for adhesions or intestinal obstructions are rarely performed as open surgery. Laparoscopic treatments of these problems are most common today. The amazing aspect of this type of surgery is the clarity of the images on the monitors employed in these procedures. The laparoscope has a camera lens that transmits pictures to monitors. Because of this, the anatomy is clearer, and the image enlargement makes even difficult anatomy much easier to figure out. Carbon dioxide gas is instilled to inflate the abdomen. This inflation allows visualization and clarity that cannot be seen in open procedures.

Most orthopedic joint replacements and other complex surgeries are done with a surgical team wearing "space suits." With these, there is coverage of the whole body including the head. A large plastic dome covers the face. Room air is pumped into the head area by a battery operated mechanism placed on the waist. Two pairs of surgical gloves are worn in most of these operations. The space suit concept results in a minimal possibility of transmission of bacteria between the surgeon and the patient, as well as preventing contamination between the patient and the surgeon. Newer developments are now in limited use. The da Vinci is a robotic surgical device remotely controlled by the surgeon. With these controls, the surgeon can perform very fine movements to ensure better overall results. Unfortunately, we are talking about a million dollars for the equipment. What the future brings to the medical profession, and especially to surgical practitioners appears to be unlimited.

Staplers have been used universally since the 60s and 70s – the refinement of the mechanisms of the staplers has been a boon to surgeons. In open surgery, staplers are used in procedures especially in the bowel, gynecologic and other intra-abdominal procedures. With the use of a stapler, surgery is performed in less time, with fewer problems of contamination. Staplers have also made it possible to remove many cancers from the lower bowel without performing a colostomy. The use of staples to close the skin has essentially replaced old-fashioned sutures which were used in days of yore. In some cases, sutures have been replaced with the use of skin glue, or by the use of very fine sutures under the skin.

Safe cautery equipment has been developed since my early years in surgery. The new cauteries can not only control bleeding but are also capable of cutting tissues with an electric discharge. In some operations, especially in extensive breast surgery, the use of cautery replaces most of the sutures previously used by the surgeon. This technique results in much less blood loss and decreases the length of the operation. In my early years when radical mastectomy was performed routinely for breast cancer, I would have to tie off scores of bleeders individually. Now, a simple, quick "zap" of the cautery is quite sufficient in stopping most of the bleeding. Of course, the larger vessels are clamped and tied by hand, using sutures.

Several new products are available in the form of implantable meshes. These are especially important in hernia repairs. Prior to their availability, it was necessary to use the patient's own tissue for repair. Because of the stretching of the tissue by the hernia, in many cases, the tissues were of such poor quality, that the patient had a significant chance of developing a recurrent hernia. Now, with the use of mesh, it is not necessary to attempt to bring weakened tissues together. The mesh replaces the tissue and is soon incorporated into the body tissue. Recurrence rates are quite low with the use of mesh.

A word about suture material… during my early surgical involvement in the operating room, the materials used to close wounds and repair tissues were cat gut, silk, and cotton. Cat gut was obtained from the intestinal muscles of animals including pigs and cows and not from cats. It was either "plain" or "chromic" depending on how it was treated. It was not a great material because of the source – some animals had better tissue than others. There was inadequate control over its strength. I read an article a few years ago about sutures. It said that if cat gut were introduced today, it would most likely not be approved by the FDA. New suture materials have been introduced using a variety of materials artificially produced. With these sutures, prediction can be made for the length of time they remain intact, and also the strength of the materials can be determined. Some sutures are made from materials that will not disintegrate. Other sutures will begin dissolving in a few days or for as long as several months. The surgeon is thus able to choose the length of time he wants the material to stay intact, on a case by case basis. It is also good that these new materials cause less reaction in the body. Silk sutures were notorious for causing reactions and frequently "spit" (rejected by the body). Because of this problem, I kept a sterile crochet hook in my office to try and "hook" these "spitters" and pull them out. Some patients wounds would not heal until all of the sutures were removed or rejected and spit out.

Ether anesthesia was first demonstrated on Oct 16th, 1846. Dr. John Collins Warren who performed surgery on a patient, Gilbert Abbott, using ether anesthesia. A bulging tumor was removed. Mr. Abbott claimed he felt no pain during the operation. The surgery was performed at the Massachusetts General Hospital in a room that is now called "The Ether Dome." Ether is rarely used now; it has explosive characteristics and is essentially banned from most hospitals. I had hernia surgery in my preteen years at Mt. Hope Hospital in North Dighton. Dr. Nunes performed the operation. Dr. Bloom, a general practitioner in Taunton, put me to sleep with ether. I vividly remember the bright lights overhead spinning as I succumbed to the ether. Nausea and vomiting were very common after surgery from the use of ether.

As was the vogue at that time, I spent two weeks on bed rest in the hospital following the hernia operation. My bed was next to the operating room door; as a result, I got to witness other people going in for surgery. At the end of two weeks, I was told to get up and go home. Not surprisingly, I fainted as soon as I got up! Wouldn't you?

Over the years machines have been developed which make the giving of anesthesia easier and safer. These computerized machines indicate how much anesthetic is given. Many parameters are measured by the anesthesia machine including oxygen level, heart rate, blood pressure, body temperature. A recent addition to the OR is the Bair Hugger. This is a forced- air warming blanket which keeps the patient warm during the procedure. Operating rooms are generally kept very cool because materials now used for "scrubs," gowns and masks, are made with artificial fibers that do not breathe. They also do not allow fluids and blood to penetrate the surgeon's scrubs. As a result, the surgeon is working in impervious materials, like being in a tent. Previously surgical gowns were made of cotton, as were the cloth sheets used to shield off the operative area. The new paper-like materials are fluid repellent.

Surgeons hand scrubbing has changed drastically. When I started in surgery, ten minutes were required for a surgical scrub of the hands. These scrubs were performed with brushes that had firm bristles. A few scrubs a day with them caused very dry skin and some skin irritation. The solutions used with the brushes were harsh as well. New brushes with a sponge on one side and soft plastic bristles on the other side have made it much easier to scrub. Less harsh solutions are embedded into the brushes which are in individual sterile packages. 3 to 5 minutes of scrubbing is all that is needed today for a good hand scrub. There is also a brush-free prep based on alcohol that requires only two minutes of rubbing on the skin. No water is necessary, and no towels are necessary to dry the hands and arms.

Skin preparation of the patient has changed as well. Ten-minute soapy scrubs were common for many years. An iodine prep called Betadine was developed which takes much shorter time to prepare the skin. Other similar products are available besides betadine. They are available as a soapy scrub and water based preps. Iodine-impregnated adhesive plastic sheets can be applied directly to the skin making an additional barrier to infection. Many new varieties of skin preps are now available, some of which depend on the bacteria killing action of alcohol.

The future of surgery is changing rapidly. An article in the July 2012 Bulletin of The American College of Surgeons entitled "21st Century Surgery" states "we may have reached the tipping point at which further innovation will jeopardize the surgeon's traditional role." As an example of the innovative treatments is the advent of radio therapy for eliminating lung cancer. There is also a non-surgical treatment called focal therapy for prostate cancer. Both of these treatments are on the immediate horizon and are completely non-invasive. An article in Business Week questions whether coronary bypass surgery should be retired, except in a minority of patients with severe diseases. Medical treatments with or without stenting may someday replace coronary bypass surgery. Non-surgical techniques are replacing a variety of procedures. Angioplasty has transformed the treatment of coronary artery disease. These new techniques are not performed by surgeons; they are performed by specially trained cardiologists. With continual developments in technology, surgery as we know it could very well disintegrate. Surgeons will have to reinvent themselves.

**Morton Hospital Executive Committee, 1985.
David F. Gouveia M.D. as President**

I am very pleased that I was able to be a part of the revolution in surgery over the last 60 years. The practice of surgery has been very satisfying, emotionally and scientifically, very challenging and rewarding. Although 90% of 5000 recently polled physicians stated, they would not encourage anyone to become a doctor. I encourage anyone interested in joining the medical profession to do it. They will be happy they did. I know I am.

SURGICAL AND MEDICAL PRACTICE STORIES

Joe and Maria from Somerville

I met Joe and Maria when I was on call at the Morton Hospital emergency room. They were injured in an auto accident while visiting friends in the Taunton area. They were in their forties at the time. Both sustained significant blunt injuries, but no surgery was required. Admission for several days was needed to ensure stabilization. Close monitoring of their abdominal injuries was necessary. It is important to note that the accident occurred before CT or MRI scanning technology. Maria probably had trauma to her liver, which did not progress to the point that would require additional intervention. Both recovered well and were discharged back to their home in Somerville. In my mind, I assumed that they would be returning to their doctor in Somerville for further treatments; however, that was not what happened.

They became patients of mine for about twenty years. If Joe was at work and unable to bring Maria to Taunton, she would take the T to South Station, and then take the bus to Taunton, and walk to my office where she would sit in the waiting room all morning. I generally did not start office hours until the afternoon. Maria would take a break from the waiting room for lunch. I saw Joe on a regular basis, but not as frequently as I saw Maria. Over the next several years both underwent elective surgery by me.

Maria loved to knit. I still wear a knitted vest that she made for me. She was also generous with items from the Azores and Portugal, as well as hand-made items she created herself. Embroidered cutwork tablecloths that she made were some of the gifts she gave to our family over the years. Maria and Joe's devotion to me was written up in a Morton Hospital brochure. It was distributed through the Taunton Daily Gazette to several thousands of subscribers. Unfortunately, I lost touch with Maria and Joe, due to his illness which required home care by Maria. My last knowledge of them came from a ward clerk on Surgical One at Morton Hospital, who occasionally would be in touch with them. Joe passed away from bowel cancer. The last I heard, Maria suffered from significant medical problems. They were a lovely couple, who had no children, but they had each other.

A Letter of Thanks and Praises for Dr. David Gouveia was written by Maria and published in "Team Talk," a Morton Hospital staff and employee monthly publication:

"Dear Mr. Porter: This letter is way overdue. On July 25, 1987, I had a bad car accident in which my husband and I were hurt very badly. Mr. Morgado was in the hospital for three days, and I was in for three weeks!

For three days I didn't know that I was in this world. The staff at Morton Hospital were the best. They helped me to get better, especially Dr. Ackil and Dr. Gouveia.

I have been in many hospitals in the past, but never have I received treatments as I got at Morton Hospital. I owe my life to Dr. Gouveia and Dr. Ackil.

Currently, I go from Somerville, MA to Taunton to get treatments three days a week. Again I say 'Thank God for your staff.'

I see Dr. Gouveia every so often for whatever care I need. I think my God is with him when he takes care of whatever is wrong with me. May Dr. Gouveia be with Morton for many, many years to come."

Thank you,

Maria Margado

P.S. Please let me know if possible that everyone knows of my thanks.

"Toe's Thumb Up"

One of my more memorable patients had an unbelievable result, which could be considered science fiction. The patient, Tom, was at work at a manufacturing plant on Weir Street. He was working on a high-pressure machine which compressed and injected plastic into a mold. The mechanism misfired resulting in his right hand being crushed and injected with multiple pieces of plastic. His right thumb was partially amputated. On examination, I found that most of the skin of the thumb had been pulled off. The bone beyond the bend of thumb was crushed, as well as partially amputated. The thought which drove through my mind - how can I save as much tissue as possible, and get some function of the remaining portion of the thumb?

Tom was a frequent golfer, who would be devastated if he were unable to return to his golf game. Returning to work as a laborer was out of the question at that point. He was close to retirement age anyway.

Because of the complicated situation, I consulted with Dr. Burden, an orthopedic surgeon who had considerable trauma experience. We decided that the first surgical procedure was to clean up the crushed tissue and to remove as much of the embedded plastic as possible from the hand. When the cleanup was completed, we decided to bury the thumb under the skin of the abdomen, in the hope that we could later use the abdominal skin as a graft to the cover the thumb. We knew that this was an old technique. Our goal was to end up with some sort of functioning thumb, even though it would not look normal.

For several weeks, Tom walked around with his right thumb embedded into his abdominal wall, and with his arm in a sling and swathe to prevent stress on the graft site. As little motion as possible was necessary for the potential skin graft to develop a good blood supply on its own. Once the graft was felt to have a good blood supply, it would be possible to use the abdominal skin as a cover for the skin lost in the accident. It also would act as protection for the exposed bone. Fortunately, the graft was pink and healthy looking. It served as a good coverage when attached to the thumb.

Dr. Burden and I consulted with an internationally recognized transplant surgeon at the Beth Israel Hospital in Boston. He told the patient about the procedure that he recommended. He proposed to transplant the outer part of the great toe onto the amputation site. To make the transplant stronger, he would fuse the bones with the thumb in a slightly bent position. This slight bend would be enough for Tom to hold onto a golf club securely. With the new "thumb," Tom would be very happy with the result.

I am pleased to tell you that the procedure healed well and was a great success. Tom played golf several days a week when he was fully recovered. He was a very satisfied patient, thanks to a new development in surgical transplantation.

Tom and his wife became and remained patients of mine for many years until his wife was too sick to travel from Fall River to my office. Tom and his wife survived for many years after the accident.

Now you know where the title of this chapter came from, i.e., "Toe's Thumb Up." Think about it. If you asked Tom about the results, he would give you a "toes thumb up."

A Single Red Rose and St. Teresa

My wife, Janice, was admitted to the hospital for intravenous fluids due to dehydration, secondary to a severe migraine attack. During her stay in the hospital, I cut a beautiful red rose, and a yellow rose from our garden to bring to her. At the same time, another patient, on whom I assisted in major surgery for lymphoma, was in the hospital. His prognosis for a cure was unknown at the time. His wife and I had worked on various projects at Morton Hospital and had spent considerable time together over the years. I gave Jan the roses, which she thought were beautiful. When I told her about the patient with lymphoma who was in the hospital and depressed by his diagnosis; Jan said: "why don't you visit him and give him this beautiful red rose, it might help to cheer him up." I took the rose to his room, as soon as he and his wife saw me, they became tearful, as well as joyful. They felt that it was a message from God. They were followers of St. Theresa, who was always depicted holding red roses. His wife felt that my gift of a single red rose was a sign that her husband would be healed. The patient underwent treatments for his illness and fully recovered. He was still alive some twenty plus years later. Is it possible that the prayers to St. Theresa of The Roses were answered? His wife mentioned my bringing of the red rose many times to me and was thankful for the gift, and overjoyed that their prayers to St. Theresa had been answered.

A Miracle at Medjugorje

A patient of mine from a very faithful Roman Catholic family might be of interest to you. I first saw him when he was in his early 20's. By that time he had undergone several sinus surgeries. His sinus infections frequently resulted in his contracting meningitis and requiring treatment at the Massachusetts General Hospital by a world-renowned ear, nose, and throat surgeon. His doctor had performed multiple attempts to prevent the sinus infections, by surgically transferring fat to the sinus areas, and by other complicated procedures. Unfortunately, over a period of time, the transplanted fat broke down, the other procedures failed, and meningitis recurred. Symptoms of meningitis are very high fevers, headaches, and convulsions. In an attempt to decrease the recurrences of meningitis, he was prescribed prophylactic antibiotics (antibiotics taken daily to decrease or prevent infection). Before my involvement, he would be transferred to Boston for intravenous antibiotic therapy.

Eventually, I spoke to his doctor in Boston, who instructed me on what dosages of medications were needed to control the infection. After that, he was treated at Morton Hospital. He worked as a disc jockey at various functions, as well as broadcasting on a local radio station. He was popular at teenage dances, and at community events. He had quite a following and took his show on the road many times to many people. Due to the failure of medical and surgical care, in this case, he decided to take a trip to the Roman Catholic shrine at Medjugorje in Bosnia, Herzegovina, where it had been reported that many miracles have occurred. He went with a group of penitents and participated in services there. On his return to the U.S., he was feeling better. To his delight, on his next visit to his surgeon in Boston, he was found free of disease with no communication evident between the sinuses and the brain. The Boston surgeon declared him healed. He was cured. His cure was felt to be a "miracle." It is my understanding that the medical cure was investigated by church officials, who agreed that this was indeed a miracle, attributed to his visit to the shrine at Medjugorje.

He went on to continue with his music ministry, as well as teaching at the high school level. Although he developed no additional sinus problems, he died at an early age of 60 from other medical problems.

The Gall Bladder that "Grew Back"

I treated a patient for what appeared to be gall bladder disease. The symptoms were correct, and x-ray studies showed an abnormal gallbladder. She was symptomatic enough that I recommended exploration of the abdomen, and possible removal of the gallbladder. She was very surprised by this recommendation because she was told in the Azores that her gallbladder had been removed. Since her symptoms continued to be a problem, she consented to a surgical exploration of the abdomen. During surgery, we found an intact gallbladder which was abnormal and contained gallstones. The gallbladder was removed without a problem, and the patient had a full recovery. The questions that came up in my mind were puzzling. Did the operating surgeon simply lie to the patient about the procedure he allegedly performed? Or did the patient not understand the doctor's conversation? We will never know since medical records from Portugal were not available for me to review.

A Tumor in the Abdomen

I saw a patient of Azorean background complaining of abdominal pain that appeared to be mostly in the back of her abdomen. This story is about medical care before CT or MRI scans were available. An X-ray evaluation showed something in the left retroperitoneal space (the space between the lining of the abdomen and the back wall of the abdomen), this was suspicious for some sort of malignancy that required exploration of the abdomen surgically. The operation is done by making a fairly large incision in the wall of the belly - big enough to look around and feel around. Once we entered the abdomen, we felt a tumor or cancer in the location, as we expected. The mass was removed, and to our surprise and delight, it was not a tumor. It was a surgical sponge that had been left in the abdomen during a previous procedure in the Azores. The medical care at that time in the Azores was not up to U.S. medical standards. The islands are small, and some had only a few doctors probably not fully trained in surgery. I was told that many procedures were done using one surgeon and one anesthetist.

During my early practice years, I was told by many patients that they would not undergo surgery because they were afraid of dying. I guess the mortality rate in the Azores was much higher than what we experience in the U.S. It took quite a while for the new arrivals from the Azores to accept my recommendations for surgery. Finally, after I performed hundreds of operations with good results, the Azorian immigrants accepted the idea that to undergo surgery was safe if performed by me in Taunton.

My practice grew quite fast, thanks to the fact that I was fluent in Portuguese. I also hired Portuguese speaking help for the office. The announcement of the opening of my office was very simple. It included my name, address, and telephone number. A note was added to it saying: "Practice Limited to Surgery," below that was "Office Hours by Appointment only." Many physicians in Taunton saw people without appointments. I think an appointment schedule makes a more efficient office.

In 1964, the medical community considered it unethical to put any other information in the announcement of a practice opening. This was not considered an advertisement. It could be inserted in the newspaper only once. You can see a major change in ethics in medicine now, in any newspaper or magazine where doctors advertise, offering services, and perhaps exaggerating their results. One physician who was in general practice in Taunton started his office hours late in the evening; he worked for a few hours after midnight at least four nights a week. These office hours did not appear to affect his practice. Patients slept in the office until being called for examination!

The phrase "practice limited to surgery" became a problem. Many older patients who knew me since birth were upset that I would not take them on as patients because they had multiple medical problems. One patient, Mrs. Medeiros, informed that she had changed my diapers many times, and knew me since I was born! She could not understand the reason that I refused to accept her as a patient. Little by little, the "limited" clause became less limited and eventually, I was recognized by several HMOs (Blue Cross, Pilgrim Health, and Bay State Health Care) and listed both as a primary care physician and a surgeon. I made certain that I did not attempt to treat complex medical problems because I was not comfortable doing that. As a result, I referred many patients to cardiologists and internists for treatment.

A Thirty Pound Weight Loss in One Day

One of four surgeons in my group was adept at surgery for the morbidly obese. Many of these patients weighed over 300 pounds. Performing an open abdominal procedure on a patient of this size was a formidable task. (Newer surgical approaches for the morbidly obese do not require such major surgery since they are performed with laparoscopic approaches). In vogue, were a variety of stomach staplings, or rerouting of the small bowel in a way that decreased the absorption of food. I was asked to assist in a bariatric (weight reducing) procedure of stomach stapling by an associate. This stapling would result in a smaller pouch of a stomach, not allowing patients to eat more than a few ounces of food at a sitting. During the procedure, the patient was prepared and draped in the usual manner. A large incision was made through a few inches of fat, and the abdomen was opened. Much to our surprise, we encountered a large cyst on the ovary which filled much of the abdominal cavity. The cyst was removed. It was so large that it filled to overflowing a large stainless steel basin in which it was placed. The cyst weighed almost thirty pounds. This truly was weight-loss surgery with fantastic results. Imagine losing thirty pounds in a few minutes of operating time!

The procedure that was originally scheduled was performed with ease. A partial stomach stapling was done.

People with morbid obesity present significant challenges to the surgeon, to the assistants, and to anesthesiologists. This patient lost 30 pounds instantaneously. The cyst was not cancerous, fortunately for the patient. An immediate satisfactory result was followed by gradual but significant weight loss over a period of several months.

An Inoperable Condition

In my early years of practice, I was called into the emergency room to treat a 19-year-old young man, who was the driver of a car that was in a collision with either a tree or a light pole. He complained of chest pain and some difficulty breathing. At that time there was no CT scans or MRIs. Regular chest x-rays showed evidence of a tear in the aorta (the main artery leaving the heart). Perhaps, if we were able to operate and repair the tear, which would require a pump to replace the heart function, the patient would have some possibility of survival. Unfortunately, this capability was not available to us at the time. If this occurred later in the 20th century, the patient might have been saved. He would be evacuated to a cardio thoracic service by helicopter for immediate intervention. Even then, the potential of survival was low.

There was absolutely nothing I could do for the patient medically or surgically. I sat with the patient, comforting him, holding his hand, and talking to him for the short time he had left in his life. This sort of problem was very disturbing to me, as you can probably understand since this happened more than 40 years ago, and I still can vividly recall it.

I understand that medical care cannot save everyone's life. Even though we are trained as doctors that death is inevitable in many cases, losing a young person whose adult life is just beginning, can cause havoc to the practitioner.

I am getting emotional just writing about this young man. An unexpected death like this can cause considerable difficulty to a physician's psyche. As in this case, there was much questioning going on in my mind. Could I have done more? Was there even the slightest chance that something could have been done to save his life? I know I am not God. Why does God allow accidents like this to happen?

Every time I lose a patient to his final reward, questions come up. Did I prescribe the right medicine? Would surgery have helped? Would surgery have made the medical condition worse?

A surgeon has to accept the fact that he is not perfect. Every procedure he does cannot have a perfect result. It is my hope that I did all I could in each and every case, resulting in the best possible outcome for my patients.

Seeing the Light

Near-death experiences, and even more extraordinary happenings are quite popular in the press and on TV at this time. Several books on similar events have become runaway best sellers on the New York Times' list. I had more than one patient undergo a near-death experience. One case is embedded in my mind...the patient was a fifty-year-old male from the Azores. He was a devout Catholic and told me that the rosary was recited every evening at his house, with many of his children participating in the prayer sessions.

"Tony" was under treatment for duodenal ulcers. Medication seemed to be effective for a long time. Unfortunately, he was admitted to the hospital with significant bleeding from the ulcer. The rapid bleeding resulted in his going into shock and losing consciousness. Aggressive resuscitation with fluids and blood replacement brought him back to consciousness. In the short period when he was non-responsive, he underwent a near-death experience, which he vividly remembered upon waking.

He was overjoyed by the situation. The description of how he felt was very dramatic and heart-warming. He said that he felt very calm. It was warm, quiet, peaceful and comforting. As he approached the bright light in the tunnel, he was in a relaxed state. It was a feeling he had never experienced, but would not upset if he had to experience it again.

He said: "I am not afraid of dying, after having gone through the passage and seeing the light. It was a wonderful feeling."

Dr. Burden's Eco-Friendly Solution

When I started a private surgical practice in 1964, I encountered a situation which I had never even thought of. The operating room on the third floor of the surgical wing had some deficiencies. The new wing was built in 1957 and was considered state of the art for its time. In my opinion, the operating rooms were smaller than I was accustomed to. The rooms were adequately air conditioned. The one exception was the orthopedic surgery suite. It never got enough cold air to be considered air conditioned. Unlike the other operating rooms, the "Ortho" room had a small window in an alcove off the main room. On especially hot days, we were forced to open the window for some attempted relief, but that was not an acceptable practice.

Dr. Burden occasionally employed an innovative cooling system that he devised. It was very simple – with a block of ice in an open container, a fan blew air onto the ice, resulting in some cooling for the surgeon and the patient. The mind of the inventor is full of many great ideas. Can you imagine the pleasure that Thomas Edison received when he invented the light bulb?

Dr. Burden is now retired and in his nineties. He has plenty of time on his hands to think up some other inventions for the orthopedic room.

A Terrible Auto Accident

One evening, in 1973, I was the surgeon on call at the Morton Hospital emergency room and was asked to report ASAP to treat a severely injured 13-year-old, who was involved in a vehicle vs. bicycle accident. On arriving in the ER, I was rushed into the room. The patient was lying on a stretcher. On lifting the sheet to examine her, I was shocked to see that her right leg was amputated from the hip down, with very "clean cuts." In the area of the amputation were the major arteries and veins – the vessels in the groin that supply blood to the leg. The vessels were in spasm, so major bleeding was not occurring at that time. To assure the bleeding remained controlled, I put on surgical gloves and applied heavy pressure on the vessels with sterile gauze pads, until additional help could be called in.

The patient was Sarah Doherty. Members of her family were patients of one of my associates, Dr. Fred Doran. He took over the case and called in other surgeons, including a gynecologist and a urologist to help reconstruct the hip and pelvic area. No reattachment of the leg was felt to be possible.

The team of surgeons consisted of me, Dr. Doran and Dr. Walter Johnson. Several hours of surgery by our team was necessary for reconstructing the pelvic organs, ligation of the vessels, and reapproximation of the soft tissues and skin. These interventions eventually resulted in complete healing without infections or other complications.

Sarah was a very determined person despite the horrendous traumatic experience. She underwent physical therapy, and within two months, she was swimming in the high school pool. I have slides of Sarah swimming in the pool.

Sarah was fitted with a prosthetic leg at Massachusetts General Hospital. She quickly adapted to her situation with the help and encouragement of friends and family. She did not expect special treatment and gives credit to her father for being a role model. Determined to live a normal life, Sarah has exceeded normality in her activities.

She is a championship skier in her class. Sarah was an alternate member with teammate Ted Kennedy Jr., also an amputee, on the U.S. Disabled Ski Team that competed in Sweden in 1986, and took part in the Demonstration Games at the 1988 Calgary Olympics. The following summer at the 1988 Olympics, the first Paralympics was launched. She has climbed Mt. Rainier, and in May of 1985 she became the first disabled person to reach the summit of Mt. McKinley – the highest peak in North America, without using a prosthetic limb.

She used only crutches to reach the top. Sarah also climbed to the top of Mt. Kilimanjaro in 2004. In 1984 she completed a cross-country bicycle trek (car-assisted) from Seattle to Boston. In 2004, she did the 490-mile walk along the El Camino de Santiago – a pilgrimage from the French Pyrenees to Galicia, Spain. She is quoted in the Anchor (a weekly publication of the Fall River Diocese) that the El Camino is a "spiritual journey" – a time for personal reflection and a chance to get away from the "grind of life."

After five years of development in 2010, Sarah and her business partner, Kerith Perreur-Lloyd, formed the company SideStix and created new models of a forearm crutch. They now have three versions of this dampen-shock system crutches available. These crutches can be fitted with attachable "feet." Some uses of the feet include snowshoeing, walking, and navigating icy terrain. The more costly Stix have moveable parts that reduce shock and increase control. With these modifications, there is a reduction of the impact of using traditional crutches.

Sales of SideStix have doubled every year. They are distributed internationally. The company is based out of Sechelt, British Columbia, where Sarah resides.

In addition to being an inventor, she is a pediatric occupational therapist and a well-known inspirational speaker. Of all the things she does, being a mother of three children is her favorite job, and first in her mind.

Sarah Doherty being praised at Retreat Center

In September of 2013, I had the privilege of attending a mini-retreat at the Sacred Heart's Retreat Center in Wareham, MA. The program featured Sarah speaking from her heart, revealing intimate stories of her life. Her background has some minor similarities to mine – her parents owned a small family-owned grocery store, as did mine. Their children, numbering nine, all worked at the store in Whittenton while growing up in Taunton.

She spoke of how her spirituality and the power of prayer helped her through the most difficult times of her life. Her belief in God was paramount in her recovery. She believes that prayer can strengthen the inner spirit to handle whatever difficulties life offers you. Those attending the sessions left there, inspired by her message, and with a heart full of optimism.

In an interview with Eleanor Gay, Director of Public Relations at Morton Hospital, Sarah is quoted as follows: "I am glad to be alive and to do the things I have been able to accomplish. I never regretted living through life with one leg. I wouldn't wish it on anyone, but my experiences certainly have opened up a lot of doors, and allowed me to meet many different people."

An Ovarian Cancer Story

Early in my practice in the late 1960s or early 1970s, I was involved in an operation which I feel is interesting enough to be included in my memoir. I certainly remember it vividly even though it was forty or more years later.

A student nurse, enrolled in the licensed practical nurse program at Bristol-Plymouth High School, was seen in my office with complaints of abdominal pain and swelling. This was prior to computerized tomography (C.T.) being available. She was booked for exploratory surgery. I asked Dr. Walter Johnson to assist in the case. As soon as we opened the abdomen, it was obvious that the patient had inoperable cancer, most likely of ovarian origin. The abdomen was filled with cancer. In fact, we were removing cancerous tissue by the handful, with the feeling that the patient had very little prospect of recovery. We removed everything we could, including the ovaries and the uterus.

Cancer-killing medications were in their infancy. Nitrogen mustard was one of the early treatments. We had heard about using nitrogen mustard directly into the abdomen but knew it was not a well-accepted treatment or even an approved treatment. Our feeling was that our patient had nothing to lose if we instilled nitrogen mustard solution into her abdomen. We left catheters in the abdomen for addition dosing of the medication. The pathology report showed ovarian cancer.

After a short recovery at Morton, she was transferred to Rhode Island Hospital, a university setting, where some experimental protocols were being evaluated for the treatment of ovarian cancer. She did not have an easy postoperative period. She required additional surgeries and other treatments which she tolerated quite well. Her recovery was amazing. Jan and I saw her many times at charity balls in Taunton, dancing the night away with her husband. She went on to live a normal and healthy life for at least thirty to forty years. She and her husband were avid skiers and frequented the North to schuss down the mountain. Interestingly, she outlived her husband who passed away somewhere in his late 60's or early 70's. You might say that this is a miracle. I am happy to say that played a small part in this wonderful story of survival.

Fifty Long-Stem Red Roses

A man from Delaware and a woman passenger were brought into the emergency room at Morton Hospital, following an auto accident. He sustained some blunt trauma to his chest and abdomen, enough so that he required observation in the hospital for a few days. His passenger was not injured and stayed at a local bed and breakfast for a few days. After admission, the patient asked to speak to me in private. He told me that he was not on a business trip, and his passenger was not his wife. She was his girlfriend, and they were traveling secretly in New England. His request was quite simple: "Please don't tell my wife that I was accompanied by someone in my car." The request was granted! The patient was well enough to be discharged with his wife, to return home after a few days in the hospital. To my surprise, shortly after his discharge, I received fifty long-stemmed red roses as a thank you for being discreet. The roses were beautiful. Occasionally, I think about the situation that I was put in and hope that all is well with him and his wife. Perhaps I helped save their marriage by being "discreet."

A Visit to Dr. Adolph Hutter
at the Mass General Hospital

A short while after suffering a heart attack in 1976, I had a consultation at the Massachusetts General Hospital with Dr. Adolf Hutter, a friend of Chris and Ann Salvo's, and a world-renowned cardiologist. For the consult with him, I took my medical records and my most recent cardiac catheterization for him to review. I spent one hour in his office, as we went over the records together. We reviewed the catheterization at length. A detailed physical exam was also performed. His conclusions were that I was in a stable cardiac condition. He recommended the following: "no eggs, no butter, and two drinks a day." The visit cost $500. But it was worth it!

The Quadruple Bypass Surgery and Complications

In the spring of 1999, I noticed increasing shortness of breath while visiting my son, David, and his family in Mahwah, NJ. I was walking near their house, which is located on top of a hill with lots of up and down roads. Upon returning to Taunton, I made an appointment with my cardiologist, Sandy Myers. I flunked all of the cardiac-related tests at Morton and was referred to the Brigham and Women's Hospital in Boston. At the Brigham, a coronary angiogram also known as a catheterization was scheduled on Holy Thursday (coronary angiography injects dyes into the arteries of the heart). I flunked that test also. Apparently, I was living on borrowed time, they told me that I had virtually no coronary artery circulation, and stated that if I didn't have the surgery, that I would probably be dead in two weeks. They scheduled emergency surgery for the next day, and I would be booked as the first case of that morning.

I knew that Charlie Collis was operated on by Dr. K, so I requested that he be the surgeon. This request resulted in snickers and giggles from the staff. They told me that I could not be his patient because he was "too busy." The next thing Jan and I did was to call Ellen Collis and ask her to intervene on our behalf with Dr. K. The Collis' had donated part of the cardiac unit at the Brigham a few years before. We had been guests of Charlie and Ellen at a Brigham dinner honoring their donation a couple of years before. Somehow, I was suddenly a new patient of Dr. K.

The Brigham was doing a study of the use of the radial artery in the arm for bypasses. I was asked to have that procedure done. Before they could use the artery, it was necessary to test circulation in the arm and the hand, by putting continual pressure on the artery, thus blocking it. With the artery blocked, they measured arterial oxygen levels electronically. The other artery in the arm, known as the ulna artery, was doing well. It was safe to use the radial artery for one of the grafts. The informed consent for surgery was more than a little scary. The usual complications were mentioned. The scary part was the "complication of death," which was written on the form in letters about ¾ of an inch in size. In the consent form was a notation that the left inferior mammary artery also known as LIMA was to be used as one of the bypass vessels. The leg vein, the long saphenous, was mentioned as a definite vein to be used. By the way, all of my intravenous lines used for the Holy Thursday test were left in place. I spent the night in bed, lying on my back with my arms out straight (Crucifixion?). It was Good Friday!

My hospital room was shared by a young man, probably in his 40's, who was waiting for a heart transplant. I had never seen anyone look so sick, and still be alive. He did undergo surgery at a later time and did well. My surgery was on Good Friday. I woke up on Easter Sunday when I heard a nurse say to me: "Doctor, I am going to pull the endo tube out of your throat (breathing tube in the lungs)." I have been told that my face looked like a basketball because of all of the swelling due to fluid retention. There was also extensive swelling of my body. John tells me that I looked like Darth Vader on his death bed! My children were aghast at my appearance and had difficulty visiting me on the first two days in the postoperative period.

Did I mention the word complications? It seems that I "wrote the book" on complications, or was the poster child for it. These are some of the problems I had following surgery:

Atrial fibrillation – (irregular, rapid heartbeat)

Severe difficulty breathing

Hematoma of the groin (bleeding into the surgical site in the leg)

Anal prolapse (lining of the bowel outside of the anus)

Left hemothorax (blood filling the chest cavity)

I was treated with "big A" [Amiodarone] for the rapid, irregular heartbeat. After a few days in ICU, I was transferred to a step-down unit. When I arrived at the step-down unit, the head nurse took one look at me and said she would not accept me in a transfer. I looked like hell, or "like a dead man dying, not walking." Back to the ICU!

ICU nurses work three days a week in twelve-hour shifts. One evening I was assigned to a very nasty male nurse. Because of blood filling my left chest cavity, it was very difficult to breathe lying down. I was more comfortable sitting up in bed, or in a chair. The male nurse told me that I had to remain in bed lying down or else. The "or else" was that he would have security come to my room and make me follow orders. I don't think I was very nice to him, as he was not nice to me. Needless to say, I slept very little that night because of that jerk. I told Jan that I would not have him take care of me the next night if he were assigned to my room. Fortunately, he wasn't!

Let's talk about atrial fibrillation, an abnormal heartbeat caused by faulty nerve conduction in the heart. I went into "A-Fib" on day four or five of post-op. A new treatment for A-Fib was available, called Amiodarone. When given intravenously, it required constant monitoring with electronic devices and the presence of a physician during the infusion which lasted several hours. I didn't revert to normal rhythm until the next day. Apparently, my heart stayed in normal rhythm the remainder of my stay at the Brigham. Unfortunately, a few days after discharge from the Brigham, I reverted to A Fib and required intravenous medications to return to a normal rhythm in the emergency room at Morton Hospital.

I have been in and out of A Fib over the last few years, and have once required electrical shocks of the heart under anesthesia known as "cardioversion." I was put on daily doses of Amiodarone orally in the postoperative period. A side effect of Amiodarone is pulmonary fibrosis, a thickening of the lung tissue, causing shortness of breath. To keep track of this complication required the use of annual x-rays and lung function tests. By the fifth year on Amiodarone, my lung functions had worsened. I was taken off of it and started on other cardiac blockers which have not been as effective in preventing fibrillation. For the five years I was on Amiodarone, I had no fibrillation.

After bypass surgery, bleeding into the groin was another problem. I was black and blue from the left groin to my knee. Swelling was present in my scrotum and genitalia. Should I have fantasized about being a porn star? Unfortunately, the swelling subsided, and my new career never happened! Just joking!

Without going into gory details, I shall mention that because of inactivity, poor oral intake, and other problems, I developed a prolapse of my lower bowel out of my anus. Treatment consisted of ice packs and gentle attempts at putting things back where they belonged. Two or three days of the treatment resulted in clearance of the problem.

Let's talk about the chest cavity full of blood and fluid. Every day, they took an x-ray of my chest. Every day, the x-rays showed that my left chest was full of fluid and blood. The surgical staff did nothing about it. Every day I was told: "Maybe we will discharge you tomorrow." My answer was: "what about the left chest collection of fluid and blood?" No answer to that question was heard, the staff just stared at me and left the room. On the day I was to be discharged, a female intern came to my room and said she was going to tap my chest to remove the fluid and blood. She looked frightened by the idea of doing a chest tap. I explained to her in detail how to perform the procedure, and was with her step-by-step as she performed something I had done innumerable times. Only once did she hurt me, when she hit a rib with the needle. The chest tap was a success. The post tap x-ray showed that most of the blood and fluid had been removed, and the lungs had fully expanded. Finally, I was discharged from this house of horrors! [i.e. .Brigham and Women's Hospital].

A side comment regarding Dr. K. His surgical ability is unquestioned, but his ability to interact with patients in negligible. He is not a people person. Anyone who trained with him is well trained surgically. I did not notice any warmth from any of his medical staff. As the saying goes "the apple doesn't fall far from the tree."

Dr. K. made daily postoperative visits to my room, a fact that surprised the nursing staff. He apparently did not visit his postoperative patients very frequently. His visits were perfunctory and unsatisfactory to me. My last medical encounter with Dr. K. was on the first, and only, outpatient postoperative visit. I had developed a collection of fluid in the left chest which would require a chest tap. To save time, I had a chest x-ray taken at Morton Hospital the day before the postoperative visit. The x-ray showed the left chest almost full of fluid. Dr. K. entered the room and did not look at the chest x-ray that I had posted on the viewing box. He turned to me and asked: "how are you doing?" I answered that I was short of breath. His response was "it's all in your head," and he left the examining room. Jan and I waited for a while in the room for someone to come in; no one came back after at least ten minutes. Jan went out and asked the nurse if Dr. K. was coming back to see me. The answer was no. So there I was with a chest full of fluid, and a surgeon who could care less. It was Jan's impression that Dr. K. did not want to have postoperative complications on his records, so disregarding them was a way of not having them recorded.

The next day I went to Morton Hospital, and Dr. McGuiness did a chest tap removing most of the fluid. The fluid has not returned. During the tap at Morton, someone was sick and vomiting in the room, I did not know who it was at first, but then realized it was Dr. McGuiness. Apparently, he was suffering from a virus but did not want to cancel the procedure, so he came in from his home in Boston to do it. That approach to patient care is certainly different from what Dr.K. did for me.

During this whole miserable adventure, my wife Janice was by my side almost 24/7. There was a chair in the room that turned into a narrow bed for her to rest. She also had a room at Children's Inn, which is just a short distance from the hospital. Brigham offered courtesy rides to the Inn for relatives staying there. Poor Jan suffered many "slings and arrows" during this time. I know I was not an easy patient, but she tried to make things better for me at all times. When I did not feel like eating, she found something I might want to eat; she helped me start walking and encouraged me when I felt depressed. Obviously, with all of the problems I had, I was discouraged and depressed, but who wouldn't be? I don't know if I would have made it without her company. My children were with me a lot in the hospital, helping me as much as they could, encouraging me to get better.

Upon returning home to 248 Winthrop Street, I had a rental hospital bed in the living room. It stayed one night and was returned. I have never felt as uncomfortable in my life, as I felt on the rental with its plastic mattress cover. The sofa bed that we had bought for our first apartment became my bed for the remainder of my convalescence. Even with the steel bar under the middle of the mattress, it was more comfortable than the plastic covered mattress of the hospital bed.

A simple form of cardiac rehabilitation was walking. I was instructed to count the outdoor light poles as I walked outside, and to increase the number of poles gradually. The first day out, I walked 15 poles and felt a little tired, but not as tired as I would feel because I had to walk 15 poles to get back home. Is this what is meant in cartoons when they show someone with a light bulb over his head, after doing something stupid? I walked daily outdoors as well as doing cardiac rehab at Morton Hospital. This rehab included exercises on various machines using both my arms and legs. My recovery was slow, but I finally returned to work three months after surgery. It felt good to function normally again. I don't think that I mentioned that Dr.K. told me that he added twenty years to my life. This meant that I should be alive until age 88! I am editing this in the summer of 2017 (began writing in 2009). It has been eighteen years after surgery, and so far the prediction has been good! Many more years to go! Deo Valente (God willing).

Jim and Agnes Almeida waving goodbye on final day in office practice

After returning to work, I was a little nervous about taking on any complicated surgery. Slowly, I limited my cases to easier procedures like hernias. Eventually, in 2002, I decided it was time to close my office completely, and just assist on other surgeon's cases.

After moving to Cape Cod in 2002, I worked exclusively with Dr. Gursewak

Farewell party at Morton Hospital operating room, 2011

Sandhu on orthopedic cases and other complicated cases one or two days a week. Working in Taunton meant waking up at 5 am, then driving forty miles to be ready to assist from 8 am to 4 pm daily. After a few years of that schedule, it was time to cut back more, and I decided to become Active Emeritus staff at Morton Hospital in 2009.

In 2003, I obtained assisting privileges at Falmouth Hospital, just fifteen minutes from my home. At Falmouth Hospital I assist on any type of surgical procedures. About 1 ½ years ago, Falmouth Hospital started an assistant surgeon program which pays participating doctors a fee for being on call. With this contract, they also paid my malpractice insurance for which I had been paying $10,000 per year. The premiums from malpractice were eating up 1/3 of my surgical fees. I have been on the staff at Falmouth Hospital for several years. It is a well-run institution, and all of the employees and surgical staff have been very nice to me. It is a pleasure to work with them. The nursing staff calls me "Sir" or "Dr. Gouveia," although most of the other surgeons are addressed by their first names. It appears that there are advantages to being a senior physician in the hospital.

MY COMMUNITY INVOLVEMENT

Community Activities

In my years of living and working in Taunton, I was involved in numerous local community activities. These included frequent appearances on Charles Crowley's weekly TV production "Old Tyme Taunton," which covered historical topics dealing with the city. These appearances usually included showing my photographs relating to the evening's topic. The programs were broadcast live, allowing for comments and questions from the listening audience. Repeat broadcasts of these tapes were common. I have had people come up to me years later, telling me how they enjoyed the reruns of "Old Tyme Taunton" which featured me.

On several occasions, I was a guest on Channel 6 (New Bedford/Providence) which broadcast the program "The Portuguese Around Us." It was moderated by Dr. Manuel da Silva of Bristol, Rhode Island, and sponsored by the Portuguese-American Federation, of which I was a member. The show was taped in the New Bedford studio for broadcast at a later time. It was also distributed to other community TV outlets to be shown in cities that had significant Portuguese populations. The show was produced in English. I will go into some detail about my experiences covering the local parades on Taunton channels.

The annual Taunton Christmas Parade was held on the first Sunday in December, one day after the "Lights On" ceremony on the Taunton Green. It seemed to me that the day of the parade was always one of the coldest of the year, as I sat on the viewing stand with the winter wind blowing. The parade was taped by the community television services and broadcast several times on later dates.

The author and Eleanor Gay announcing the 1993 Christmas Parade

Eleanor Gay and I did the commentary for the parades. We were given the parade lineup as a guide. Eleanor would write some information about the participating organizations and groups which were helpful in describing the units as they passed - we had to ad lib much of the chatter. There was no real script to follow. The two of us would individually view the floats as they lined up prior to the parade start. We also interviewed marchers and float workers, which resulted in good ideas for comments, as the floats passed. We had small monitors, so it was easy to be confused when the parade was in full swing. To make things more difficult, the floats passing live in front of us were not always what showed on our ten-inch monitors. The taping was done at different locations and by cameramen walking around on foot.

Competitions for "Best of Parade" for floats, marching bands, etc. were announced before the end of the parade. Groups vied for award ribbons. The grammar school entries always demonstrated a lot of imagination and obvious parental participation in constructing the floats. The high school entries were more complex and had more sophisticated themes.

The Christmas parade was a great adventure for many youngsters. They marched, smiled, and waved enthusiastically to the crowds along the parade route. Commercial floats, political groups, Veterans of War groups, police, and the wailing of the fire department's sirens added to the fun. The older generation of parade participants looked very comfortable, happily riding in convertibles supplied by local auto dealers.

Miss Taunton waved and smiled to the crowd, as she rode by in a convertible. Each year the new Miss Taunton was always a true beauty. Participating in the parade was an opportunity for people from all walks of life to enjoy. It was a typical American tradition for a variety of people and organizations to be viewed in public. Local marching bands from both Taunton high schools and the Taunton City Band were always enjoyable. Many out of town marching bands also added to the procession.

The author and Eleanor Gay working together on The Centennial History of Morton Hospital

For at least eight years Eleanor Gay and I sat in the freezing temperatures of the open viewing stand. Eventually, Eleanor decided it was time to move on. I announced the parade for a couple of years with another co-host but decided to also step down from broadcasting the parade.

Eleanor and I knew each other well. We worked together

on several projects for many years including being associate editors of the "Centennial History of Morton Hospital and Medical Center." There was chemistry between us. During the parade broadcast, she understood that I would make a controversial or perhaps a nonsensical statement. I understood that she would always smooth things out with her well-thought responses.

Eleanor and I were Taunton-born and bred. She was one year ahead of me at Taunton High School. Her brother, Leonard Menice was a classmate of mine.

Eleanor worked most of her life in positions dealing with the public. She worked as a reporter, columnist, and cartoonist at the Taunton Daily Gazette. Her husband, Edgar Gay Jr., was Managing Editor of the Gazette for many years. She was also employed for several years by the Reed and Barton Silversmiths as Managing Editor of "The Silver Lining" (Reed & Barton's company magazine). She also produced commemorative issues for Reed & Barton's 150th anniversary. In 1980 she edited a publication for the Diamond Jubilee of St. Paul's church. At the time we worked together, she held the position of Director of Public Relations at Morton Hospital.

The cover of the 1989 history of Morton Hospital, drawing by J.S. Conant & Co. Boston, MA. Circa 1889

She lived in Taunton for most of her life. In contrast, I was away for fifteen years before returning in 1964 to start my surgical practice. Eleanor knew everything about Taunton and its residents. She knew who was married to whom, who had children, what their occupations were, etc. It took me a long while to even come close to her understanding of how the city functioned and what the local politics were. She was more diplomatic than me in the views she expressed. I was more of a free thinker and was not reticent to express opinions that were not always acceptable to some people. I think that our different attitudes and ideas made for more interesting TV presentations. This is not meant to say that we were ever hostile to one another, we were not. When Eleanor and I announced that we would no longer cover the Christmas Parade, many people told us that we would be sorely missed. People would mention how they always looked forward to our TV chatter. It is my feeling that we were two hometown kids who were proud of Taunton's heritage and enjoyed presenting it to the public.

A Historical Note – Taunton was widely known as the "Silver City" due to it having more than twenty manufacturers of silver products during its history. It is also called "The Christmas City," a title it received for its annual decoration of the Taunton Green. In December 2013, Taunton celebrated "One Hundred Years of Family Memories" with a well-received lighting display of the Green.

The author as Paul Revere and Janice as Betsy Ross in the Bicentennial Celebration

Photography by David F. Gouveia

Taking pictures has been my hobby since pre-teen years. My first camera was a Kodak Box Camera. It had no flash ability, making it a good outdoor camera, but not ideal for indoor photos. Later my folks bought me a 35mm camera which accepted a flash attachment. The flash was a four-inch reflector which used one bulb at a time and required screwing in a new bulb after each picture was taken. A few years later, Sylvania came out with the "Blue Cube" which rotated and allowed me to take four consecutive pictures before changing the "Cube."

My wedding gift from Janice was a Contaflex 35mm camera with a nice shiny brown leather case. It was my first single-lens reflex camera. The lens was a superior Carl Zeiss 50 mm. Manual focus was necessary. I think this camera made me feel like a real photographer. I don't remember all the details about the Contaflex, but I just loved that camera. As my collection grew in future years, I owned Nikon, Leicaflex, Fuji, and other cameras with interchangeable lenses. Currently, I use a digital Sony Alpha 100 as well as a small Canon pocket camera. Film is no longer necessary although some purists only use film. With digital cameras, I have the ability to see the photo immediately. If I am unhappy with it, I just take more shots.

My earlier photos were black and white. Eventually, color film became available. Since color prints were expensive, I turned to color slides, as did many photographers. With the cost of slide film and processing, the price per slide was as little as ten to twenty cents per image. I estimate that in my lifetime, I have taken fifty thousand slides. On many vacations, I would take between twenty to thirty rolls of Kodachrome or Fujichrome film, each with 36 exposures.

In the past few years, I have started to wean my slide collection. I stopped counting slides when I reached 25,000 slides. With slides, it was common to bracket exposures by taking more than one slide, to assure proper exposure. During the weaning, I have destroyed more than ten thousand slides – some were duplicates, others poorly exposed, and some with no lasting interest in the subject.

Over the years, I have donated a few thousand slides to the Old Colony Historical Society. They depict special events in Taunton during the past forty years. There are more to be donated, but I have not found the time to identify and date them.

I have dabbled in oil coloring of black and white pictures. This technique was used prior to the evolution of color film. I remember doing one for my aunt,

Esther. Photos done with oil paint remain quite acceptable after many decades have passed.

While living in Georgia from 1962-1964, Jan and I had several occasions to travel around the beautiful American Southeast. The antebellum homes and the glorious gardens were such a pleasure. One could spend days in each city – Savannah, Charleston, Natchez, Atlanta and New Orleans, among others.

Taunton celebrations and gatherings were always put on film. In the late 1960s, I started photographing many community celebrations and historical events. The American Bicentennial provided me with an abundance of activities to record. The 350th anniversary of Taunton's founding resulted in a plethora of photo ops. With slides, I was able to set up programs and present slide shows to organizations, churches, and small clubs.

The Old Colony Historical Society was my favorite venue. My slide shows there were many and frequent. The last major involvement with the Society was a series of programs called "Taunton – Then and Now." In this series, I chose old and antique photos from the Society's collection and compared them with new photos of the same location, as they were at the present time. There were, of course, many changes over the years. Some locations had three or four different structures built on them, from the time the original photo was taken. It was a tour down "memory lane" for many in the audience. Most of these historical slide shows were well attended to the point of being "standing room only."

On the subject of the Historical Society, I will bring up a major publication by it in 2007. After several years of research and writing, Dr. William F. Hanna completed "A History of Taunton Massachusetts." This book was a fresh approach to the history of the city. It was the first historical book about the city since S.H. Emery authored the "History of Taunton" (1637-1893). In the Hanna publication, it was decided to include photos of significant objects in the Society's collection. I was more than pleased to be asked to take the photographs to be included in the book.

My interest in photography involved a variety of activities which will be listed in the following paragraphs. Some of the chronology may not be in order, because of the intermingling of some events with other events.

I had two forays into outdoor art festivals, at which I sold framed photos, displayed on metal racks. I participated in the Newport Outdoor Art Festival for two summers, and my photos competed for juried awards. In 1981, I was given the "Best of Show" award at Newport for one of my favorite pictures taken on

Exhibiting at an outdoor art festival

vacation, entitled "Windmills of Portugal." I also won the "Best Color Photo" award given by the Falmouth Artists Guild for "Foggy Morn, West Falmouth Harbor" a few years later.

Bermuda Rooftops

The early 1980s were busy years for me and my cameras. I mounted a one-man exhibit at the Taunton Art Association where 42 photos were displayed in frames constructed by New England Picture Frame Co. in Providence, R.I. Prices ranged from $45 to $125. I recently scanned the guest book from the exhibit and found 120 signatures. One of the signers was Marilyn F. Hoffman, Director of the Brockton Art Museum (Fuller Memorial), who wrote me a letter asking me if I would donate a copy of "Bermuda Rooftops" to the museum. As a result of the donation, I was listed in the International Museum Index of American Photographic Collections under "Brockton Art Museum – Fuller Memorial."

In celebration of Morton Hospital's 100th Anniversary in 1989, I was asked to review the hospital's archival photo collection to prepare a permanent display of historical photos. After choosing the photos for display, I had a professional photo laboratory make four by five-inch negatives of them. With these negatives, it was possible to enlarge the photos up to thirty by forty inches. I chose about twenty images to display in various sizes from 8x10 to 30x40.

The exhibit has been in place in an entrance corridor for about twenty-five years and continues today to be enjoyed by visitors to the hospital. Mr. Arthur Bert of New England Picture Frame helped me with the framing and hanging of the exhibit. He made the task a lot easier than I expected. Arthur Bert was very supportive of me and my photography ventures. He showed my works to a Providence interior designer, Andruzzi, who placed several of my photos in client's homes.

Ken Swartz of Swartz Office Supply in Taunton specialized in retrofitting banks, new bank construction, and interior decorating. I was very pleased to accept an assignment to photograph important structures in Taunton, Rehoboth, and New Bedford. Photos taken of these sites were framed and used as part of the décor at a bank in each city. The banks were branches of the New Bedford Institution for Savings.

Eleanor Gay and I were associate editors of "The Centennial History of Morton Hospital." It was written and edited by Edward F. Kennedy, Jr., a well-respected local historian. My main assignment was as a photo editor. I believe that copies of the book are still available, for sale, at the Old Colony Museum.

For many years I submitted framed photos to be displayed at the Annual Members Exhibit at the spring meeting of the Massachusetts Medical Society. The photos and other artwork on exhibit were the works of society members and their relatives. It was an opportunity for them to display their artistic abilities. Many of the works on display were sold on the silent auction table.

In the years 1990 and 1991, I submitted images to the Pfizer Laboratories for an annual calendar contest featuring award-winning physicians' photographs. In 1990 an "honorable mention" was given to me for a photo taken on the beach in Nazare, Portugal. It showed the very unusual Nazare fishing boats, which were characteristic of the area. The scene included the boats, the sandy beach, and very high cliffs behind them. A small copy of the photo was printed on the Honorable Mention page of the calendar with a short biography of me.

The 1991 version of the Pfizer calendar used my photo of a lion tamer of the Moscow Circus, which was touring in the US. The photo was used for the month of February page. A portrait and a short biography of each winning photographer were included on a separate page.

Receiving award-winning plaque by Pfizer representative

In the early 2000s, I entered a contest held by Pilot Press and Twin Light Publishers. The contest was for both amateur and professional photographers. The goal of their books was to present a "photographic portrait" of several New England areas, taken by various local camera buffs. They had previously printed ten books of various locations, with which they had success. My involvement with the publishers started with the "Upper Cape Cod" edition. Eight of my works were chosen for publication in the hard bound volume which retailed for $24.95.

The next year's production featured "The Mid and Lower Cape" – from Cotuit to Provincetown. My photo of a shingle-covered windmill was used for the front cover. Several of my other photos were included in the book. For the release of this book, we held a book signing at Borders Books in Hyannis. Over the next three years, additional volumes of the series were produced in Boston and throughout New England. I made a few contributions to these.

For several years, the Falmouth Chamber of Commerce printed my photos in its annual visitor's guide. These booklets were distributed to thousands of subscribers of the Falmouth Enterprise newspaper. A large number of these guides were also distributed at the Chamber's office and were available for free at business outlets throughout Falmouth.

The Massachusetts Film Office held the "5th Annual Photo Exhibit," a competition for pictures to be used in a calendar. One photo of mine was accepted and displayed at the State House on Beacon Hill in the Gallery Lobby outside the House Chambers.

I tried starting a camera club in Taunton. It met in my office waiting room for a few months. Enthusiasm was not obvious when we met monthly. I decided not to continue with the club. The Brockton Camera Club was said to be a great one to join. After a year, I stopped attending. Members of the club seemed to resent the intrusion of an "out-of-towner." They were not friendly and were very competitive to the point that I could not accept.

About ten years ago several interested photographers got together and became original members of the Upper Cape Camera Club. The club first met in the basement of the West Falmouth Methodist Church. The club later moved to the West Falmouth Library, which served it well for a few years. The popularity of the club and its increase in members forced the club to move to a larger meeting room at the Falmouth Artists Guild. Keeping up with the current changes in photography, the club held many of its competitions in digital presentations. I was usually among the top three contestants annually in print competition, but I decided to stop competing in the digital world. The important reason causing me to stop was that I started writing this memoir in 2009. Writing has taken up considerable effort and time. I occasionally attend the camera club meetings for some of the educational programs only. As you have probably figured out, I had an amazing time photographing the world for most of my life.

350th Parade in Taunton

In 1989 Taunton celebrated the 350th anniversary of its founding, with over thirty special events. The 350th parade was the most spectacular event ever seen in the city. It was called "The Grand Procession" and started in Westville (a section of Taunton), and passed by my house at 248 Winthrop Street, as it marched to downtown Taunton. My family and friends, sitting on our lawn, had front row seats to the spectacle. An estimated 50,000 to 70,000 people viewed the parade. Over 160 groups participated in the three-hour event. As many as 2000 people also participated in the parade itself.

Eleanor Gay and I narrated the parade, with coverage sponsored by our community cable TV company. She and I sat on top of the TV van which was situated at the intersections of Taunton Green, Weir Street, and Main Street. Access to the broadcast site was obtained by climbing a ladder, to the dismay of Eleanor, especially when she was descending. Our viewpoint was excellent. The cable company supplied us with a new large monitor (at the Christmas parades our monitor was only 8 to 10 inches in size). This new large monitor was about 14 inches in size, but at times it was not bright enough to clearly see the action being taped. We had no booth or overhead coverage, so the brightness of the day made it somewhat difficult to see the monitor. We sat on folding beach chairs. At one point I moved and got too close to the edge of the van. I was barely able to prevent a 10-12 foot fall onto the street. We quickly moved to the middle of the van to avoid a disastrous injury.

The parade was led by Mayor Richard Johnson, who served as the Grand Marshall. Sitting with the mayor was his wife Jean, and their daughter. They rode in an open carriage pulled by the Hallamore Clydesdale horses. The weather cooperated until the ninth and final division reached the railroad tracks on Winthrop Street, at about 4 pm. At that time, a significant downpour occurred. Rain started soon after a Native American performed a dance in front of the viewing stand. Eleanor and I wondered if he performed a rain dance. If he did, it was very successful.

It is not possible to list all of the wonderful units that passed before us, but several stand out in my mind 25 years later. I will elaborate on a few of them. The largest group was the Polish American Community Club which presented an outstanding display. Their unit was comprised of several parts which included a dancing group of women dressed in authentic outfits from many regions in Poland. They had a band performing polkas and the most outstanding float in the parade – composed of 25,000 red and white paper flowers, hand-made by members of the club. Each flower was placed by hand onto the float which also featured the red eagle – the Polish national symbol. It certainly deserved the first place award in the Social-Civic Division. (A total of fifty floats were entered).

The Cohannet School entry was the first place winner in the school division. The theme was "Children Are the Future of Taunton." It had children sitting at school desks, dressed as various professions. Each profession was identified on a banner on the desks.

The Morton Hospital float was a large eight-foot multi-layered birthday cake in celebration of the hospital's opening in 1889. On the corners of the float were Leslie McNulty, LPN; Cathy Scott, RN; (an Oncology nurse and employee of the year); and Mrs. Phillipino, Volunteer of the Year. Julia (Jackovitch) Bik was the fourth representative. She had been affiliated with the hospital for 41 years. She was instrumental in starting the Licensed Practical Nurse program in Taunton and was a graduate of the Morton Hospital School of Nursing in 1929.

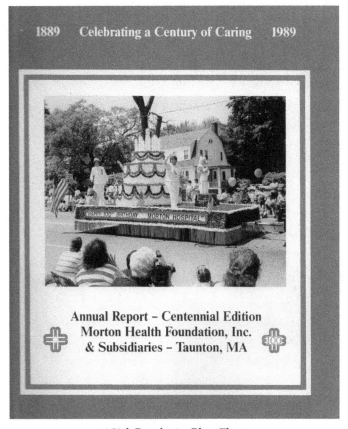

350th Parade, 1st Place Float

Parade music was supplied by the Shriner's band, many various school bands, and the Comedy Clown Band, to name a few.

The most exciting and entertaining units were the Mummers Bands – one from Brumal, Pennsylvania, the second from Palmyra, N.J. I was interested to find out that on New Year's Day in Philadelphia as many as twenty thousand participants perform in the Mummers parade. The parade has been a phenomenon since 1901. The bands are a family affair with performers ranging from pre-teens to those over seventy years of age. Members play string instruments, brass instruments, percussion, etc. Mummers wear a variety of masks, and their costumes are elaborate – bordering on Mardi Gras type outfits. There was an abundance of white feathered costumes, and large feathering fans in the two groups we viewed. The Mummers have to be seen to be believed.

The largest horse unit in the parade, the Budweiser Clydesdales was removed due to the heavy rain which started as they approached the viewing stand. It is common to take the horses out of a parade for their protection. The most important reason is the safety of the horses – a bad slip or fall could result in injury to these beautiful and valuable animals. The Budweiser vans always follow the horses in a parade, in the event bad weather should occur.

People scattered quickly when the downpour started. We had to stop broadcasting to prevent damage to the valuable equipment used in the broadcast. Despite the rain, the parade was beautiful and exciting. It was a wonderful experience to be involved in the Grand Procession.

Taunton was a very proud city that day.

Let's Go On with the Show

Since my years in high school, I have been in involved in several aspects of the entertainment field, mostly as a member of the audience, but sometimes as a participant in the production. I have had no formal lessons in music or singing, but I joined the Taunton High School Glee Club and discovered I liked to sing.

At the high school, we performed at least two choral concerts each year in the auditorium. As an offshoot of the chorus, I sang two solos at the Old Colony Historical Society in a program depicting the 100th anniversary of the 1849 Gold Rush.

At Tufts, I became involved with the Tufts-Jackson Chorus. (Jackson College was a separate institution for women, affiliated with Tufts). Jackson was on the same campus, and the women attended co-ed classes at Tufts. Several years later the two schools formally combined.

Dr. Thompson Stone was the conductor of the Tufts-Jackson chorus. He was a taskmaster, but a wonderful man to work with. He also served as the director and conductor of the Handel and Haydn Society. The Society is a very prestigious Boston choral group that is known for its annual Christmas production of Handel's Messiah. The Society recently celebrated its 200 anniversary. In my junior year at Tufts, Dr. Stone asked me to audition for a place in the Handel and Haydn Chorus. I was honored to be asked but had to refuse. My primary reason for being at Tufts was to get into medical school. With so many laboratory afternoons and extremely difficult classes, I had no time to dedicate to the choral society.

As the librarian for the Tufts chorus, it was my job to assemble the song books for about a hundred chorus members. When new songs were chosen, I would take the MTA into Boston, pick up one hundred copies of each new piece, and insert them into the songbooks.

The concerts we gave were in formal attire - men in tuxes, women in long dresses. My favorite classical piece was Faure's Requiem which we performed in its entirety in Latin. We also performed several lighter pieces including a Gilbert and Sullivan number that goes like this:

Go you heroes, go to glory
Thou you die in combat gory
You shall live in song and story
Go to immortality

Go to death and go to slaughter

Go, and every Cornish daughter

With their tears, your graves shall water

Go to immortality, go you heroes, go to immortality.

Tarantarah rah, Tarantarah, rah

The Tufts chorus sang each year at Tufts Night at The Pops in Symphony Hall. We performed in many other venues around Boston. Our concert at Boston's Jordan Hall was such a pleasure. The acoustics at Jordan Hall are said to be the best in Boston. Speaking about acoustics, I must tell you about the concert we performed at Boston's John Hancock Hall. We were one of the first groups to sing there. After our first number, it was obvious that the audience was having trouble hearing us, even though we numbered one hundred voices. Dr. Stone pointed to his big smile – telling us to keep smiling and continue with the concert.

After this concert, the John Hancock organization decided to improve the hall's acoustics. Some of the difficulty could have been from the amount of cloth covering the walls, in addition to the fact that the chairs were covered in sound absorbing material. As they say: "the best-laid plans are?" I don't know who laid the plans for Hancock Hall, but I hope they hired someone to improve the situation.

Prices have changed a lot. College students were able to get 2nd balcony seats to the Boston Pops in the 1950s, for a mere 50 cents. Each spring we performed at Tufts Night at The Pops. It was such an honor and a privilege to meet Arthur Fiedler in the Green Room. Fiedler was the conductor for the Boston Pops for decades and responsible for its prominence and success.

I had a minor foray into musical directing at Alpha Sigma Phi, my Tufts fraternity. Alpha Sigma Phi had never participated or competed in the annual Tuft's "Christmas Sing." I convinced a dozen fraternity brothers to join the competition. We sang "Go Tell It on the Mountain," and I thought we did well. We were rewarded with an Honorable Mention. Not bad for beginners, or my first time directing a chorus.

During my college years, I went to New York City to do some touring. At Radio City we were offered a choice to tour the Radio City Music Hall or attend a live performance of the NBC Symphony Orchestra conducted by Arturo Toscanini. I chose the Music Hall tour, but if I had to do it all over again, my choice would be to see Toscanini, in person, conducting his orchestra.

I developed an avid interest in live stage productions over the years. The first play I remember seeing was "Brigadoon." It was performed in a small community theater in Somerset, MA. "Brigadoon" is a simple but glorious story with a magical theme. It served as a stimulus for my interest in the theater.

Tufts had a small theater where students majoring in theater could improve their singing and acting ability. It was called the Tufts Arena Theatre, an in-the-round playhouse. Many of the plays performed there were deep and somewhat disturbing. Other performances were much more uplifting. Comedies and musicals counteracted the depressing plays by Chekov and Pinter.

During college and medical school days, I could rarely afford to attend legitimate theater. There was little room in my budget for this type of extravagance.

One play that I attended was a pre-Broadway run of Leonard Bernstein's "Candide." For that performance, I took a girl named Bobbi, who was Jan's "Big Sister" in Nursing School at Cambridge City Hospital. Bobbi was extremely well-endowed and always stood out in the crowd. As we walked down the balcony stairs to our seats near the front, I really enjoyed watching the men's reactions, eyes bulged, heads jerked and necks twisted to catch a glimpse of Bobbi. We saw the same reaction when we left the theater before the completion of the show. Because the nursing school had a midnight curfew, (and the play was three and a half hours long), we had to leave early long before it was over.

Pre-Broadway auditions in Boston sometimes tried different songs to see what should be included in the final version of the show. Candide obviously was having a problem with the length of the show. By the time the show got to New York, many of the problems had been fixed, but it remained a lengthy production. It became a huge success and in recent years was revived on Broadway. Unfortunately, neither Boston nor Hartford are now used for pre-Broadway try-outs, as they had been for several decades. If the show didn't make it in Boston or Hartford, it would not make it on Broadway.

My attendance at live stage performances waned a great deal over the next five years, as I struggled through a one-year internship at The Ohio State University and a four-year residency at St. Elizabeth's Hospital in Brighton. In Columbus, I managed to see one ballet and a performance by Danish comedian Victor Borge. Columbus was a "crazy for football city" but not crazy for finer entertainment.

During my residency, I got married and became the father of two children in less than two years. There was neither time nor money to go to the theater.

While living at Fort Stewart, my time was taken up with other activities. I was active in the Fort Stewart Bowling league, and even recorded the highest single-game score of the season.

I was not bitten again by the theater bug until a couple of years into my private medical practice in Taunton. For a few years, while living in Taunton, we were members of the Boston Theatre Guild. The Guild sponsored new shows and traveling companies from New York City. Our seats were located at the right center of the aisle, and just a few rows back from the stage. On opening nights, we sat behind Elliot Norton, the famous theater critic from the Boston Globe. By watching his reaction to the performance, we could predict whether a good or bad review would appear in the paper. He left most performances a little early, giving him time to write the review for printing in the morning's paper.

As the years went on, we decreased the number of stage shows we attended. Winter snowstorms were a real problem. Also, getting home around midnight, meant we were not at full speed the next day. Babysitters posed another problem, because of our late return from Boston.

For many years in December, I took a course on "New Developments in Surgery" at New York University School of Medicine. The courses were given at the Grand Hyatt Hotel at Grand Central Station. I would go to the city for the first days of the course and Jan would join me on Friday for the weekend. Off we went at night for great dining, and an evening at the theater.

On one of our visits to NYC, we were able to get tickets to Barbra Streisand's remarkable Broadway debut performance in "Funny Girl." We were so excited by the show that we hung around the stage door for a long time hoping to see her up close. Apparently, she sneaked out a back entrance to avoid the crowds at the stage door.

We were able to get tickets to sold-out shows because of our connection with Jack Krauss, owner of American Cord and Webbing Company in Pawtucket, R.I. Hedy, my mother-in-law, was the forelady at his manufacturing plant for many years. Jack lived in NYC and knew whom to call for hard-to-get tickets. As I recall, Jack also gave us tickets to the Music Man with Robert Preston, and to My Fair Lady with Rex Harrison for our honeymoon.

Some of the many shows we have seen include, Hair; Equus; Fiddler on the Roof (with Harry Goz who was the stand-in for Zero Mostel); Cats; A Chorus Line, etc... The list is endless. We enjoyed Les Miserables three times, the first at the Pantages Theatre in Hollywood when our son-in-law Peter gave us front row seats. The seats were so close to the stage that at times we felt "spit on" by the performers. We loved Les Miz so much that we have taken every family member to see it.

Being solo in New York City, I was able to purchase a ticket to any show on the day of the performance. The major reason that I was able to attend so many great Broadway performances was that many times there are single seats available at the box office, before show time. My all-time favorite performer was Angela Lansbury in "Auntie Mame." It was her first night back from vacation, and she looked excited to perform. Perform she did, she was so fabulous that I had to call Jan after the show to tell her about it. I roused her from sleep to share the joyous feeling I had after seeing Lansbury at her best. (She has received a total of four Tony Awards for best actress in a musical category, and one Tony for best supporting actress in a play. Only the late Julie Harris has received more Tonys – a total of six.)

My single seat at "Jesus Christ Superstar" was in the front row just behind the orchestra pit. Unfortunately, the kettle drum was right in front of me and was loud enough to almost rupture my eardrums. Jesus Christ Superstar was a legendary story of the hippie movement and broke several rules regarding propriety on stage.

Over the years Jan and I have seen many of the most famous stage performances – Ethyl Merman in "Gypsy;" Roberta Peters (my other favorite Broadway performer) in several productions. We have seen Shirley Jones (Mrs. Partridge from The Partridge Family show) perform with her husband, Jack Cassidy. Others include – Mary Martin; Ben Vereen; Donny Osmond in "Joseph and the Technicolor Dreamcoat;" Harry Belafonte; Mandy Patinkin; Hal Holbrook; Mae West and Eartha Kitt. Another outstanding performer was Pearl Bailey in an all-black production of "Hello Dolly" in which she ate an entire roast chicken on stage every night, and admitted that she gained weight during the show. Other major performers include Van Cliburn at the Kennedy Center; ballet stars Martha Graham, Edward Villela, and Rudolph Nureyev.

At Great Woods in Mansfield, we attended many performances, while it was still the venue for the Pittsburgh Symphony Orchestra. There we enjoyed Michael Feinstein and violinist Joshua Bell (very early in his career). As President of the Portuguese-American Federation, I held a reception and dinner at Great Woods for Elmar Oliveira, a son of Portuguese immigrants. I shook Elmar's hand but had to be gentle because his hands are very valuable. You may not recognize his name, but he was one of the premier major concert violinists in the world.

His musical ability led him to be the only American violinist to win the Gold Medal at Moscow's Tchaikovsky International Competition in 1976. He has since performed worldwide with numerous prestigious symphony orchestras. He is also a recipient of the Order of Santiago, Portugal's highest civilian honor.

At the Warwick Music Circus, we were entertained by many artists including Englebert Humperdink, Tom Jones, Don Rickles, Billy Crystal, the flamboyant Liberace, and Steve and Edie Gorme.

Jan and I spent a great weekend in New York City with Ellen and Charlie Collis, and Lisa and Amir Missaghian. We took the Acela into the city and checked into the Helmsley Palace on Central Park South. Leona Helmsley owned many hotel properties in NYC but spent years in for jail for allegedly committing tax fraud. When we arrived at the Hotel, she was there holding her little dog and overseeing the employees.

Our visit to NYC was only two months after the 9-11 attacks on the World Trade Center. The city was in a depressed mood, still recovering from the shock, but we were not. We took advantage of the special pricing in many restaurants (prices were reduced city-wide to encourage tourism which was suffering after the attack). On Saturday we had tickets to "The Full Monty" which had many off-color themes. Ellen looked at me early into the show with disdain, thinking that I had taken her to an X-rated production. As the show progressed and got funnier and funnier, Ellen was the one who was laughing the hardest, even during the full male nudity parts (rear-view only). We were all in a good mood after the finale.

We took a cab back to the hotel and were laughing loudly about the show. The cab driver was happy to see tourists in a good mood. He said we were the first group of people to ride in his cab in such a spirited mood since 9-11.

Saturday night we had dinner at The Grand Circle Restaurant at the Metropolitan Opera. The food was great. The production of La Boehme was a visual spectacle. The scenery and costuming were amazing, the singing thrilling. The entire day was a wonderful experience we will never forget.

After Sunday Mass, we went to the Plaza Hotel for its famous (and fattening) brunch at the Palm Court. We ate delicious gourmet food for about three hours. A strolling violinist entertained us, as we ate like gluttons. The desserts were to kill for. A bargain at $65.00 per person. The Plaza has since been renovated into condominiums with only a few floors remaining as hotel rooms. It is my understanding that the brunch has been re-established at The Palm Court.

All good things must come to an end. We went back to Providence on the Acela – full of good food with two couples who have been life-long friends, and part of our extended family.

Morton Hospital Follies

In 1982 the idea of Morton Hospital employees doing stage shows came from Eleanor Gay, the hospital's Director of Public Relations. Others who joined her in developing the concept were Carol Gonsalves as Choreographer, Kyle Sepersky, and several others from the hospital community.

The first program that I remember was a fashion show at the Coyle and Cassidy High School auditorium. Many of the medical staff walked down the runway dressed in various outfits. Clothing was supplied by Fosters and other Taunton clothing stores. My outfit was for the weekend skier, and I went on stage carrying skis on my shoulders, dressed in a warm outfit including a scarf, gloves and a knit ski hat. That was the only time in my life I was a skier! I guess my Mother's protective influence on me became obvious as I got to be in my mid-thirties and early forties. I avoided activities in which I might get injured. Who would pay the bills if I couldn't work?!

My first solo performance for the Morton Follies was in 1984. Roseland Ballroom on Broadway was set up like a nightclub with tables and chairs. Drinks were available at the bar. The show was called "The Cabaret Capers" and featured a variety of singers and dancers. I found it difficult to get into the part of Tevye in "Fiddler on the Roof" – the wonderful play about changing times in Russia, during the reign of the Tsars in 1905. I think my family became very tired of listening to me rehearse "If I were a Rich Man." By listening to tapes of Zero Mostel's performance, I picked up some of the accent and annotations needed to sing the song successfully. My outfit included pants tucked into boots, a loose fitting white shirt and an open vest, similar to how a peasant would dress in Russia. I enjoyed performing this role very much, and I trust the audience enjoyed it as well.

Another year we did a skit based on Saturday Night Live's newscast parody. Ours was based on current events in Taunton and around the country. On the afternoon of the performance, I received a phone call from one of the hospital employees, recommending that I not wear "good" clothing for the skit. I thought that was an unusual request but went along with her advice. The skit included slides of current events shown on a portable slide screen. At the end of the newscast, I was hit in the face with a cream pie by the girl who called to warn me. Some of the whipped cream landed on my slide screen and stained it. It was great fun performing this skit. The best part was being able to read our scripts, and not have to memorize lines.

Another year, the head of hospital security and I did a scene from the movie "The Odd Couple," written by Neil Simon, where one of the characters says the word "enter" several times in response to the knocking on the door. No one came through the door despite the character's repeated requests to enter. It was not well-received and was a flop. In anticipation of the audience's reaction, I set up members of my family with plastic fruit and vegetables to throw at me and my cohort at the end of the skit. Several of my family members rose from their seats, booed, and yelled, as they bombarded us with plastic food. At least that was funny.

My favorite solo performance was in a scene from "The King and I" in 1986. I had a few months to get ready for the show. My family again had to suffer through repeated rehearsals at home, and with multiple viewings of Yul Brenner performing in the movie version. Costumes for the performance were designed by Connie Ross, wife of the hospital administrator. Sewing the costumes was done by the mothers of the Siamese children. My outfit included a shirt made of shiny, satin material and loose fitting knee length pantaloons. I wore sandals with straps around my ankle. Under my open shirt was a t-shirt depicting a muscular chest and six-pack abs.

Author as the King of Siam with his children

To look more like Yul Brenner, I shaved my goatee and wore a skin-toned skull cap. My wife Janice was not aware of my shaving off my thirty-year-old goatee. My appearance changed so drastically that when I appeared on stage, Janice said to one of our children, sitting next to her in the audience – "that's not dad." She was not happy that I was clean-shaven.

There were three musical numbers from the show – "The March of the Siamese Children," "Getting to Know You," and a parody of "Shall We Dance?" titled "Do I Shave?" The first scene included seven beautifully dressed Siamese children entering the stage to the music of "The March of the Siamese Children." As each child approached me, he or she bowed. I acknowledged them with a slight bow, and announced that the golden rule is "in this country no one's head should be higher than the king's." I playfully began to bow, lower, and lower, and lower, with Mrs. Anna and the children's heads still bowing lower than mine. Next, I went on my knees and then sprawled onto the stage with my face to the floor. The children laughed and giggled as they assumed the position. We stood up, and I sang the parody of "Shall We Dance?" titled "Do I Shave?" as the children bowed and backed off the stage. I then danced off, twirling Mrs. Anna who became so dizzy, that I almost had to carry her off the stage. I didn't know that Evelyn Irby, RN (Mrs. Anna) suffered from vertigo caused by excessive twirling. The next day's performance we slowly danced off, with no twirling.

Author as Tevye, performing from Fiddler on The Roof

It was a fun performance for all, and the highlight of my brief stage career. I recently bumped into a woman, whom I had not seen in 25 years. During our conversation, she asked a question that surprised me – "are you still active in the performing arts?"

My final performance for the Morton Follies was in 1987 in a scene from the musical Zorba. In that show, I sang "I Am Free" which was originally performed on Broadway by Herschel Bernardi. Zorba was a man who was a free thinker. The song expressed his philosophy of life with lyrics – "I have nothing, I want nothing, I am free." The song was followed by a vigorous Greek circle dance. The characters shouted "Oopha" as we twirled around the stage. The dance was proposed by a friend, Steven Kardamis who was proud of his Greek heritage. I think he was pleased with the performance.

As you can see from the numerous stories above, I have had a variety of experiences involving the performing arts. As they say "Let's Go on with the Show."

Old Colony Historical Society

My involvement in community affairs and functions in Taunton was quite extensive. The organization to which I gave the most time and effort was the Old Colony Historical Society (OCHS). Just a short brief history of the Society: The OCHS was founded May 4, 1853. Originally it met in a house near St. Mary's Church on Washington Street. A larger building was acquired on Cedar Street which allowed exhibit and storage space in a stone building that was later used as a movie theater when I was growing up. In 1926, the OCHS moved to its current location on Church Green. It moved into the Bristol Academy building which was designed by renowned architect Richard Upjohn in 1852. Upjohn also designed St Thomas Episcopal Church and Pilgrim Congregational Church in Taunton. The Bristol Academy building is in Taunton's Church Green National Register District of Historic Places. I consider the building an architectural gem, and I was honored to be involved in carrying out its mission. The 2012 Annual Report of the Society states its mission is to: "collect, care for, and interpret the history of the Taunton region, collaborating with the community to share meaningful connections between the past, the present, and the future, to this end containing books, documents, artifacts, and decorative arts relating to the region's history."

Postcard photo by the Author, circa 1985

My earliest contact with OCHS was in my senior year at Taunton High School. The high school history club celebrated the 100th anniversary of the Gold Rush by writing and performing a play about the era. We researched the Society for names of people who went to California at that time. These names were used in the play. My part in the play was to lead the cast in two songs of the period – "Oh Susannah" and "My Darling Clementine." Perhaps you could call this my debut as a singer?

The most memorable lines in the play were performed by Fay Louison (sister of Leonard Louison, a friend and a lawyer in Taunton for many years). Faye, portraying a woman who was joining the Gold Rush, stated "Farewell to Taunton, home of swaying elm trees and Taunton High School," as tears fell from her eyes.

My next contact with OCHS was when Jan and I joined as members in 1972. I was encouraged to join by the President of OCHS, Dr. Jordan D. Fiore, Professor of History at Bridgewater State College. Jordan was a dear friend and confidant, as well as a lifelong patient. Later in 1984, I became a member of The Board of Trustees. In 1998 I was elected Vice President. On April 20, 2000, I was sworn in as the 12th President of OCHS, a position I held for six years. I now hold the title of "honorary trustee."

Over the past years, I have given many illustrated programs at OCHS – many of them to capacity audiences. Since moving to Falmouth, I have had time to review more than 25,000 slides taken over the previous forty to fifty years. These slides included scenes of many events and celebrations that have occurred since 1964. I continue to review slides. There are still countless numbers of slides to be identified and then added to the collection of images at OCHS. During my tenure as President, I established the "Photographic Preservation Fund." Donations to the fund were originally to be used for preservation of the thousands of negatives and photographs in the collection. The funds have also been used to purchase supplies and equipment to preserve images on all media. Donations to this fund are a wonderful way to honor or memorialize someone. Donations are gratefully appreciated, and acknowledgment of the donation is sent to the honoree or the next of kin. It is my hope that donations will continue for future generations.

In an attempt to summarize my activities for this memoir, I searched through Annual Reports and Quarterly Newsletters. Fortunately, I found that my OCHS President's Report of 2005 included most of the highlights of my presidency, I have decided to include that report in its entirety in the pages that follow:

Annual report 2005
Old Colony Historical Society
Church Green
Taunton, Massachusetts

As outgoing president, I would like to take you on a brief trip down memory lane during my six years in office. In 2000, a review of our investment holdings showed that as years went by our stock portfolios contained only a few companies, due to mergers and buyouts. The Board selected Mellon Private Financial Asset Management to take over our investments and to diversify our stock portfolio. This proved to be a very good move. Of the many exhibits and programs in the year 2000, the exhibit of framed Civil War photographs from the collection of the Medford Historical Society "Landscapes of the Civil War" was a standout success.

Recognizing the large number of Portuguese Americans in Taunton, the Old Colony presented an exhibit "Presepios Acorianos," a collection of ceramic figures representing the nativity and religious festivals in the Azores. The exhibit was loaned by the Museo de Presepio in Lagoa, San Miguel, the Azores. Our society was given considerable exposure to the numerous Tauntonians of Portuguese descent who are an integral part of the community, and a group to which I am proud to belong. In 2001, in addition to very diverse presentations at our regular meetings, a major exhibit was "Work and Play." The Lives of Children in Taunton, 1870 to 1920. We added two new employees to our staff, Raymond A. Gagnon, caretaker and Fred Robinson, museum assistant. The choice of these men has proven to be a great asset in the maintenance of our building and collections.

In 2002, we celebrated the 150th-anniversary of our own venerable Bristol Academy building designed by Richard Upjohn. The Pilgrim Congregational Church was also built in 1852 and designed by the same architect. These events were celebrated at a joint meeting of the organizations with a slide lecture about Richard Upjohn. The presentation was followed by an organ concert on the newly restored Johnson and Sons organ. Our finances improved greatly as we became the recipient of a sum of money from the estate of George Soper. We also received the National General Operating Support Grant totaling $36,842 over two years from the Institute of Museum and Library Services, the ninth time we had received that award. Old Colony Historical Society entered cyberspace in January by launching a website, opening our organization for review throughout the world.

In 2003, our Sesquicentennial year was very exciting. The Board made available a significant amount of money to support several well-attended and successful events. Starting in January, an open house was held. At that affair, the winner of the logo contest was announced - Ms. Kendra Dooley, a student at Taunton High school. This logo was used on all 150th-anniversary materials. On May 4, 2003, the exact day of the founding of the society 150 years before, we held an anniversary party on our grounds. Several groups performed throughout the day - a barbershop chorus, Portuguese music ensemble, Native American storytelling, a traveling medicine man show, and Irish step dancers were enjoyed by our members and guests. Much ice cream was eaten along with popcorn, soda and large slices of birthday cake. A color photograph was taken at the celebration showing schoolchildren dancing around the Maypole graced the cover of our 2003 annual report. It was enjoyable to watch an old tradition being revived thanks to the leadership of Mrs. Eleanor Calvin.

In June we conducted a very well attended "Tour of Homes of Distinction and Houses of Worship." On October 16, the society presented award-winning filmmaker Ken Burns, who enthralled the audience at Taunton High School with American subjects – "The Civil War, Baseball, and Jazz." Mr. Burns was the guest of honor at a society reception following the lecture. On October 25, over 350 people participated in the Mount Pleasant Cemetery walking tour. Eighteen costumed interpreters brought people to life who were interred there. For a brief period, the many important people buried there were able to talk to our visitors.

In 2004, progress was made in planning renovations to our building. Evaluations of our building by members of the architectural firm of Menders, Torrey, and Spencer of Boston resulted in a two-volume master plan for the Society. This document will serve as a blueprint for the Society's property management for the next twenty years.

The scope of this project would result in considerable expense. Because of this, the Board commissioned a feasibility study by the well-respected museum consulting firm of Case and Mann. After their interviews with twenty-plus citizens concerned with Taunton's history, they felt that a major capital campaign was not practical. The board decided to approve a renovation project in phases starting with our priority handicapped access. The funding for this renovation included a matching grant of $100,000 from the Massachusetts Historical Commission, and two Community Development Block Grants totaling $50,000 from Taunton's Office of Economic and Community Development. Additional funding from Col. Ruby Winslow Linn had been received over several years specifically for handicapped access, and another anonymous donor came forward to honor the memory of Arthur J.F. Tutton.

Charles Collis donating a $25,000 gift to The Old Colony. Jane M. Hennedy as Director, far right.

A former Tauntonian, Charles A. Collis, donated a gift in the amount of $25,000 to be used at my discretion, and in my honor. With some of these funds, the portrait of George Washington was restored. In addition, audio and visual equipment was purchased. Another former Tauntonian, Mrs. Mary Shaub of Northhampton included the society in her estate in 2004. The gift included an endowment fund named after her father Elliott B. Church; the fund was more than $1 million. Additionally, important Taunton furniture was willed, including a tall case-clock made by Abner Pitts who resided on Church Green, only two doors away from our building.

I'm finally getting to 2005. It was a year full of activity and excitement. I will mention some of the programs and activities. In January, a lecture on diners was presented by Richard Gutman, titled "Meals on Wheels – The Diners of Taunton," in association with an exhibit by guest Curator Emily Milot, "Dog Carts and Owl Wagons – Taunton's Night Lunch Wagons from Galligan's to Hickeys." For the April annual meeting, Louis Ricciardi's talk was "Payable on Demand, Paper Money, and the Broken Banks of Bristol County." He also generously loaned several rare Taunton area banknotes for the accompanying exhibit.

In October the family of Richard De Wert donated to our permanent collection the Congressional Medal of Honor given to Navy Medical Corpsman Richard De Wert, posthumously, for valor shown during the Korean War. The medal was instituted by President Abraham Lincoln. Only 3,441 individuals have ever received one. Richard De Wert's Medal of Honor now has a permanent place in our military history room. A presentation ceremony was held at which Richard De Wert's relatives and servicemen who served in the same Marine unit with De Wert (Dog 7 Company) participated. A major exhibit by curator Jane Emack-Cambra entitled, "Daring, Dauntless, and Defiant: Richard De Wert and the

**Old Colony Historical Society Board of Directors, 2003. Courtesy of
Old Colony Historical Society, photo by Dick Arikian**

Korean War" was well received, as was a program about Corpsman DeWert, given by archivist Andrew D. Boisvert.

The groundbreaking ceremony for our handicap ramp was held on September 2, 2005. This started the first phase of our Master Plan. By the end of 2005, the new roof was almost completed. Work on the cupola was in progress. Interior changes including accessible restrooms, a new office for our director, and improvements to the front office and hallway were nearly completed. The accessible ramp and brick plaza were shaping up well.

It has been an honor to serve as president of this Society for the past six years. My term 2000-2006 was made an easy task by a very cooperative Board of Directors, by the hard-working members of various committees of the Board, and by the countless volunteers who gave freely of their time to the Society. I would be remiss if I did not mention the following individuals without whose efforts we would not have a successful Society: Former Director Kathryn P. Viens, current Director Jane M. Hennedy, Assistant to the Director Elizabeth M. Bernier, Curator Jane Emack-Cambra, former Archivist Greta R. Smith, Archivist Andrew D. Boisvert, Caretaker Raymond A.Gagnon, and museum Assistant Fred J. Robinson.

I am proud to leave the society with a considerably improved financial status and with an improved physical plant. I wish the incoming President success in his or her endeavors and look forward to the future implementation of the next phases of our Master Plan.

Sincerely yours,

David F. Gouveia

An Evening with Ken Burns

In 2003, The Old Colony Historical Society celebrated its 150th Anniversary. The Board decided to sponsor an event featuring, internationally known personality, Ken Burns. We did this as a community gesture by presenting a program by this historian and filmmaker. His fee was quite high, but we were able to negotiate the price down and reduce the cost somewhat with his agent. The Taunton High School auditorium which seats 1000 people was reserved for the presentation. We also planned to have a VIP reception at the Society after his lecture. The reception was a fundraiser, with hors d'oeuvres and wine, as well as a chance to meet and speak with Ken Burns in person. On arrival at the Old Colony, he was given a tour of the museum by the staff and appeared very impressed by the museum's collection. As President of the society, it was my privilege to escort him to the high school where there were approximately 700 people in the audience.

Before we arrived at the high school, I drove Ken around historic areas of Taunton, informing him on the city's historical background. I pointed out significant architecture and mentioned various types of manufacturing that had a major effect in making Taunton what it was. His program discussed American culture and history. Topics covered were baseball, the automobile, and the Civil War. It was a pleasure to see the positive reaction by the audience for this program. At the end of his talk, he came backstage and asked if I knew a quick way out

In celebration of our
Sesquicentennial
Anniversary

Old Colony
Historical Society

is pleased to present
documentary filmmaker

KEN BURNS

*From Lewis and Clark
to Frank Lloyd Wright:
Ken Burns on American Culture*

Thursday, October 16, 2003
Taunton High School
6:30 – 7:30 p.m.

Ken Burns from 2003 Sesquicentennial Anniversary program

of the auditorium. He felt that if we went into the crowd, out front, that we would not get to the reception at a reasonable time. I knew the inner workings of this high school and its "secret" exits.

He and I walked down an unlighted corridor to a loading platform, where we could easily get to my car and drive to the Historical Society. The reception went well, and Ken was a big success. He was friendly to speak with and made a lasting impression on our members. I have discussed other celebrations of the Sesquicentennial of the Society in other areas of these writings.

The Massachusetts Medical Society

I don't have the exact year when I joined the Massachusetts Medical Society (MMS). It was during my residency at St. Elizabeth's Hospital. My chief of surgery, John Spellman M.D., was vice president of the Medical Society at that time. He encouraged his residents to become members of the Society. One definite advantage was the malpractice insurance made available to its members. Medical Protective Insurance Company offered coverage for $25 a year. I continued with that insurance for many years into my private practice, but rates climbed quite a bit in the 1960s.

To become a member of MMS, it was necessary to go through a personal interview with a "Censor." My interview is still clear in my mind. The interview was held at the headquarters of the Society at 22 The Fenway, Boston. I was interviewed by an elderly gentleman dressed like a "Proper Bostonian." It was not a comfortable position to be in. 22 The Fenway was an impressive brownstone building with a very formal interior and dark wood-paneled walls. Membership was treated somewhat as an honor, rather than the current attitude that any medical doctor or osteopath is eligible, assuming he or she has no criminal history.

After my two-year U.S. Army appointment, I returned to Massachusetts and became active in the Society. Dr. C. Nason Burden encouraged me to join the local division of the MMS, the Bristol North District Medical Society. He was also instrumental in having me appointed to the Council, and to various committees of the Society.

The Council of the MMS, now called the House of Delegates, meets twice a year to discuss and vote on matters pertinent to the practice of medicine. The format for the House of Delegates is similar to the American Medical Association (AMA) deliberations. The meetings also include educational sessions. As president of the Bristol North District for two years, it was my responsibility to book meetings and choose appropriate speakers for the meetings. Dr. Barbara Rockett was president of the MMS for two terms from 1985 to 1987. She was the first female to be elected to the position.

I invited Barbara, who was a classmate and friend at Tufts Medical, to be the guest speaker at our meeting at Wheaton College. Many more members came to the meeting than had made reservations. The kitchen ran out of the main course. Barbara and I had to wait for whatever was available in the kitchen. What it was, we were not certain, let's just call it "mystery meat." It was terrible. We had a good laugh over it, but I was embarrassed that the President of the MMS had to share an inedible meal with me.

Customs have changed a lot. In the 1970s and 1980s, cigars were distributed after the meal. Many members smoked cigars after dinner. Jan was not happy when I came home because I came home smelling of cigar smoke. All our meetings are now smoke-free. We believe the Attorney General's warning that smoking is harmful to our health.

For several years I was involved in the American Medical Political Action Committee (AMPAC). AMPAC meetings were held in the evening in Auburn, Massachusetts, about an hour and a half away.

AMPAC was involved in legislative matters pertaining to the practice of medicine at the national level. Activities of the group included visits to US Senators and Representatives in Washington. I found it interesting to be intimately involved in the political process.

One year, I went with Dr. Burden to the AMA meeting in Chicago, where I was an observer of the House of Delegates. One evening, we were to meet with other members for dinner at a local restaurant. We got the directions but went out the back of the hotel instead of the front door. Dr. Burden and I walked in South Chicago for quite a while. We recognized our mistake, returned to the hotel and went out the correct front door, finding the restaurant immediately. For those of you who are not familiar with Chicago, South Chicago was basically a combat zone. Fortunately, we did not get into to any altercations.

I have been a member of the Nominating Committee for many of my years of membership. In that committee, I have been involved in choosing officers of the society and, AMA representatives. I am proud to say that I was instrumental in nominating Dr. Burden for President of the MMS from 1976 to 1977.

Another appointment was on the Committee on Legislation, where I was an alternate to Dr. Burden. We met at the Harvard Club on Commonwealth Avenue in Boston. Parking was a problem there, but the biggest problem was snowfall. It seemed that the winter meetings were always accompanied by a blizzard. We had some hazardous trips back to Taunton.

During the early years of my belonging to the Council, we met at the Park Plaza Hotel in the Park Square, Boston. Our meetings were held in the elegant ballroom. Lunch was always the specialty of the house, broiled scrod. It was a gourmet's delight. May I add that we were also served Boston cream pie for dessert.

My main contribution to the MSS was being a member of the Committee on Ethics and Grievances. I served as a member for five years, following which I was recommended to be the Chair by the outgoing Chair, Dr. Leonard Morse of Worcester Massachusetts. Dr. Morse is a prominent figure in the field of ethics and has been very involved in the AMA deliberations on ethics.

Mass Medical Ethics Committee members and legal advisors

I chaired the committee on Ethics and Grievances for five years and was honored with a plaque that reads:

Massachusetts Medical Society

David F. Gouveia, M.D. In appreciation for 10 years of dedicated service as a member of the Committee on Ethics and Grievances. Including services as Chair since 2011.

May 11, 2006.

Since the late 1970s, I have held the position of Secretary of the Bristol North District Society. It became time for "young blood" to take over. My resignation will take effect in May 2015. It has been a good long run.

I intend to remain as a Delegate to the House of Delegates at MMS and attend the annual meetings in May, and the interval meetings in early winter.

Appreciation plaque with Alan M. Harvey, M.D.

GHOST STORIES

Ghost Stories Introduction

Taunton, Massachusetts was the site of settlements in 1637 and was founded as a town in 1639. As a member of Taunton's 350 Anniversary Committee, I organized a "Tour of Houses and Churches" in September 1989. Included on tour were several homes of significant historic architecture, as well as 18 churches opened for viewing.

Two of the houses on tour had histories of abnormal occurrences that suggested paranormal activity.

The following stories are based on details that I was told by occupants of the homes visited during the tour. I have also included the story of a third building that was not on this tour but had considerable historical importance.

A fourth story is included of unusual activity occurring at Morton Hospital's Nurses' Home.

I do not rule out the possibility that ghosts occupy other locations in Taunton since I have not had the occasion to discuss the paranormal activity with their owners.

The Pie Lady in the Window

In a pastoral New England setting, sits an antique Federal style house. This extremely well-preserved property was built in 1805 and was featured in the 1989 Tour of Homes. There, we heard the story of the "pie lady in the window." Over the years, people going by the house reported seeing a lady, holding a pie, in the front window of the second floor. This was reported not just one time, but there were many times the vision was evident to those who passed by the house. Our curiosity was piqued by this story, so we climbed the stairs to the second floor and stood at the window where the pie lady had been seen. I think imaginations can run wild under these conditions, but I definitely experienced a strange feeling in the room.

Two happenings verified the strange feeling. The first one involved a blind man with a seeing- eye dog. He and the dog climbed to the second floor. Contrary to the dog's training, he left his master behind and fled down the stairs, leaving the house completely. Incidents of this sort do not happen often. Seeing-eye dogs are trained to stay with their masters at all times. What caused the dog to flee? Was the pie lady involved? I leave that to you to make the decision.

The second strange occurrence had to do with my camera. As I may have said previously, photography has been a big part of my life. I have owned and used a variety of cameras since my pre-teen years. As usual, that night I took many photos in the house. When the photos returned from the processor, most of the photos were clear and well exposed. However, all the pictures taken in the pie lady's room were clouded and blurred. I have no explanation as to why this happened. Is it possible that the pie lady was frightened by the flash from the camera, and did something to ruin the photos? Again I leave you to make the decision.

Another Ghost Story

A well-educated couple purchased a historic antique colonial house in North Taunton, near Field Street. Both worked out of town. She was employed by the legal profession. I don't recall what the husband's occupation was, but he also was out of the house during the weekdays.

It was their intention to start a weekend bed and breakfast inn, specializing in honeymooners who were interested in colonial times. They hoped to cook meals for their guests using colonial cookware in their large stone fireplaces. The home was one of the several buildings of architectural significance on tour. For our tour, they dressed in authentic colonial clothing, as they would for honeymooning guests.

I talked to them for a long time about the house and its well-preserved architecture. They told me a story about the first few months of ownership of the property. Shortly after moving into the house, they were aware of strange noises including loud banging and sounds of footsteps in the attic on weekend mornings. (They were not at home Monday through Friday during the day). It scared them a little. They felt there was a possibility that the attic could be haunted. They thought about it for a while, not knowing what to do about the noises. They decided to do some research on how to rid their home of possible ghosts. After considerable research, they decided to take a friendly approach to rid the ghosts, and solve the noise problem. It was their hope that being nice to the uninvited visitors would gain good results, and stop the problem.

One particular Saturday morning, there was considerable activity in the attic. They climbed the attic stairs and spoke loudly, offering an interesting solution. With statements like – "we are the new owners of this house. You are welcome to stay where you are; however, the noises are quite irritating. We would appreciate it if you could be quiet on weekends when we are home." After several similar weekend conversations, the activity in the attic ceased, and no further problems occurred.

This procedure sounds like a good solution to a puzzling situation. How would you have acted under similar circumstances?

A Possible Visit by a Very Old Ghost

History tells us that one of the first recorded murders in Taunton occurred at the McKinstry House. Built in 1759, the house has served as the rectory for the St. Thomas Episcopal Church since 1908.

In 1763 Dr. McKinstry's sister, 28-year-old Elizabeth, lived with the family. A slave named Bristol had been with the family since age 8. He was asked by Elizabeth to heat some irons in the fireplace so that she could do some clothes ironing. As she checked the irons, Bristol struck a severe blow to the back of her head causing her to fall into the hearth. He then dragged her unconscious body down the stairs to the cellar. There he took an axe and with both hands split her skull with it. She died about 24 hours later. The inscription on her headstone in the Plain Cemetery reads – "basely murdered by a Negro Boy."

Although he was deluded into thinking that the act would gain his freedom, he was hanged in the "hanging ground" at Plain Cemetery, near where his victim was buried. He was represented in court by Robert Treat Paine, a signer of The Declaration of Independence from Taunton.

St. Thomas Church, a Gothic Revival building, was designed by noted architect Richard UpJohn. It was built 1857-1859. In the 1970s and 1980s, Reverend Thomas Crum was the pastor at the church. Jan and I were friendly with him because of our involvement with Morton Hospital, where he was on the Board of Directors, and President of the Board of Trustees for two years.

Many of our close friends attended St. Thomas Church – the Betz family, the Pollards, the Marstons, the Millers, and the Russell family, among others. Over the years we attended several functions at the church, especially its annual fair, where we purchased beautiful items, some from other older Taunton families. There were also several dinners served at the Parish Hall. These dinners were prepared by various family members including John Pollard, who served up his famous chicken dish.

Reverend Crum and his wife Sarah, who was employed in administration at Wheaton College, invited Jan and me to dinner one evening. During the meal, served in the dining room next to the kitchen where the murder occurred, we had an interesting conversation about Elizabeth's murder. The Crums mentioned that unexplained events have happened in the house which caused them to question the possibility that a spirit could be the reason for these actions. As we enjoyed our meal, the lights went out for no apparent reason in the dining room. It was quite scary to sit in the dark and to consider the possibility that a spirit could have caused the blackout. The electricity returned spontaneously in a short time. A sigh of relief could be heard when the room brightened. Was the ghost of Elizabeth responsible for the loss of power?

Again, I ask the question – what do you think?

The McKinstry house was featured in the Tour of Homes of Distinction and Houses of Worship. This tour was held in celebration of the Old Colony Historical Society's 150th anniversary in 2003.

Morton's Ghosts

After I had written some of this topic, I found a two-page letter from Eleanor Gay with additional information on the Nurse's Home. Therefore, I have made alterations to my original thoughts.

But first I would like to give a little history of Morton Hospital and its student nurse programs. Registered nurses were graduated from Morton from 1889 – 1937 and 1941 – 1952. The program was discontinued because of increased requirements for an R.N. education that could not be met in a small community hospital environment.

In 1941 the Nurses Home at Morton was built as a dormitory with both classrooms and laboratories. After 1952, the building morphed gradually into an administrative building. As the years passed, the hospital had over 200 patient beds, and increasing administrative space was necessary to run the hospital. The Nurses Home became the answer to increasing needs for more office space.

The hospital was founded in 1889, in the home of the former governor of Massachusetts, Marcus Morton. The impetus for establishing a hospital came from Silas D. Presbrey, M.D. who started a subscription program of ten dollars per year for five years to help finance the project. One hundred and twenty-five subscribers and seventeen societies pledged the money to provide funding for the hospital.

The first patient was admitted in late 1889. The original hospital had only ten beds.

Now that I have given you a brief history founding of the hospital, let's look into the possibility of the Nurses Home being haunted. I became interested in that possibility after I spoke with the last person to live in the property. She was convinced that a "friendly ghost" shared the building with her. She detailed some of the unexplained events that she was aware of.

My friend, Eleanor Gay, and I discussed the situation, and she sent me her thoughts on it. Now that the Nurses Home has been torn down, where did the spirits go?

Eleanor Gay writes in her letter –

March 4, 2004

Dear Dave,

I apologize for the delay in getting back to you regarding Morton's friendly ghost in the Administration Building's 3rd floor.

After addressing the Morton Hospital retirees at the December meeting as well as asking several employees if they had heard or encountered the "ghost," it was evident that some had. However, they were in the minority.

This began when Colleen McGann called you to ask if you knew about the "ghost," as you are a historian. She thought it might be recorded at the Old Colony Historical Society. So then you followed up and got in touch with me.

Colleen works with Mary Kostanza on the 3rd floor. Mary not only felt a presence but saw a shadow. She told Colleen about it, and I can't remember if Colleen felt a presence. Cindy Reagan (Dori Bingham's PR assistant) who also works on the 3rd floor said she too had felt a presence, or someone looking over her shoulder.

I experienced the ghost while working Saturday mornings. I was alone, yet doors kept slamming, and footsteps could be heard running up and down the three flights of stairs. There are three floors in the building. I worked on the first.

One morning I decided to see who had brought kids in, or just what was going on with the commotion. I went from the basement (Personnel) to the 3rd floor calling out to anyone who might be working. No answer, just complete silence. When I got back to my office, the doors started slamming, and the running footsteps resumed.

I asked the hospital chaplain, Father Lagoa, the following Monday if he had come into work that Saturday. He said no, but he had heard about a "friendly ghost." I was never afraid, but when I found out the possibilities, I just locked my office door on Saturday mornings.

Sandy Seekell, the manager of the Anesthesiology office, said she too was aware of the ghost, a playful one when her office was in that building.

Sandy and her co-workers recalled their adding machines would suddenly start up, the computers would flicker, and the doors would slam shut. Sandy said they'd holler, "Hey, stop fooling around and do some work."

From the information I gathered from various conversations, the ghost was a student nurse whose boyfriend was killed in WWII. She committed suicide by jumping off the roof of the school. This would have made the Taunton Daily Gazette, so it's doubtful that it actually occurred. I have heard other stories that the friendly ghost is a retired nurse who was allowed to live on the 3rd floor until she died.

Dorie Cabral Borsari recalled an incident when the Nursing School's Class of '51 went out to celebrate their graduation and upon their return found their rooms in disarray. Clothes, books, paper, everything was scattered around the room. Nothing was stolen, so they decided it was a prank. Dorie had told Eileen Friary about my call, and both agreed it could have been the ghost that ran rampant in the rooms. Dorie and Eileen worked on maternity after graduating.

There is another story told to me by Lorraine Tonry. Lorraine said on some nights a nurse in a rocking chair could be seen on the roof of the Administration building. A couple of retirees said that they either witnessed or heard about it and that it was visible from the old operating room. That was before the mansion was demolished. (That one kind of gives me the creeps!)

There's also a story about the rack holding stethoscopes. One stethoscope would start swinging, and the others would follow.

Barbara Baskas told me that she lived in the old Nursing School before finding an apartment when she first came to Morton. Barbara had never heard of the ghost.

As a retired Director of PR & Development, I wouldn't want people to be afraid to come to Morton because it might be haunted. However the Administration building is separate from the Hospital and judging from the stories I have heard, there are "believers."

I received a Christmas card from Wendell Buck. He retired as a special assistant to Larry Ross. Dell said that if I wanted more information on the ghost to talk to George Ferreira.

Let me know what you plan to do with the "friendly ghost" if anything!

My best to Jan.

Eleanor.

Addendum by DFG: Since this letter was written, the Administration Building (formerly the Nurse's Home) has recently been torn down.

"Whither goest the ghosts?"

TRAVEL STORIES

Auschwitz – Birkenau

The following information about Auschwitz was adapted from a book I wrote, based on information that I put on tapes during a tour of Poland in 1990. These tapes were transcribed by Vicky Andrews, my typist, who had to struggle as much as I did, trying to spell Polish words and names of locations. I also referred to Wikipedia for additional information.

Jan, Hedy and I went on a three-week tour of Poland, with a group of Polish-Americans from Rhode Island and Massachusetts. During our travels, we saw many beautiful farms in the countryside. It was said that Poland could raise enough food to feed all of Europe. Most of the major cities in Poland were totally destroyed during the WW II bombings and fires. Only Krakow was not destroyed. The cities now consist of newly constructed buildings, done in such a way that they appear centuries-old. Fortunately, photos and architectural plans were available to enable workmen to rebuild accurately.

On June 9th, I left the tour group and took an English-speaking bus tour to Auschwitz. We drove through the very pleasant countryside between Krakow and Auschwitz, with pastoral scenes leading to the concentration camp. On arrival at the "factory of death," we were shown a 30minute film produced by the Russians in black and white, as an introduction to the camp.

The film stated that 4 million people were killed there. Rudolf Hess testified at the Nuremberg Trials, after the war that up to three million people died there. 2.5 million were gassed. Five hundred thousand died from disease and starvation. Around 90% of the victims were Jewish. Others executed groups included 150,000 Poles, as well as Romas (Gypsies), Soviet prisoners of war, Jehovah's Witnesses, and homosexuals. These victims were brought there from 29 countries, under the pretense that they were being relocated.

The exact number killed will never be known. Many registration records at Auschwitz have been destroyed. In addition, many thousands were killed before even being registered. Any person, weak or ill, was not registered. They were killed on arrival. Children under a certain height were killed. It is said that children who knew about the height requirement would stand on tip-toes and extend their neck hoping to make the height requirement. So much tragedy happened there that even in a 90-minute tour, it might take pages to summarize. After watching the introductory movie, we started the tour in the pouring rain. We went through the famous gates with the German slogan "Arbeit macht frei" – translated "work makes you free."

Some of the Auschwitz buildings were destroyed by the Nazis prior to their downfall, but enough stand to vividly portray the horror. We were shown registration certificates of people from many countries, including one man from Chicago who was apparently visiting for the Holy Days. Jews from as far away as Greece were brought to Auschwitz. In the museum, many photographs, measuring at least 4x6 feet demonstrated the activities in the camp. Our guide explained things quite well. She showed us the living conditions for thousands of people crowded into small quarters. We saw one room filled with human hair, all of it gray, a result of the poisonous gas exposure.

After death, the hair was cut off and sent to Germany, to be woven into cloth, or used for other items such as shaving brushes and hair brushes. Other rooms contained over 110,000 shoes. Only the shoes of poor condition were kept. The good shoes were sent to Germany to be worn. In the exhibit of suitcases which numbered close to 4,000, was the suitcase of Anne Frank's father. Other rooms contained empty canisters of cyanide salts. Thousands of eyeglasses were exhibited. All gold, silver and precious stones were kept by the Germans. Gold teeth were removed from the dead. One room was filled with hundreds of prostheses taken from people before incineration.

Auschwitz was also a site for major medical experimentations. Experiments including sterilization of men and women were performed with the hope of finding a permanent means of sterilization, thus ensuring that only one "superior race" would endure.

Dr. Joseph Mengele was known as the "Angel of Death" experimented on identical twins, and on dwarfs. He would use drugs on one of the twins, and then autopsy both twins to evaluate the effects of the drugs. Interestingly, according to information on the internet, some drug companies bought prisoners to use as guinea pigs for testing new drugs.

In the basement, we visited various prison chambers. We saw a stand-up chamber in which four men were crowded in a small square just big enough for them to stand up all night. They then returned to heavy labor the next day. This process was repeated until they died. We saw the rooms where the prisoners undressed, and then went out to the firing squad. Those to be shot, stood in front of symbols indicating their crimes (being Jewish, a Gypsy, or homosexual).

We visited the prison cell where Maximillian Kolbe died. Kolbe was a Franciscan Friar who was imprisoned at Auschwitz. He volunteered to die in the place of a married stranger, who was scheduled for execution. For his work at the prison, and for sacrificing his life, he was canonized in 1982 by Pope John Paul II. Wikipedia says that he is the patron saint of drug addicts, political prisoners, females, journalists, prisoners, and the pro-life movement. He is honored in the Roman Catholic Church, the Lutheran Church, and in the Anglican Church. I have read his biography, and recommend it to anyone who wishes to be inspired by a holy man's actions.

Before taking us to the gas chambers, our guide pointed out the gallows that were used to hang the German, Rudolph Hess, in 1970. He was convicted of being involved in so many atrocities.

In the gas chamber, which was partially underground, the tour participants were informed that in this location, prisoners were told to take their clothes off to take a shower. Just as the prisoners were treated, we were suddenly in total darkness. I don't know if my imagination took control of me, but I heard a hissing sound consistent with gas being blown into the room. For that brief period, I was horrified. The lights came back on, and we were taken into the incineration room. Two incinerators had been reconstructed, using plans found at the site. Also, some of the incinerator parts were left behind. Going into the incinerators were two narrow-rail tracks on which were two large metal bins. These bins looked big enough to carry several dead bodies at a time into the incinerator.

In the last summer of Hitler's reign, about 20,000 people were killed at the camp daily. The crematories were unable to incinerate all of the bodies after they were gassed. To solve this problem, large ravines were excavated on the camp, into which dead bodies were thrown, then doused with benzene and set on fire. Survivors reported that the flames flew upwards, and the sky turned red, as the massive fires burned.

We then took a bus ride to Auschwitz II, also known as Birkenau. The original Auschwitz was in series of brick barracks built for the Austrian military in the 1920s and 30s. Auschwitz II consisted of wooden structures (barns, etc.) brought there by the Nazis. Living conditions were worse in these buildings – wooden beds on which six to eight people slept, were stacked four or five high. There was only one toilet for thousands. The toilet was nothing more than a hole in the floor. In both camps, underwear was only changed once in a few months, allowing diseases like typhus and scabies to run rampant.

Of interest is the fact that our guide had worked there for 18 years. She had promised her father-in-law that she would continue his work as a guide until she died. Her father-in-law was a former prisoner at Auschwitz. Our bus driver was a prisoner at Auschwitz, and our bus guide had relatives imprisoned there. This was a day that I will never forget. The world should never forget these atrocities.

I did not join our Polish tour for dinner and merriment. A visit to Auschwitz is too draining an experience. I returned to the hotel, sitting in the dark, eating fruit that I bought from a street vendor. I spent the evening trying to sort out thoughts in my head about the horror that I witnessed that day.

A Visit to Mexico

Jan joined me in Houston, Texas, where I was attending a surgical conference in 1972. Our plan was to fly to Mexico City to do some touring. We looked up hotels in the area. One hotel seemed to be the right one for us. It was an older hotel. Our travel agent gave us the information – it was one of the original hotels in Mexico City. It had Spanish architecture and was known to be very charming. It did not seem charming when we went to our room. What a disaster! The room was too small with one window that opened and provided the only "air conditioning." The view was of rooftops occupied by hundreds of pigeons cooing. In our bathroom was a dilapidated, dirty and broken toilet seat, and a visiting pigeon. There were no screens on the window, and pigeon droppings were everywhere.

Although we had prepaid for three nights, it didn't take Jan and me long to gather our luggage and get out of the hotel! "Keep our deposit" we yelled as we left the lobby and hailed a cab to a modern-looking hotel that we had seen on the way to the "Mexican Charmer." We checked into the Sheraton Maria Isabella and were pleased with our accommodations. Mexico City at the time suffered from a real smog problem. The sun was rarely able to penetrate the pollution. We walked around the city and at no time did we feel unsafe.

The highlight of the city for us was the National Museum of Anthropology where we saw the famous stone of the sun, also known as the Aztec Calendar. The museum had extensive displays of Aztec and Mexican artifacts. The National Museum was the most visited museum in Mexico.

At the National Palace, we were in awe over the massive murals by artist Diego Rivera, depicting scenes from the Mexican Revolution. Rivera was married for a short while to Frida Kahlo who was recently the subject of a popular movie.

One day, we hired a driver with another couple to take us to the pyramid sites, to Tasco and Guadalajara. Tasco was a "silver city" with literally hundreds of shops filled with sterling silver jewelry. Although Tasco was famous for its jewelry, we felt that the quality and the variety was not to our liking. We purchased very little in Tasco, which resulted in the unhappiness of our driver, who would have received a significant kick back, based on our purchases. In the jewelry shops in downtown Mexico City, we had seen better quality jewelry and silver artifacts. While shopping in the downtown area, Jan purchased a sunburst pendant with a green stone in the middle. She wears this piece occasionally, and each time receives comments on it.

The short trip to Guadalajara was exciting. The city is an ideal location for retirees. It has an ideal climate and is a city bursting with Spanish architecture. The best part of this day trip was our visit to the pyramids (Teotihuacan). The couple with us were a bit younger and more reserved than we were. This impression was obvious at the pyramid site – neither of our wives was willing to climb the pyramid. The men were more aggressive (or so I thought). The climb was difficult due to the narrowness and depth of the steps. The pyramid was at least ten stories high. We did not turn around until we reached the flat area at the top. At that point, our wives looked like miniature humans. After looking around for a while and viewing the other pyramids, it was time to go back down. What goes up, must come down. There were no ropes or banister to hang onto. The man, with whom I climbed, turned to me and asked: "can you carry me down?" He apparently suffered from a fear of heights and was very scared of descending the narrow stairs. I suggested that he sit on his butt, and descend one stair at a time – which he did. I carefully walked behind him taking one slow step after another. We reached the bottom without my companion dying, but his color was a pale green.

This day of touring was very satisfactory, and we returned to the hotel unscathed. On another day, we went to a minor league bull fight where training was held for prospective toreadors. It was all pomp and circumstance enhanced by the playing of appropriate music. Beautifully dressed toreadors in training added to the atmosphere.

The spectacle began with the bull being released into the arena. Picadors attacked the bull and eventually cut into the neck muscles of the bull to weaken his ability to attack. The toreador entered the rink waving his red flag to attract the bull and try and kill him. At one point it looked as if the bull would win the battle. Because of the inexperience of this toreador, he was lifted by the bull's horns and thrown into the air. The look on the rookie toreador's face is hard to forget. It was one of terror. Would he be killed by the bull? The picadors eventually rescued him and killed the bull. It was our understanding that the bull was used for food. Although it was a violent performance, it was interesting to be involved in a local, cultural experience, even if many people object to and try to stop bullfighting in Mexico altogether.

On a religious note, we went to Catholic Mass at the Basilica de Guadalupe in Mexico City. It is on this site where a peasant named Juan Diego saw a vision of the Virgin Mary in the 16th century. The building was completed in 1709 and houses the original cloak on which is the image of Our Lady of Guadalupe. Because the building has been sinking into the ground, it has recently been replaced with a new basilica, next to the original, which still stands but is tilting.

We sat just a few feet away from the original cloak. It is beautiful and revered by millions of Catholics worldwide. At Mass, which was in Spanish, we sat near the lector, as he read from the Bible. It was just a few months after the death of my father, John F. Gouveia. The lector could have been my father's twin. He had the same skin color and similar facial features. His general habitus was also similar to my father. If I believed in reincarnation, I would say that this man was my father's return to life. My emotions were hard to describe. I can still visualize this man whom I saw for just a few minutes, more than forty years ago, in the Basilica.

Because of stories we heard about getting sick on food and water in Mexico (Montezuma's revenge), we drank only from bottles that we opened. We avoided fruit that we could not peel. We ate no raw vegetables or salads. I even brushed my teeth with Sprite! On the last night in Mexico, I made a faux pas. I had a fancy rum drink with ice cubes. What a mistake! The next day we were scheduled to return to the USA, I woke up with an upset intestinal tract. To make matters worse, we were informed by our airline that only one seat was available on our flight back. Apparently, it was vacation week in Mexico, and all flights were filled. We had not reconfirmed our seats in time. I let Jan go home on our scheduled plane. I was offered a seat on a subsequent flight that was to arrive at 4-5am in the US. The flight was fine, but my gut was not. It was a common joke that planes leaving Mexico had a very large number of restrooms, compared to those arriving in Mexico.

We landed in the middle of the night, meaning that customs agents had to work overtime. They were not happy to see us. They were rude, abrupt, went through all of my bags, before allowing me access to my homeland. Little did they know, I was wearing several sterling crucifixes around my neck!

A Visit to Harry Winston Jewelers - 718 Fifth Avenue, N.Y., N.Y.

Harry Winston Jewelers is one of the most famous jewelry firms in the world. It has been in business since 1932 specializing in the most exquisite diamond jewelry. It has been made famous by the clientele it serves – the rich and the famous. Only the "upper crust" could afford to buy a Winston offering.

In 1958, Harry Winston donated the Hope Diamond to the Smithsonian. This large blue diamond is known for its rare color, perfect quality and large size. It was once owned by Louis XIV and stolen from him during the French Revolution. It is thought to be stolen, originally, from an idol in India, and it is said to have a curse, bringing bad luck and death to its owners and all who touch it.

It originally was 112.3 carats; it has been cut at least twice and is now 45.5 carats. On a trip to Washington, D.C., Jan, I, and our children were in awe of the size and beauty of the stone at the Smithsonian.

In 1963 Harry Winston also donated the "Portuguese Diamond" to the Smithsonian. This gem is 127 carats with faint yellow and blue fluorescence in an antique emerald cut.

I bring up Harry Winston because of an episode that occurred when we were in New York City with Susan, David, and Hedy and Walter Such. Strolling down Fifth Avenue, we passed by Harry Winston Jewelers. There was an armed guard at the door. The door was locked. I decided we should go in. This was not the usual jewelry store with glass enclosed cases displaying multiple items for sale. There were no display cases. The only displays along the walls were glass-protected jewels displayed in cubicles about 16 inches in size. Jan and I were the only people in the store since Hedy and Walter decided to stay with the children on the sidewalk.

We were approached by a salesman who asked: "what can I help you with." Jan was a little setback, the tone of the man's voice was haughty. Jan said she was interested in seeing opal jewelry. His answer was: "we only carry precious stones!" I asked if Myron was available, I was acquainted with his aunt who had been a patient at my office, and who was very proud of her nephew in New York City. She even recommended Jan, and I stop at Winston's and say hello to Myron.

Soon a gentleman came out of the backroom and introduced himself as Myron. He was very accommodating and suggested that my in-laws and our children come into the store. He then proceeded to take us into a private room with chairs and tables, where diamond jewelry was presented to potential clients. We were obviously not buyers who would be considering a purchase of such expensive jewels.

Our visit with Myron was brief and cordial. We discussed his aunt and his cousin Shoshana Garshick from Raynham, MA. The motto – "It's not what you know but who you know" applies to this situation.

I Googled Harry Winston and found some interesting reviews. I reviewed some 3 and 5-star reviews, but many of the comments were 1 star. Comments included - "I have never been in a store that made me feel so uncomfortable or out of place. The staff is extremely rude and pretentious." I know how that reviewer felt in our first minutes at Harry Winston's, but we became welcomed when I mentioned Myron's sweet old aunt.

MISCELLANEOUS

Bats in the Attic

People who are plagued with bats in their home usually don't talk about it. There is a certain "hush, hush" about the problem. We had bats in our attic at 248 Winthrop Street. All attempts at removal of them failed. We tried an exterminator, but his solution did not work. We placed moth balls in the attic to no avail. We purchased a sonar emanating machine run by electricity, but it didn't work. When checking the attic one day, I found that a bat had eaten through the wire and apparently committed "Kamikaze." We tried sticky fly paper to no avail. We knew that the bats "hung out" near the chimney. We knew this because of the collection of guano in that spot on the floor. Bat guano was selling for ten dollars a pound at that time, but who would buy it?!!!

Every once in a while, I would clean up the guano pile but was not successful in trying to sell it. Several times a bat got into the house. We were not certain what its point of entry was. One thing we knew was that leaving potpourri around attracted them. There was a feeling that the weather made the difference. I found out that bad lightning storms caused problems with their sonar, and in confusion, the bat would come into the house from the attic. Pandemonium struck each time we had a bat in the house. The children were petrified, Jan was anxious. Especially scary was the swoosh, swoosh sound as they flew around the house. We tried catching them in butterfly nets! We tried chasing them around. One time my father-in-law, Walter, pursued them with a broom and was quite happy when he captured one. Walter also used a tennis racket to kill another bat in David's bathroom. We eventually found a solution to get them out of our living quarters. The solution? Close the room off, keep the lights on, and open all the windows. When we did this, in the morning we had no bats. The brightness of the lights caused their departure. Another reason for their leaving was that we had no bugs for them to eat!

Bats are necessary to keep our food supply abundant; they eat insects that would otherwise damage the crops. On our cross-country trip, we didn't see the largest ball of twine; we did, however, visit the largest collection of bats in the country. To get there, we drove one complete day through Texas and New Mexico to Carlsbad, New Mexico, which is very near the Mexican border. We toured the Carlsbad Caverns where approximately 700,000 bats lived. Talk about guano! At dusk, we sat and watched the bats leave the caverns. They flew out in a counter-clockwise fashion as they departed the cavern for the night. Before dawn, they would return after eating insects all night. We were told at the caverns that the great southwest vegetable and fruit farms would not exist if it were not for the bats. They were unwelcomed guests to us at 248 Winthrop Street, but they were the salvation of the farmers of the Southwest.

Goldy's Obituary

The following is a great parody on the passing of "Goldy." Goldy was my mother-in-law, Hedy Such's car, a Buick Century, which apparently was the "official car of senior citizens." Before Lisa and Peter obtained the vehicle, "Gram" had not driven the car for some time, due to illness.

Goldy had very low mileage. It was not a stylish vehicle and in some circles was called a "fart mobile." It served Lisa and Peter well when they were in this country on vacation.

Her demise is described quite well in the obituary below. It seemed appropriate that during her Memorial Service, I heard the nicest words expressed, "doesn't she look good."

Obituary:

1995 Buick Century (Gold) Nick Name, Goldy. Deceased in this City of East Falmouth, Massachusetts on February 7th.

Goldy, the Levesque family's beloved 1995 Buick Century, passed away on Monday, February 7th after a brief illness. She was ten years old.

Goldy was purchased by the Levesque's via an inter-family transaction for an astounding $1.00 in August of 2001. The car was in service as the official Logan Airport shuttle ride, for most of her four years of service.

An aesthetic masterpiece, as well as a mechanical marvel, Goldy was capable of reaching speeds up to 55 miles per hour, before developing a gut-wrenching front axle shimmy that would render the driver helpless and at times, incontinent. Recovery from this otherwise fatal control maneuver was only possible by rapidly increasing the forward speed to 75 mph, causing a subtle nose down attitude, correctable with proper control inputs, using the car's sophisticated trim tab system (opening the trunk at high speeds could often achieve the same result).

Goldy took a turn for the worse in the recent snow storm activity on the Cape. She developed a serious cough that grew worse when her rear window was shot out with a BB gun! She spent weeks under the snow and ice, and despite a daring repair attempt on the window, using the finest duct tape and Johnny Walker Black Label cardboard, the damage was fatal.

Goldy was traded in at 530 pm on Monday, Feb 7. We told the children that Goldy was going to a place where she could run free with lots of other cars, and where she would be loved and tuned regularly. The children couldn't have cared less.

Viewing will be at the O'Hara Motors Auto Dealership in Falmouth on Saturday, Feb 12th. Calling hours will be 2-4pm and 7-9pm, followed by dinner. In lieu of flowers, please make donations to the "New Jeep Payment Fund" c/o Peter Levesque, 19 Eli Road, East Falmouth, MA. 02536

Please also note that the Town of Falmouth has determined that with the removal of Goldy from the neighborhood, property values have officially increased another 50% - so you can all expect a new assessment very soon.

Sincerely,

The Levesque Family

Some Games We Played at the Cape House

UpWords is a board game similar to Scrabble. It's similar to Scrabble, but it is played in three dimensions. During the game, players are allowed to place tiles on top of each other until the stack numbers five. Each additional tile has to make up a new word. Each player has a certain number of tiles to get rid of in order to win. When a tile is placed down, the player picks up a new one, until all of the tiles are used up from the bank. At times, no additional plays are possible, so the person with the fewest remaining tiles is the winner. Because players are allowed to challenge a word, we kept a dictionary on the table to check for accuracy. One night, while playing with the grandchildren, Sarah put the word "mead" on the board. I challenged her but lost the challenge. Mead is an alcoholic drink made from grains. A few days later Sarah was in a class in which the teacher used the word mead. She asked if any students knew what the word meant. Sarah's hand went up fast since she knew the answer. The teacher was surprised. Sarah called me that day to tell me about the class. So, I guess one could call UpWords an educational game.

One day in Boston, at The Games Store in Faneuil Hall Marketplace, I noticed a game called "Fact or Crap." We were with David and Nancy's family. I mentioned it would be a great gift for my birthday. When my birthday came around, I received the game as a gift. Fact or Crap is played as follows – one player reads a statement from a card, only he/she knows whether or not it is a true statement since the answer is on the card. The other players hold a paddle which on one side it says "Fact" and the other side says "Crap." Each player has to choose an answer. The players with the right answer get a plastic coin. The losers have to put a plastic coin back in the bank. The goal of the game is to get as many plastic coins as possible. What I found interesting about the game is the reaction from players who are adamant that their answers are correct. My most fun is reading the statements, and watching the reactions from the players, especially if they argue against what the card says is correct. So many facts that we take for granted in our daily activities are not what you think they are. Is this statement, that I am making, "Fact or Crap?!"

Other games played with the grandchildren include Kings in the Corner. This card game is also a favorite. The game requires skill similar to Solitaire; each participant has to assemble a column of cards from the king and queen down the line with the Ace being the lowest card. It is a game of luck, but it requires some ability to manipulate cards. Five or six-year-old children can play this game and win. All they need to do is keep an eye on the open lines and not miss any moves. Once you learn the concept of the game, you can become a real winner. As you know, youngsters love to win, and I enjoy letting them do it.

We also played Dominoes frequently. This game is easily learned at an early age and does not require difficult decisions. Jan and I have tried other board games and games of skill. But it is hard to beat UpWords, Fact or Crap, Kings in the Corner, or Dominoes. If you don't have these games or other favorite board games, please buy them and play with your children or grandchildren. It is something that will give them many good memories over the years, as well as giving them something to write about in their memoir.

PEOPLE STORIES

Pat and Norris

Pat and Norris in the playroom at 248 Winthrop Street

Just thinking about Pat and Norris Marston brings a smile to my face. We had so many exceptional times together. We were friends for most of our time together in Taunton. Pat (Patricia Slade Marston) was in many of my classes at Taunton High School. Pat was very tall; she didn't come from a vertically challenged family as I did. 5' 7" was the maximum height of my family. Pat was over 6 feet tall. I would describe her as "fun-loving" and boisterous. She was hard to define. She was fun to talk to in high school. She always had something to say, and she was the kind of girl you would like to see at a party. She knew how to enjoy herself.

Norris was an airline pilot with Delta Airlines, flying both nationally and internationally. He was full of hilarious stories about overnight stays at some of the cities that he flew to. One of his most memorable stories was a stay in downtown Detroit, where he went alone to what he thought was a restaurant. When he sat down, he was handed a menu that he had problems understanding. Rather than a restaurant, he had walked into a house of ill repute. The meals on the menu were codes for his choice of the evening's entertainment. When this was explained to him, he kindly excused himself.

After graduating in 1949 from Taunton High, our classmates went off to colleges in many parts of the country. I had no contact with Pat until after returning to Taunton in 1964. By that time she was married to Norris, had seven children, a macaw named Sebastian, a llama, and a variety of goats. She sold and gave away goats milk. She was especially generous giving away goat's milk for babies who were unable to tolerate cow's milk.

Let's talk about Sebastian, the Macaw. Macaws are native to Mexico, Central, and South America. In the wild, they like savannah type habitats. They are omnivores. They live eighty to one hundred years in captivity. According to the

National Geographic, owning a macaw requires a commitment to their long-term welfare including making arrangements for them, when the owner can no longer care for them. They bond deeply with their caregivers who take the place of the lifelong partners they might have had in the wild. Sebastian was not caged; his domain was the entire large entryway and the front parlor to the right of the entryway. A tree in the entryway served as his perch. He was allowed access to any room in the house at any time. He had an excellent speaking ability; he essentially was the doorbell for the house. Sebastian announced anyone entering the house with loud screeches "Pat! Pat! Pat!"

Pat and Norris had made arrangements to take care of him until his demise. I borrowed Sebastian for my 50th birthday party. The theme was "Hawaii 5-0." Guests were asked to wear Hawaiian clothing. Sebastian fit into the celebration quite well. Floral shirts and shirts with bird motifs were everywhere.

Tom Filkorn, an army friend from Chicago, helped us in roasting a pig with an apple in its mouth. Many Hawaiian type dishes were served to the guests. Over Eighty guests enjoyed themselves, and the party was a great success. After the party, Jan, Tom and Annie, his girlfriend, and I were sitting in the living room. Tom asked Annie to marry him. He was not on his knee, but she accepted. Tom was also very excited about having Sebastian at the party and became very friendly with him.

Getting Sebastian out of the house the next morning became quite an adventure. He had been locked in the playroom overnight and made the playroom his own habitat as well as his toilet. When I opened the playroom door, Sebastian flew onto my right soldier. I didn't think much about his being on my shoulder until I tried to get him off of it. Each time I tried to get him off me, he dug a little deeper to the point where I was afraid that my skin would be penetrated. Sitting in my kitchen, I tried to have him move to a perch on a chair. He would walk down my arm and stop near my hand, then walk back up to my shoulder. Jan and I were getting desperate. My arm and shoulder were beginning to get painful, so we called Pat and Norris to rescue me! The only lived about a mile away, so they arrived at the house very quickly. When Sebastian heard their voices on the patio, he got very excited flapping his wings and making noises. He immediately went to them, Praise the Lord.

Sometime later, Tom Filkorn was on a Delta flight when the crew was announced. Captain Marston was the pilot. Tom sent a note to the captain asking how Sebastian was. Soon Norris came into the cabin out of curiosity of as to who knew his macaw. They had a short and pleasant reunion.

More than once their llama and the goats escaped out of the backyard, and were seen parading down Weir Street during the night. A lot of people in Taunton had police scanner radios. They were amused by the police report of a menagerie walking down Weir Street. There was no question as to who owned the escapees. The Marstons were the only people with a llama and goats in the downtown area.

During the warmer weather, the Marstons went to Annisquam, a small town near Gloucester. Their land was on a high point overlooking the Atlantic. Their complex consisted of the main house and several outbuildings. The prior owner was an ironsmith. He had a forge in one of the buildings. Most of the hinges and locks on the property were made at the forge. To accommodate their expanded family, they converted two of the structures and a stone silo into housing for their family. Their animal family was allowed freedom on the complex, so it was not surprising they would break out of the backyard in Taunton, and amble down the roads. If you have not had any contact with a llama, let this be a warning: don't get too close to him. They are prone to spitting in your face as a protective action. It is an unpleasant and messy experience.

Pat and Norris hosted a new years' party to which we were invited in the 1990s. Most of the guests were of a similar age, around sixty years or older. I still think the party started too early, by ten pm we were getting tired. Someone hatched a plot to advance the clock in the living room by more than an hour. Olde Lang Syne could be sung, and champagne sipped prematurely. Pat noticed that the time had gone by very fast, and she caught on to the ruse. It was a good idea, while it lasted. Tired or not, it was a great evening with friends like Jean and Arthur Miller, and Audrey and John Pollard, and other friends of theirs who attended St. Thomas Episcopal Church.

As a pilot for Delta Airlines, Norris was required to follow federal regulations which forbid pilots to work after their 60th birthday. His retirement was coming up, and Pat planned a retirement party at Logan Airport on the day of Norris' last flight. She was under the assumption that he would fly on his birthday. We were all excited and planned to attend the gala. A wrench was thrown into the plans when Pat learned that Norris could no longer fly because the rule stated that he could not fly after obtaining age 60. The party was canceled, and Norris retired. He did not take retirement at first very well. It was rumored that he did not get out of his pajamas for several days. Norris had a great career – his family traveled a lot, because of the perks allowing family members to fly anywhere at a minimal cost.

Pat's happy life came to an abrupt halt when she was diagnosed with leukemia. She fought a great battle for many months. I mention this because of an incident that follows. I was in a grocery store in Raynham. A person came up to me, whom I did not recognize at first. She was a fairly tall woman with no hair. As soon as she spoke to me, I knew it was Pat. Her appearance was disturbing. She had lost weight, and her face was very edematous. We talked for a long time. She did not appear depressed. She was a fighter and determined to live as long as she could. Jan and I attended her funeral service at St Thomas' Church. We were sad to lose a person who was so much fun to be with.

As I look back, I am so pleased that Jan and I were a part of her life. She was an original, free-spirited, full of ideas, open to suggestions, and generous with her time. Several times she and Norris helped us with cleanup after parties at our house. One night we watched the sunrise as we finished the dishes. It is my hope that Pat continues to see the sunrises in her eternal rest. Amen.

The Blizzard of 1978

Jan and I have fond memories of the blizzard of 1978. The three to four days of the blizzard and its aftermath was actually a lot of fun. Life was like a Currier and Ives print. People were walking around and talking to each other in the streets, and taking their children on sleds to the grocery store. The storm occurred February 5th, 1978. The least amount of fallen snow was about two feet, some areas such as Lincoln, R.I. got 50 inches of snow. The storm was a great lingering event, very slow moving, allowing a large accumulation of snow. Along the shoreline, some areas had four high tides of the new moon over two days. The winds were very high; Boston reported wind gusts up to 83 MPH. The storm broke every record in the book. At times snow fell at 4 inches per hour.

On the coast, the blizzard lasted 40 hours. Many houses were lifted off their foundations and floated away. It was estimated that 11,000 homes were destroyed by the flood tides. For the 35th anniversary of the storm, WCVB (Boston) showed a program covering the storm. There was also a video taken in 1978 of a report by television broadcaster, Harvey Leonard. He predicted the catastrophic storm several days before it hit, but he was not taken seriously. Photos showed people and cars stranded on route 128, making it look like a parking lot. Highways had drifts as high as 15 feet. It was reported that at least 56 lives were lost due to the storm. Estimates of damage were more than 1 billion in dollars.

Let's go back to "Currier and Ives in 1978." People were walking everywhere. We went to Shaw's Market, pulling a sled behind us. Our son John, and his friend Jason Pollard were with us. They climbed and posed on top of plowed snow piles, easily 15 to 20 feet high. Everyone we passed greeted us. We saw neighbors we had not seen in months. Winthrop Street, Route 44 in front of our house, was fairly well plowed. People were able to walk in the streets because of the motor vehicle driving ban. I had no choice but to my drive my car to the hospital. I was stopped by the police, but a short discussion with the officer solved the problem. Driving a car was not forbidden for healthcare workers, especially the surgeon on call. It took days to dig all of our vehicles out from under the snow. The roofs of our cars were barely visible from the second-floor windows.

Isn't it amazing how well we can get along without electricity? Isn't it great how well people respond to disasters?

Sol and Mae Berk

Our next door neighbors at 252 and 248 Winthrop Street were the Berks at 250 Winthrop St. Sol originally had a jewelry manufacturing business on Oak Street, in one of the many brick buildings which were once part of the Mason Machine Works. My godmother, Josephine Lawrence, worked for him in the jewelry plant for many years. Sol opened up a retail store at the Oak St. address. Eventually, he established Berk's Shopping Center which is said to be the first discount store for jewelry, appliances, and other merchandise in the Taunton area. Berk's was in Raynham on Rte. 44, about a ¼ mile from the Taunton line.

The land on which our home and office at 252 Winthrop Street were built, was originally owned by Sol Berk and sold to my cousin, Joe Lawrence, of Royal Builders. Joe contracted with us to build a house with an attached office at 252 Winthrop. The space that was to be a garage in the original plans became the office space.

Back to Sol and Mae Berk. Sol was a very kind man, thoughtful and generous. Lisa was very attached to him and was known to visit him at age 3. One day she rang Sol's doorbell. When Mae answered, Lisa, asked, "Can Mr. Berk come out and play with me?" I think Mae was a little surprised by the question from such a little girl. The Berks lived in the house that originally belonged to Ms. McKechnie, who was one of my teachers at Herbert E. Barney School.

Mae was a short statured lady who loved jewelry. Her diamond was about three carats in size, in a beautiful setting. Both Sol and Mae were patients of Dr. Myer Bloom, whom I may have mentioned elsewhere in this book. Mae suffered from insomnia. Nothing seemed to help the problem. I mention Mae's diamond because of the following story – I promised Jan that since we originally had no money for an engagement ring, that by our tenth anniversary, she would get a diamond ring. What better place to buy the ring but at Sol's store? I went to the store one day and told Sol my interest in buying a "rock" for Jan. He asked about what size diamond she would want. I answered the same size as Mae's ring! Sol's look was one of great surprise. I don't think he expected that. Within a few days, Sol came to our house with a cloth sack full of diamonds. He spread out the jewels on our kitchen table, and we chose a good size one. It was a little less than three carats, but caused a few looks of surprise among our friends. Our granddaughters would like to inherit the ring, but with all of the female grandchildren we have, I am not certain who will be wearing the ring in the future.

Let's go back to Sol and Mae; Sol had a stroke with some residual one-sided weakness. He was hospitalized and then went to a rehab center. While he was ill, Mae and her daughter-in- law from Brockton, decided that Sol could not return to the home that he loved so much. His wife and daughter-in-law felt that Sol could not climb the outside stairs or up the second-floor stairs. So Mae put the house up for sale. She bought a condo on Church Green so that Sol would not have to climb stairs. He could ride in the elevator. The irony of this story is this: Sol recovered well from his stroke. One of the major parts of his rehab therapy was climbing stairs, which he did very well. Sadly, he was not allowed to return to 250 Winthrop Street. He so loved the house and seemed depressed by its sale.

Sol and Mae eventually moved to the Los Angeles area to be near their son Howard Berk. Howard was the author of the book titled "Hero Machine." He was involved in the movie and TV business and wrote scripts for several series on TV, as well as being involved in some feature films. Mae predeceased Sol. We visited Sol on our 1978 cross-country family vacation. To our surprise, Sol was a delivery man for a photo processor in the Los Angeles area, despite having had a stroke. Jan and I could not believe that he could drive the California freeways and into downtown Los Angeles at his age. Additionally, at our meeting, he brought his female companion, a lovely lady, who made it quite clear that they maintained seperate apartments - a proper decision for the times. My, oh my, the times have changed. By the way, Sol's hair was in a ponytail.

Sol returned to Taunton for a visit a couple of years later with his companion. I am sorry to say that his properties were not in good condition. His home on Winthrop Street was poorly maintained by its owner. Berk's Shopping Center had also seen better days. Sol was unhappy that he came back. It is often better to maintain a fantasy than it is to face reality.

Margaret and Louis Stone's "Yard Sale"

Margaret and N. Louis Stone lived on the corner of Highland and Winthrop streets across from our home at 248 Winthrop. Louis was an industrialist, who at that time was a co-owner of Harodite Finishing Company in North Dighton. The Stone family was well known and quite wealthy. In fact, there is a building on Commonwealth Avenue in Boston named in their honor at Boston University. The Stones were Jewish. Margaret was a Christian. She was the daughter of a silversmith and artist. Margaret said that her family moved to Taunton so that her father (August Charles Miller) could work for Reed and Barton Silversmiths. He was a well-known a silver- design artist, as well as an excellent oil painter. In fact, Margaret gave us one of his paintings, a beautiful winter scene that hangs prominently in our house. It was said that he was involved in designing many of Reed and Barton's sterling silverware (but I digress, as I frequently do). The Stone family home had beautiful landscaping with several valuable specimen trees surrounding their one-story brick house.

Louis Stone suffered from Guillain-Barre syndrome. This disease made it difficult for him to stay at their home on Highland Street - he was one of the five to ten percent of victims of the disease who did not fully recover from it. The Stone family decided to sell their home and move to the new condominium on Church Green. Margaret was able to have her unit custom built, with higher ceilings on the top floor to accommodate some of her beautiful furnishings. Jan and I were invited to the condominium for a tour by Margaret. It was a beautiful place to live. The foyer of the condominium had a wonderful crystal chandelier, which was originally at the Park Theatre in Taunton, and can be seen at night as you pass the building. The Stone's original house was moved to Sherwood Lane in Raynham and was lived in by Attorney Roster and his wife, Joan.

Prior to the move, Margaret was selling some of her furniture and asked if we were interested in purchasing any of the pieces. I had the feeling that she was so proud of her belongings that she wanted to make certain that they went to people who would appreciate them. Jan and I would definitely appreciate them since we had recently moved into 248 Winthrop Street with its high ceilings and spacious rooms. We ended up buying a Chippendale sofa now in our den at 68 Governor Bradford Lane, Falmouth. Other items purchased include silver and pewter fireplace set, an iron fireplace fender, a wrought iron garden table with glass top and four chairs, a lamp table that was a marriage of two furniture styles. I believe the sofa was only $25. Bill Frazier, a dentist from Boston, who married one of Jan's nursing school friends, was visiting one Sunday when we went across the street and carried the sofa on our backs to 248 Winthrop. We must have looked funny crossing the street. The fireplace fender was made of fenestrated polished iron. It came with papers from Hammer Galleries in New York City, authenticating its provenance. It is unique and probably quite valuable. It is now in our Cape Cod house in storage. We also received a set of four small chairs made of writhen wood. Jan made needlepoint cushions for them.

Some of the trees on the Stone's landscaping were very unusual as well as unique. Unfortunately, the developer was in a hurry to build King Phillip Condos on the property, so they were all cut down, and we lost the chance to have some spectacularly beautiful trees on our property.

Margaret and N. Louis Stone were well known as philanthropists, and very generous to Morton Hospital. The meeting room at Morton Hospital is named in Margaret's honor, for all of the contributions she made to the hospital, in kind, and in financial support. In addition, an area on the ground floor of the hospital was dedicated to N. Louis Stone. They were a dashing and glamorous couple.

Ernest Lopes

Ernest Lopes was a distant relative – his maternal great-grandmother and my great grandmother were sisters, I figure that Ernest and I were third cousins. His uncle was Joseph Fresta of Dighton Avenue. I was born in the home owned by the Fresta's, on the second floor of an apartment rented by my Aunt Josephine and Uncle Manual Lawrence, who were my godparents. Joseph Fresta was my confirmation godparent. The Fresta's and my maternal grandparents were from Villa Franca da Serra, in northern Portugal. If I ever finish my family tree, you will see how these facts breakdown. But I vary from my main theme of this writing.

Ernie was a friend of mine. His house was about a quarter-mile away from 986 Somerset Ave. He was a couple of years older than me. He was born with a cardiac problem – a "leaking valve" as it was called. He had frequent episodes of what was probably heart failure. His activities were limited because of the heart problem. That meant he couldn't join the Costa kids and me when we played at their house, just a few houses away from him. At times his lips were blue, and he was bedridden.

I frequently stopped to visit him on my way to the Costa's home (originally owned by my Netto grandparents). We would just sit and talk – remember that this is the 1930s and early 1940s. Radio was the only game in town.

One day on a visit to Ernie, his sister, Lily Lopes, and I were on a home-made see-saw. Don't ask me why, but I panicked on the upward stroke. I jumped off and broke my right wrist. Dr. Nunes set it at his office. It healed well with no deformity, and no X-Rays were needed.

South End Club Folk Dancers. Ernest Lopes is center of photo

Unfortunately, a short time later, Ernie died. I think he was just under sixteen years of age. The sad part of this story is that if Ernie were born later in the 20th century, his heart problem could be repaired, and he could have lived a normal life, physically and emotionally.

It is just amazing what can be done now. Medical science has advanced so rapidly. New and innovative techniques have revolutionized medicine. So many people have lived long lives which would not have happened without these scientific breakthroughs.

Maybe Ernie is one of the reasons I decided to become a doctor. And I am glad I did.

Clara and the Hoky

Clara Fitta Duarte had no children of her own, but she raised several of her sisters and brothers in a moderately- sized home at 1070 Somerset Avenue, just a block away from my family home. Her mother died in childbirth, delivering her nineteenth child. Clara was a wonderful, friendly lady, active and very religious. Clara was married to a barber. As far as I know, there was no additional income to help support the children. In those days, everyone grew vegetables and fruits on a small farm on their property. People did a lot of canning at home, giving them the ability to feed the family with better food in the winter months. I am not certain if welfare programs were available.

Carol Staples' mother was one of Clara's adopted children. She was age two at the time of her mother's death. Another brother, Ernie, is the only surviving child that Clara helped raise. He is in his nineties. Ernie was a frequent visitor to Gouveia's Cash Market, where I hung around since early childhood. When I was very young, and just learning to talk, Ernie liked to squeeze the toes of my shoes. When he did this, he would say "Sapato" – the word for shoes in Portuguese. At that time, all I would say in response was "Papu," which is now what my grandchildren call me.

In her later years, Clara lived at the Presbrey Court Apartment complex for people over 55 years of age, conveniently located a few yards away from Our Lady of Lourdes Church. I occasionally visited her at her apartment. As the years passed, Clara became less mobile, and she had some difficulty walking. The apartment was perfect for her. It consisted of a large room with living area, kitchen and an eating area. The bedroom was small but adequate, and the bathroom facilities were handicap friendly. I mention Clara's infirmities to introduce the story of the "Hoky."

A Hoky is a vacuum-like sweeper often used in theaters and restaurants. In private homes like Clara's, it is a Godsend. It picks dirt up and requires no electricity. It is people-powered. It reaches under furniture and has a rotary brush and a cushioned bumper to help protect walls and furniture.

Clara demonstrated her Hoky for me. While sitting on her couch, she could roll the sweeper back and forth and around to clean most of the room without getting up. An additional feature of the Hoky is that it hangs and folds flat. (This Hoky information was obtained from a "Home Trends" catalog.) The Hoky now sells for $69.99. The front cover of the catalog shows a photo of the Hoky and a prominent announcement in very large letters. "Hoky Is Back!"

Clara was a member of the Holy Ghost Society at Our Lady of Lourdes Church and was involved in its activities. Portuguese Catholics, especially those from the Azores brought their own traditions of "Festas" (religious and social feasts) to this country. The most popular Festa is the Holy Ghost Festival. Since 1920, these feasts have been held annually in many cities where Portuguese are present in large numbers (Taunton, Fall River, New Bedford, and Falmouth). The Festa is held on any weekend from the week following Easter until the mid-summer. Seven families are chosen from the members of the Society to display a crown for one week at their home. Queen Isabel of Portugal, wife of the poet King Diniz (14th century), instituted a cult called the "Coronation of the Emperor." It is said that the characteristics of this festival are based on that cult. At the homes of the seven members chosen, a room is made into a chapel to display the crown surrounded by flowers and candles. Visitors honor the Holy Ghost crown by praying and leaving a donation. Each weekend at Sunday Mass, a member of the host family is honored at the crowning ceremony. The donations received at the home are given to the Society. Several social affairs occur on the seventh weekend. A procession follows the Mass, followed by a free dinner called "Sopas." After the meal, auctions of donated items – homemade Portuguese delicacies and religious items are sold. Festivities for the rest of the day include band concerts and music for dancing.

A very popular dance is the chamarita (I can still see Clara dancing the chamarita, and calling the steps of the dance at the South End Portuguese Club). The dance starts with couples dancing to waltz music. The couples then line up and join hands to dance in a circle. Next, the couples waltz off separately. Each woman dances half way around her partner. This move is followed by the partners hopping around in one spot. The waltz is resumed, and these different steps are repeated throughout the dance.

In other chapters of this memoir, additional information regarding Portuguese feasts has been mentioned. They are very popular, and attendance at some of the feasts total in the thousands.

Some of the information above is adapted from the thesis: "The Portuguese: Life in Taunton, Massachusetts from 1860 to 1930" - a thesis by Shirley Ann Rebello, submitted to the Graduate School of the Bridgewater State College, Masters of Arts Program, 1983.

Mayonnaise and Whiskey

I have never been a fan of mustards, but I have always liked the creamy feel of mayonnaise on my palate. I have heard about other uses of "mayo," but the kind I am writing about is probably the most interesting. It came up when I decided that I should photograph my aunts and uncles in the natural environment of their homes. I wanted them clothed as they would normally dress – casual, not dressed up for a formal portrait. I gave them no warning. I just showed up, unannounced, at each house to do the photo shoot. That's how I did it the day I decided to photograph Aunt Mary Marques and Uncle Joe Marques. I arrived at their home on South Street in Raynham early in the afternoon. Aunt Mary had just washed her hair – and this is where the mayonnaise story begins.

After shampooing and rinsing, Aunt Mary applied mayonnaise to her hair and then covered her head with a shower cap. She felt that this method would condition her hair and make it more manageable. As I said previously, I wanted a candid photo! The picture of the two of them was just perfect - shower cap and all.

Before taking the photo, I was sitting with them in the living room of their antique home. Uncle Joe offered me a drink, which I accepted. You should know that he was a man who was fond of liquid spirits for his entire life. He came back into the room with a tall glass, at least 12 ounces in size. It was filled with straight whiskey, no ice, no water. When Aunt Mary saw the drink, she shook her head at me, indicating that I should not accept the drink. Uncle Joe thought that he was acting generously, and doing me a favor. At this point in his life, he was having some problems related to his age. To him, a large drink did not seem too much. I gladly took the glass from him, but I did not drink it. I would have been comatose if I had that much alcohol.

The visit was a pleasant one, we talked and reminisced for quite a while. Fond memories of Aunt Mary and Uncle Joe are permanently etched in my mind, thanks to mayonnaise and whiskey.

An Unexpected Phone Call

While I was at my billing service to check on some business matters, Charlene, the billing service owner, informed me that she had received a "strange" phone call from an ex-patient of mine. She was not certain if it was a serious call or just a crank call. She had kept the information – patient's name and home telephone number to give to me if I wanted to return the call. I was anxious to find out the reason for the call.

The patient's name was Richard, a long-time patient of mine who had moved to Florida with his wife and five children many years before and settled in a city near Cape Canaveral. He was very surprised that I returned his call. He told me has was retired, and over 65 years of age. His children were all grown and doing well. He told me the reason for the phone call. Apparently, he was thinking of me, and the care that I had given him. The purpose of the call was to thank me for all I had done for him and his family. Specifically, he wanted to thank me for saving his life – in 1967 he had a major blood clot that I diagnosed and made the appropriate medical referrals to resolve the problem at Tufts Medical Center.

Before we ended our long conversation, he again said that he never expected to hear from me. He repeated that he was forever grateful for my care. That day, I thought about the long hours that I worked on a daily basis – operating in surgery, making hospital rounds, holding office hours, and spending many evenings returning calls to patients. This phone call gave me great satisfaction.

Richard's comments elevated my spirit, and reinforced my hope that I did as much as I could to help the thousands of patients, whom I treated for almost forty years as a surgeon, and in my role as a primary care physician.

The Edmund Rego Story

My sister, Chris, was Edmund Rego's girlfriend. Edmund and his widowed mother lived on the hill behind Gouveia's Cash Market. Edmund was her only child. During WW II, Edmund was drafted into the Army. He served in a combat zone and was unfortunately killed in battle, as was his neighbor Antone Medeiros, who lived only a few hundred feet away from him. There were two Gold Star mothers living on, or just off Baker Road.

Edmund's death was devastating for Mrs. Rego. Her neighbors and friends were very helpful in getting her through the mourning period, but nothing could bring back her son.

A while after Edmund's death, our postman asked if he could leave a little box at the store. The box was for Mrs. Rego. It was from the Department of the Army. It was no bigger than 4x6 in size and was thought to contain Edmund's personal effects. To this day, I don't know why I was asked to take the box to Mrs. Rego. I was probably 12-13 years of age.

Obviously, she was devastated when I showed up at her door with a little box containing the personal effects of her only son. I did my best to console her, but what can a teenager say to an adult in this horrendous situation?

Mrs. Rego did fine, eventually. In later years, she moved to California to be near her few relatives. I believe she came back to Taunton once or twice to visit. She lived with her family for many years in California before her demise.

The "Pop Tart Couple"

One day, on Emergency Room call, I treated two patients who were celebrating their 50th wedding anniversary. As a gift to each other, they went on a hot air balloon ride over Taunton. Getting into the gondola was difficult because of their ages. Getting out was much easier. The hot air balloon got into trouble and crash landed in a field. The couple told me they were like "pop tarts" popping out of a toaster, as they flipped out of the bucket and landed on the ground. They were laughing a lot about being "pop tarts." Fortunately, they sustained no serious injuries. This was definitely a memorable balloon ride, and an unexpected ending to their celebration. Thanks to Kellogg's breakfast foods, they had a day to remember.

Mary and the Belly Button

This is a tale about a woman named Mary, who lived a few houses away from my parents. I was familiar with her and her family but was not ready for what occurred after she became a patient of mine. During an exam on her, we began talking about the belly button (the umbilicus, technically). I guess I stimulated her interest in that anatomic site and was unprepared to receive an unsolicited variety of humorous cards, jokes, and appliances for the umbilicus.

Over the years, I received belly button cards in the mail. The cards were always unsigned, but I knew who sent them. The variety of cards was surprising. Mary went out of her way to find these cards and other items related to the belly button. Some of the sayings on the cards were bizarre. It was fun receiving the cards.

She was also able to find items that enhanced the utility of the belly button. One day. I received a beautiful red faceted jewel about an inch in size. Its purpose was decorative and was meant to be inserted in the belly button as an attention-getting gem. The most useful gift from her was the "Belly Button Salt Cellar." It came with a wide screw-in base and was meant to be used when lying in bed and eating celery. The instructions were to fill the bowl of the cellar with salt. While lying in bed, one could stick celery into the bowl, making for a pleasant appetizer. The idea was interesting, but I never tried it! I have lost the cellar in one of my moves, but I can say that I don't miss it.

Another clever gadget that she gave me was a brush to sweep out lint so that it would not collect in the umbilicus. There is nothing more disgusting to a surgeon than an accumulation of belly button fuzz, which requires removal during the preparation for an abdominal procedure.

If you are interested in obtaining more information on this topic, I suggest going on the internet and Google "belly button stuff." You might be surprised by what comes up!

And when you eat celery, think of Mary and have a chuckle over her shenanigans. It makes me smile just to think about her.

Kale

You may recognize my Aunt Mary Marques' name if you have read the "Mayonnaise and Whiskey" story in this book. Aunt Mary was a champion for the eating of kale. My wife, Jan, heard her say that anytime she did not feel well, felt weak, or tired, she would eat kale for a few days, and bounce back to resume her normal activities. Eating kale to her was the answer to many physical problems. My other aunts, Josephine and Lucy, as well as my mother, had similar thoughts on the value of eating kale. At our house, kale soup was frequently served.

All the Netto sisters, except Esther, grew kale in their gardens. For the winter, they had a winter version that they could pick any time when they needed it. Kale tolerated freezing weather well.

What was the magic of kale? I went to the WebMD site and found information that surprised me. Kale is ranked the number one leafy green vegetable – "A nutritional powerhouse!" It is an excellent source of vitamin C and vitamin K. It also has a good amount of calcium and folate. Kale is also high in anti-inflammatory antioxidants. The quercetin in kale protects against arthritis and memory loss.

The calcium and potassium in kale help keep bones and teeth strong, and it contains several other nutrients which help maintain healthy eyes, hair, and skin.

Bottom Line Health recently said that spinach and kale are the new "brain foods." In a ten year study of almost one thousand older adults, it was found that those who ate just one or two servings of kale or spinach per-day, had the cognitive abilities of people eleven years younger.

As you can see from the advantages of eating kale, Aunt Mary was right. Eat kale. Make kale soup. Enjoy it and stay healthy.

For any readers who would like to make kale soup, here is one of Aunt Mary's soup recipes. Kale soup is a classic Portuguese soup or "Caldo Verde" - green soup:

Ingredients: 1 pound of finely chopped kale, not winter kale. Remove ribs from leaves before chopping. Half a pound of linguiça. One large onion chopped. Four medium potatoes cut into small pieces. Half a can of chickpeas (may substitute chickpeas with elbow macaroni or one cup Campbell beans, or half a cup of white rice). Okay to use frozen kale - 1 pound if no fresh kale is available.

Directions: In a large pot add chopped kale to 1 1/2 quarts water. Add linguica, chopped onions, cubed potatoes, and chickpeas. Simmer above ingredients for 20 minutes. Add two tablespoons of olive oil. Simmer 20 minutes more. Add some water, if soup looks too thick. Add salt and pepper to taste.

As the Portuguese say "BOM APETITE!"

Joseph and Mary Marques wedding, with over 40 family memners.
Photography by Boutin Studios

Susan and David's Joy Ride in Lexington, Kentucky

On our trip from Fort Stewart to Taunton in July 1964, we stopped to visit John, and Julie Preneta in Lexington, K.Y. John Preneta was my mother-in-law's brother. He was staying home to take care of his wife, Julie, who was seriously ill, suffering from inoperable pancreatic cancer. In addition to spending time with them, we were treated to a short ride around Lexington to view the large green grass farms where racing horses are raised and trained. We also stopped at the "Man O War" bronze statue of one of the best racing horses of all time.

John and Julie's house was on the top of a very steep hill. The hill and its consequences are the reason for writing this little story. Our daughter, Susan, was four. David was three years old. Neither had any experience driving an automobile, obviously. That fact didn't seem to bother them much. It certainly didn't stop them from driving a car. The car was parked on a flat area on the top of the hill. We thought it was in "park." Somehow Susan and David got the car into neutral. As we sat in the living room, we saw our car rolling down the driveway, across a busy roadway, and stopping when it hit some bushes.

We rushed out, in a panicked state, to see what had happened. David was behind the steering wheel. Susan was on the passenger front seat, apparently telling David which way to turn the steering wheel. Fortunately, they were not hit by a passing car, nor did they hit any cars. Damage to the neighbor's property was minimal. We were very fortunate. Jan and I read them the riot act to them. They didn't drive again until Driver's Ed class.

Susan

Our first child Susan was born on February 1, 1960, at Saint Elizabeth's Hospital in Brighton Massachusetts. She suffered from ear infections early in her life, resulting in her having tubes inserted in her ears to relieve the pressure. She was one of the youngest patients in the practice of my former college roommate and fraternity brother, Dr. John Kurkjian.

She attended Our Lady of Lourdes School from first to fifth grade, and Catholic Middle School from grades six to eight. During her middle school education, she had two major medical problems. The first major medical problem was an attack of Bell's Palsy (facial nerve paralysis). She was seen in consultation by more than one neurologist. The general recommendation was "let the disease take its course." In desperation, she was treated with oral prednisone with no significant improvement. The symptoms lasted a few months, again quite a difficult problem for a teenage girl to go around with a one-sided facial deformity similar to that of a stroke patient. She was fortunate to have recovered completely from the facial weakness. On occasions when she is tired, I can notice a little facial weakness. There still is no specific medication for Bell's Palsy.

Her second major problem was a finding of spinal scoliosis, which was felt not to be correctable with bracing or casting. A consultation was held with prominent back surgeons who recommended spinal fusion. The operation was performed in 1973 at the Massachusetts Hospital School in Canton, MA. Dr. Arthur Carriere was the primary surgeon. During the long postoperative period, it was necessary for her to be kept in a full body plaster cast for healing to occur. As a patient in a hospital school, she was able to attend classes. These classes (grade appropriate) resulted in her not losing that year at school.

Although she was lying flat in bed, she was able to use prism glasses while attending classes, reading, or watching television. As healing progressed, she was allowed to come home on most weekends. Jan's uncle Jim adapted a wooden door, which served as a stretcher. It was necessary to use the front door into our house to get Susan in. The door was wide enough and went straight into the central hallway. The experience of undergoing a spinal fusion was quite an ordeal for a young teenager. She was a trooper during the entire postoperative period.

Most high school sports were not reasonable for her to engage in after a spinal fusion. For all her "growing up" years, our family belonged to the Edgewood Swim and Tennis Club in Raynham. Susan spent many summer days at the club. As a member of the swim team at Taunton High School, she was able to compete in athletics, and served as a co-captain of the swim team with Sarah Doherty, who is the patient in the chapter "A Terrible Accident."

After high school, Susan entered Curry College. However, because the nursing program was new, it had not yet received accreditation, so she left Curry and completed her RN program in the hospital where she was born - Saint Elizabeth's. Over the next two years, she worked at Saint Elizabeth's and Cardinal Cushing Hospital in Brockton from 1982 to 1984 on a part-time basis, while she was a full-time student at Boston College. She received a Bachelor's of Science in Nursing from Boston College in 1983. She also worked on a part-time basis at St. Luke's Hospital in New Bedford. Her full-time employment was mostly at Morton Hospital in Taunton Massachusetts.

For seven years she left her hospital employment to work as a visiting nurse for the VNA in Taunton, Freetown, Berkley, and Lakeville. Her last full-time career position for 20 years has been in the operating room at Morton Hospital. Morton has recently been sold to the for-profit company Steward Healthcare. Most of her time at work is in the operating room. She's also a part-time teaching nurse for the surgical services. She has been offered the position of Operating Room Supervisor but has refused the offer for family reasons.

Her marriage to Frederick Thomas on October 5, 1985, became a complicated affair. Fred had a major injury two days before the wedding. The accident happened when Fred and a friend were jogging on a road in Whittenton. Fred noticed a car coming towards them and pushed his friend into the bushes at the side of the road. Fred jumped away from the car, but unfortunately, he could not jump high enough to avoid being hit. He sustained significant fractures of the right hip, pelvis and left knee.

Although he was an inpatient at Morton Hospital, he was able to attend the wedding with the help of his private nurse, Arlene Brown. Arlene dressed him in a tuxedo and brought him to the wedding service at Our Lady of Lourdes Church in a wheelchair. The wedding reception was at Wannamoisett Country Club in Rumford, Rhode Island. Fred remained at the reception for a short time. For the formal photos, he was supported by members of the wedding party. If you ask him, he will tell you that he has very little memory of the day's happenings.

The honeymoon was canceled. Fred returned to the hospital. Susan came back to 248 Winthrop St. and stayed in her own old bedroom on the third floor. After a long recovery, Fred returned to work as a plumber. It became obvious to him that he could not physically work as a plumber for the rest of his life. He became a part-time student at Northeastern University, where he received a degree in Mechanical Engineering.

Many years after his accident he underwent a right hip replacement with very good results. He now works for a major Boston construction company where he designs plumbing, fire protection, and heating and cooling systems, which are used in the construction of large projects in Boston and occasionally in New York City.

Susan and Fred have two children, both of whom have finished college. Christopher graduated from the University of Vermont with a degree in economics and a minor in philosophy. He is currently working for Prudential Financial. He is very busy studying and taking advanced tests, so he can eventually become a registered investment advisor. Christopher is currently living in Boston's North End.

Kerrin graduated from Curry College, magna cum laude, with a B.A. degree in early childhood education in 2015. She is living at home and has done some substitute teaching in Taunton schools. Kerrin will start in a full-time teaching position as a kindergarten teacher in New Bedford at the Alfred Gomes School, beginning in the fall of 2015.

Susan and Fred originally lived on Ashland Street in an American Four Square home, which they restored beautifully. Fred's sister Marilyn and her husband Lee bought the home from them. Susan and Fred moved into a new development in Segregansett Woods in North Taunton. They have a newly built colonial house on Cara Circle.

David

I have mentioned previously about David's precipitous delivery at Saint Elizabeth's Hospital on March 29, 1961. I don't think he has slowed down since then. He has always been very busy and a great talker. It has been said of him that he is so glib that he could talk dogs off a meat wagon. His education is similar to Susan's.

He started school at Our Lady of Lourdes in their kindergarten and primary schools. His middle schools were Taunton Catholic Middle and Martin Middle. One day, we were called to Catholic Middle by the principal for a conference. Apparently, David was seen kissing a girl (Sue Johnson). This behavior was not allowed at Catholic Middle.

David had a brief foray into ice hockey. Fortunately for Jan and me, he did not continue playing hockey. At the time there were no ice rinks in Taunton, so we had to shuttle him out of town, sometimes in the wee hours of the morning. His competitive nature was expressed in tennis. At Edgewood Club, he was very active in tennis competition. At age 14 he won the club championship against very strong adult tennis players who were at least twice his age.

Another sport David played was Little League Baseball which he did for about five seasons. One of his teammates was Steve Turner, also known as "Swish Turner," a nickname he was given for his actions as a batter. Steve Turner's mother was the favorite fan of the family members in the stands. Her name was Verna Alice Turner, a longtime telephone operator at Morton Hospital. Her popularity was enhanced by the large cowbell that she rang to stir her son's team to victory. The cowbell was accompanied by loud and encouraging noise from the crowd.

At Taunton High School, he was the star of the tennis team and reached the semifinals in the Massachusetts State Competition in his senior year. He also competed in out-of-state games at the Mount Hope Tennis Club, and the Johnston Rhode Island Racquet Club. After a difficult year at Boston College, he transferred to Bridgewater State College for additional courses before going to Johnson and Wales University in Providence Rhode Island for three years. There he met the girl who would become his wife, Miss Nancy Kashtan. In 1985 he graduated from Johnson and Wales and on July 4, 1986, he married Nancy.

The wedding reception at Singer's Wedding Hall was an extravaganza not to be missed, and one certainly not to be forgotten. It was a New Jersey wedding with all the trimmings. The reception was as follows: the guests entered a large room where hors d'oeuvres of all kinds were offered on several tables. Caviar with frozen vodka was one of the choices. Hot and cold canapés were devoured - there was so much food and drink that the guests thought that this was the main course. After an hour or so of drinks and hors d'oeuvres, a door was opened into a larger room which was set up with dining tables, a dance floor. A band named 3M provided the music for dancing.

Several courses of food were placed in front of us, all very generous and very tasty. I would be remiss if I did not mention the wait servers and their assignments. Every time someone got up to dance, or to socialize during the reception, a fresh napkin and fresh utensils were placed on the table. That kind of attention is not common in New England weddings. Prior to the dinner being served, Nancy's grandfather, Max Kashtan, performed the ceremonial cutting of the bread followed by a Jewish prayer.

David and Nancy moved to Taunton and rented an apartment in our office building at 89 Washington St. In 1987, they bought a house at 8 Spring St. where they lived until moving to Mahwah NJ in 1994 with their two daughters, Sarah and Alyssa.

David's first job was with Sysco food distributors out of Norton, Massachusetts. He later had sales positions at Capital City Products and Bunge Foods. For about the past 20 years, he's been employed by a Midwest firm, Dawn Foods, where he has been the leading sales person almost every year. He currently has a Director's position in the wholesale division. The job requires considerable air travel. He had refused this position for many years because it required travel and overnight stays. Now that his children have grown, he is more comfortable being away from home for short periods. He has become a member of the American Society of Baking and participates actively in its annual meetings.

He doesn't play much tennis presently but has been doing well on the golf course. Downhill skiing, which he occasionally did during "ski seasons," has been hampered by a ski-related accident in which he fractured his left knee. Since then he has avoided the slopes. Guitar playing and singing remain popular with David. We occasionally join him in guitar sessions in the great room at 42 Thunderhead Place in Mahwah. Their split-level house has a large cathedral ceilinged great room that is perfect for family gatherings. In warm weather, his in-ground pool is a favorite for family members and guests.

Their home is next to Nancy's parent's house. Her parents are Barbara and Murray Kashtan. Murray is an electrician and a great home handyman. Murray taught shop at Mahwah High School. Barbara was an early childhood educator.

David and Nancy have three children. Their oldest daughter, Sarah, has a Bachelor and Master's degree in psychology and is studying for a PhD. Their second daughter, Alyssa, has an Associate's degree, as well as a real estate license. She works for a legal firm which specializes in bankruptcy cases. She continues her education as a part-time student, and may eventually go to law school. Alexandra recently graduated from Mahwah high school. She demonstrates many artistic abilities and is a fine jewel craftsman working in precious metals and stones in Manhattan, designing rings and jewelry.

David has strong religious beliefs. His large Bible, which was previously owned by Walter Such (his grandfather), is always open on a table in the dining room. He is a weekly attendant at Catholic mass, and also belongs to a Christian men's group that holds weekly Bible study meetings.

Lisa

Lisa was born at Morton Hospital in Taunton on September 24, 1965, several months after we moved into 252 Winthrop St. She had a happy childhood, attending kindergarten, first, and second grades at Our Lady of Lourdes School.

These years were followed by two years at Bennett School and one year at Maxham School where she finished her elementary schooling. During her middle school years at Maxham School, she was introduced to music and played the flute. At Martin Middle School, she was active in the band, choir, and stage productions. Her music teacher was Mr. Ken Almeida. He was very enthusiastic about music. Enthusiasm struck Lisa and most of her close friends. Members of the school chorus performed in productions of "Annie" and "Oliver." I can still remember Lisa and her friends on stage with their faces smeared with dirt, as members of the cast of the two musicals.

Lisa remained active in extracurricular activities, in the chorus, and as a member of the swim team at Taunton High School. Flute playing lost its glimmer, so she stopped playing it in her senior year. She vividly remembers performances by Marie Schumacher and by one of our neighbors, Tommy Goren. Lisa was also in high school cast of "Dolly" starring Sharon Sikorski.

From Simmons College, she received a Bachelor of Arts in business management and marketing. On the last day of finals at Simmons, she met a Taunton boy, Peter Jon Levesque, whom she started dating in May 1987. Peter was a mortgage consultant at Bristol County Savings Bank on Broadway in Taunton. Peter had been friendly with two priests since CCD classes. Father Edward Byington was in charge of Catholic education at St. Paul's Church in North Taunton. When Peter was in the fourth and fifth grade, a lifelong friendship developed between Peter and Father Byington, and with his close friend Father B.R.L. Connerton. For many years Peter had dinner with the two priests every Thursday night (also called "holy night.")

When Peter and Lisa announced that they were marrying, Father Byington became involved in making the arrangements for the religious part of the day. The wedding gift from the priests was a concert at the church before the ceremony, and during the mass by a Gregorian choir from Rhode Island. The singing was beautiful.

An elegant wedding reception was held in the top floor ballroom of the Biltmore Hotel in Providence. The food and service were excellent. The only problem we had was that several guests commented on the loudness of the music, making it difficult to carry on a conversation. Jan and I spoke to the bandleader more than once, asking him to lower the volume. The answer was that if we complained about the volume again, the band would stop playing, and leave the hotel. The discussion ended, but the volume remained a problem.

After a honeymoon at Walt Disney World, Peter and Lisa moved into a second-floor apartment on the driveway side of 89 Washington St. About six months later Peter accepted a sales position in the shipping company, Navieres, headquartered in Puerto Rico. The job was in Long Beach and Irvine, California. Off they went to the West Coast. They remained there for a short period. They then moved back to the East Coast where Peter worked for American President's Line (APL) in New York City.

After living in an apartment for some months, they bought a home on Springfield Avenue in New Providence, New Jersey. I think you could call this home a "money pit." Much DIY work was performed in its interior. The exterior was painted with the help of Sean and Annie Maguire. The house was quite improved, but renovations were not completed by the time they sold the property and moved on to another assignment for Peter.

Lisa had a major reaction to shrimp while jogging in New Providence. She'd eaten some leftover shrimp before going for a run. She became quite weak as she approached the house and collapsed on the front lawn, where she was found by Peter who called 911. She was resuscitated and treated at a local hospital with good results. Interestingly, she is no longer allergic to shrimp.

Their next move was to Texas with American President Lines. They purchased a beautiful red brick house in a new large development in Plano Texas, where most of the homes look the same. Fortunately, Peter did not drink enough to confuse his home from other homes on the street. During these many moves, Lisa worked in a variety of positions, mostly in restaurants where she eventually became part of management.

Alas! In 1996 after 18 months, a position was offered to Peter in Hong Kong for 2 to 3 years. It is now 2016, Peter, Lisa, and the family still live in Hong Kong. Jan and I visited them in Hong Kong where they lived in a large development (everything in Hong Kong is large) called Parkview. It had wonderful panoramic views of Hong Kong from the terrace. Hong Kong is a thickly populated city with many high-rise apartment complexes which rent for very large amounts of money. Parkview had marble floors, solid brass fixtures, and wonderful interior features.

Their apartment was a two bedroom, with two baths, and with a very spacious living and dining area. Monthly rent was $18,000. Fortunately, much of the rental expense was covered by Peter's employer. During this period, Peter attended Kellogg School of Business in Hong Kong. He received his Master's Degree in Business Administration.

In 1998 Lisa returned to Taunton to have her children there. She lived with us at 248 Winthrop St. Catherine was born in August 1998 by cesarean section. Dr. William Watson was her obstetrician. Catherine attended Mullen Hall School after graduating from the West Falmouth Preschool and the Sandpiper School.

Paul was born in 2000 by normal delivery. While Peter was establishing a new company named V-Logic in Hong Kong, they decided to purchase a house at 19 Eli Lane in East Falmouth in 2001. Paul attended Friendship Garden Preschool. He and Catherine later attended the Hong Kong International School when they moved to Hong Kong. Lisa lived at 19 Eli Lane with Catherine and Paul. Peter visited frequently for two to three weeks at a time during the five years that Lisa and the children lived in the United States.

A third child Matthew Hin Levesque was born in Hong Kong on October 20, 2009. Mr. Hin became part of the family at age nine months. Adoption from China was finalized in July 2010.

All three children have had the advantage of living in a foreign country and attending the Hong Kong International School (HKIS).

Catherine really enjoys studying Mandarin at HKIS. For many years throughout the seventh grade, she had classes in gymnastics which she enjoyed. She's also in Girl Scouts. Lisa was the head of the Girl Scouts counsel for Hong Kong. Catherine now participates in competitive soccer, field hockey and rugby. As an ambassador at HKIS, she meets new students and their families giving tours and answering questions about school.

HKIS runs trips to various locations. Catherine has worked in an orphanage in China, a school in Laos, Vietnam, and in South Africa, where she worked in a school teaching English for 45 days. These trips expose students to the history and culture of other countries. Paul David Levesque has been active in sports over the years. He is playing baseball and basketball. He was also a member on the rugby team. He volunteers for food banks in Hong Kong. And in the six grade he toured Beijing with the school. He anticipates going to foreign countries to do charitable work, as Catherine has done. Paul spends a lot of time hanging out with his buddies and watching sports on television. Cooking is his favorite hobby.

He has worked as a member of the kitchen staff at the American Club, where he was photographed wearing a tall white chef's hat. Paul and a close friend make complete meals for the family in the kitchen in their TaiTam high-rise.

Matthew Hin Levesque now six years old is the charmer in the Levesque family. His smile and his friendly attitude are amazing for his age. He is active in tennis and swimming. Riding his two wheel bike is one of his favorite pastimes. His most favorite activity could result in his being named a Lego engineer. I have seen him finish a Lego project, building trucks and tanks in as little as 20 to 35 minutes, this includes moving parts functioning properly. Like most children his age, he is addicted to television shows. Another activity at the Cape is his brewing coffee in his small child's play kitchen. The coffee is caffeine-free since it is just water. Matthew is also seafood lover. He does not like beef or chicken, but he loves to eat especially at Eulinda's ice cream shop.

Ex-Patriots can stay in Hong Kong because of financial incentives that most businesses offer. Incentives include paying part or all of the rent. They also pay part or all of school expenses. Other incentives are "home leave" with travel expenses to their native countries either as plane tickets or vouchers for plane fare.

Hong Kong is a great place to live. Lisa is very comfortable and happy there. She remains very active in charitable events. She's been involved in the American Women's Association and in the Hong Kong International School, where she is a volunteer and Board Member of the Parent Faculty Organization (PFO). These organizations do a lot of charitable work for the benefit of poor people in Hong Kong and mainland China. Frequent activities of this sort keep her very busy. She also plays Chinese style mahjong occasionally and enjoys working out with her friends.

Peter has been involved in many activities in the community and professionally. He has been President of the American Club and is now president of the American Chamber of Commerce of Hong Kong. He is an employee of the Wharf Company serving as Chief Commercial Officer. In these positions, Peter and Lisa attend functions and banquets for prominent international visitors and major political visitors from all over the world. All of these activities are made possible by their current "Amah" – a full-time live-in helper named Roseminda, who is from the Philippines. Lisa and Peter live in a high-rise apartment in the TaiTam section of Hong Kong directly across from the American Club, which is the center of the social life of American ex-patriots. They hope to return to the Boston area once their stay in Hong Kong has ended. They have lived a life that only a small percentage of people could ever experience.

John

John was born in Morton Hospital on July 18, 1970. Jan was attended by Dr. Bruce Willetts, who was assisted by Dr. Steven Rosenbaum.

Delivery was difficult because John was in a transverse breech position intra-uterine. Manipulations were required to allow a footling delivery safely and without complications. John was born a few months after our moving to 248 Winthrop St. He was the first child to be brought up in that home.

His introduction to education was at Brick House School and was followed by five years at Maxham School on Cohannett Street. After a brief time at Martin Middle School, we transferred him to Taunton Catholic Middle School, for the rest of grade 6. Conditions at Martin were a problem for John, so we recommended a switch of schools. Moses Brown School (MB), in Providence, was his education from grade 7 to graduation from grade 12. We were fortunate to have Dr. Brezinski in our carpool. He took the morning run which allowed him to start his dental appointments on time. There were two afternoon trips, one at 3 PM, and one at 6 PM to pick up the children involved in athletics at Moses Brown. These trips were done by the Donahues, the Murphys, the Nowaks, and by my wife, Janice.

John was very active in soccer, playing in the local spring, summer and fall leagues from age 6 through ages 18. He was a team member with some very talented players including Ricky Robbins, George Pinto, Mark McGuire, David Simas, and many others. In the spring, he was a member of the traveling team selected for Southeastern Massachusetts Soccer Association, which competed against teams and several regional locations throughout the state. While playing at the University of Massachusetts at Amherst, six days prior to his brother David's wedding, he and an opponent collided with their heads during a header, the impact was very loud – many of the games going on in other surrounding fields stopped play because of the noise and commotion. At the hospital emergency room, a major concussion was diagnosed, and John was examined and x-rays obtained. John's team eventually won that semi-final game but lost in the finals without his tenacious defense.

On the ride back to Taunton there was no question that he had a concussion. He was talkative and constantly repeating "David is getting married, David is getting married" followed by some laughter and applause. The kind of repetitive comments are not out of the ordinary following a severe concussion.

At Moses Brown he was active in soccer and lacrosse in which she sustained a second concussion, being cross-checked from behind by an opponent from another school. John was also in the 1988 production of the "Music Man" as a member of the barbershop quartet. He would later become involved in theater. Jan suggested that if he became successful on stage, he could change his name to "Sterling Babcock."

John was accepted at Wheaton College in Norton Massachusetts as a member of the first co-ed freshman class. Wheaton women may not have been psychologically ready for male students. The men on campus were not originally accepted. Coed dorms were a challenge. Co-eds even had to share dorm and bathroom facilities. Signs of anti-male feelings were evident campus-wide. Some of the walks on campus were decorated with pro-feminine symbols. Attitudes towards male students dramatically changed over time. By the end of his sophomore year acceptance of members of the opposite sex by female students was the norm.

John met Ashley Arbaugh, his wife-to-be in 1991 at Wheaton College. She was a member of the Class of 1993. He graduated in 1992 with a double major in English Literature and Theater. The Theater degree was partly based on his training and experience at the Eugene O'Neill Theatre in Waterford, Connecticut in 1991.

His first full-time job was as a sales executive at the Boston Phoenix, a free weekly newspaper and radio media company with information of interest to a large number of college students in greater Boston. From 1994 to 1996, he started a company with Judith Garbarini, his future mother-in-law, on Gingerbread Lane in East Hampton Long Island called East End Delicacies. He sold and distributed gourmet bakery desserts to retail stores in Manhattan and Long Island - some of the shops included very high-end food emporium's such as Dean & Deluca, Gourmet Garage and Balducci's. Judy was very supportive of John and gave him a place to live for most of the time they worked on the business together. They worked well together, growing the business from 1994 through 1996 which was eventually sold and became East Hampton Gourmet Foods – still in existence today. I was told she would call him "the son she never had."

From 1997 to 1999 he was employed by Katz Media Group and worked in New York City and Boston. It was here that John would come up with his software idea, DirectRep.

John and his wife were married on August 21, 1999, and after a Honeymoon in Rome and Amalfi Italy, they moved into a one-bedroom apartment in Washington, DC on Connecticut Avenue outside of Cleveland Park.

John and his schoolmates from Rhode Island founded a software company called DirectRep, Inc. The software enabled buyers and sellers of media – TV, Radio, and Cable to negotiate and purchase time over a web-based platform, eliminating paper and manual processes. The idea was evolutionary and revolutionary in the Media Industry at that time. They had an angel and other investors help launch and support the company's development. DirectRep had a tremendous five-year run, but was not acquired by CMGI or Donovan Data Systems and could not continue to operate. They ceased operation on 9/1/03.

Their first child Isabel was born in Georgetown Hospital on June 16, 2002. Their next move was to Bridgehampton, NY where they remained until early 2004, after which they relocated to Wilton Connecticut and rented a carriage house on 221 Westport Road in Wilton. A year later they bought a home just down the street from the carriage house at 229 Westport Rd., Wilton, CT.

The purchase was made possible by a sum of money which John received from the sale of Gouveia Realty Trust, and money that his wife had inherited from her deceased mother, Judith.

John's next appointment was with MediaSpace Solutions in New York City. He commuted to New York from 2004 to 2007.

Child number two, Jude, arrives around Thanksgiving at 456 pm on November 20, 2006, at Stamford Hospital in Connecticut.

Marital strife resulted in a separation from his wife in the summer of 2008, followed by an attempt at reconciliation. They, however, were unable to solve their marital problems. Divorce proceedings resulted in the final decree in the winter of 2010.

For about 18 months starting in 2010, John was a consultant in the software industry. During this time, he developed a software program for IDSN, (an internet based food safety software company) that was put in place to handle the recent government's food safety initiatives in 2009. John presented to the heads of the USDA, FDA, and Capitol Hill; and to various Senators, while he searched for grant money to continue the expansion of the software. John also presented to David Acheson, former head of food safety for the FDA. This program was meant to find deficiencies in tracking contaminated food products that would result in illness if they were consumed. Such food must be taken off the market before any further damage was done.

A member of the committee which evaluated the proposal was Tom O'Brien, the son of our Falmouth summertime neighbor Richard O'Brien. After a full review by the committee, the recommendations were rejected due to the inability to get grant funding.

His last full-time employment was as a chief marketing officer (CMO) for a company named PerfectSoftware in Wilton. In 2014, the business was purchased by another corporation. Despite his vast experience in software, he and other employees were let go from their positions for corporate reasons and transformation.

Despite the turmoil in the divorce, John has maintained a great relationship with his two children. Isabel is fifteen and Jude is ten years old. Isabel is active in several activities, she's been involved in musical theater and singing. Her major activity is being a goalie in soccer in Wilton which competes with other Fairfield County teams in her area. She is a smart, strong-minded, aggressive young lady who I think will do very well in life.

Jude has a much more relaxed personality, he and John have an excellent relationship and enjoy watching sports on television, especially baseball and football. John and Jude become couch potatoes for weekend NFL contests. Jude played soccer on John's Holland and Japan teams but was not happy with the game or coach John! He is very active in baseball and plays 3rd base, and pitches. John has coached and managed for both Jude and Isabel's soccer teams. Jude is also a very good student. He enjoys playing games on the computer or iPhone. His personality is that of a gentle person, reminiscent of his great-grandfather Walter John Such. Jude has the appearance of Jan's Polish side of the family as well, and John calls him a "little Polack."

The job losses, the divorce, separation from his children, and financial struggles have all had significant negative effects on John. It has been a difficult struggle to accept these many interruptions in his way of life. It is my hope that the future will be one of his involvements in ventures for which he is capable, knowledgeable and fulfilled.

More than 50 Years of Jan and Dave

It all started at Cambridge City Hospital in 1956. Janice was a student nurse at the hospital. I was a third-year student at Tufts Medical working every 4th night and every 4th weekend at the hospital. My stipend was twenty-five dollars per month, plus room and board. The position as a lab technician was to draw blood and perform lab tests on an emergency basis. That is how I met Janice, who was a patient who needed laboratory work. I drew the blood samples. What a way to start a romance!

Janice Ann Such, age 3, 1940

The flame of love grew stronger over the next year but was cooled by my appointment to an internship at Ohio State University Hospital (OSU) in 1957. Many letters between us kept our romance alive. For a few days in the fall, Janice visited me in Columbus. Our relationship was sealed during this visit. Since I was not happy with the program at OSU, I planned to return to Boston's St. Elizabeth Hospital for a surgical residency. My chief of surgical residency was Dr. John Spellman, brother of Cardinal Spellman of N.Y. When Dr. Spellman retired, his position was assumed by Dr. Richard Stanton.

Janice received an RN degree in 1958. She was employed as a registered nurse at the Pawtucket Memorial Hospital. We were now only 40 miles apart, and still very much in love. One evening while sitting on a bench in Boston Public Gardens, I proposed to Janice. She accepted! Her family approved, and a wedding date was set. On April 18th, 1959, Janice Ann Such, R.N., daughter of Walter and Hedwig Such married David F. Gouveia, M.D., son of John and Patricia Gouveia at St. Theresa's Church; Pawtucket R.I. Vows were blessed by Father Patrick Hunt.

Our first apartment was at 9 Wallingford Road, near the corner of Commonwealth Avenue in Brighton. It was a two-story brownstone about a mile from St. Elizabeth's Hospital. The apartment had an entry way which we used as an

Janice Ann Such, engagement photograph

Wedding Day

eating area, and as a space for an office desk. We had a living room with a fireplace and French doors, which when closed gave us some privacy in the adjacent bedroom. There was a small kitchen with a white enamel table that we bought at Sears in Cambridge for 10 dollars. The bathroom was off the kitchen. It was obvious that the bathroom was an addition to the back of the house. It had no connection to the heating system. The living room furniture included a sofa which opened into a double bed, two maple end tables, and a maple coffee table. The total cost of all these pieces of furniture was $1000.

Surprise! Jan was pregnant. Susan was born February 1st, 1960. The entry way became the nursery. Jan was working as a private duty nurse before delivery. She was to deliver at St. E's, where she was working. After a couple of months, Jan was able to return to work on weekends with Hedy and Walter taking care of Susan. They slept on the hide-a-bed in the living room. It might interest you that I made $100 per month as a resident. Our rent was $98.00 a month.

Lo and behold, Janice was pregnant again. There was no room for two children in our Wallingford Road rental, so apartment hunting we went. We moved into a house with three bedrooms, a kitchen, a living and a dining room at 37 Dearborn Road, Medford Hillside. The apartment was a short walk up the hill to Tufts, where I spent four years in college. The kitchen at Dearborn Road had a wallpaper of an interesting and

246

A day at the Beach

unique pattern, with multiple cows depicted. Unfortunately, the way the paper was hung, the cow's heads were separated from their bodies, even if you were sober. Uncle Bob Robertson, a life-long teetotaler, considered drinking after seeing the wallpaper.

One icy cold night, March 29, 1961, Jan called me at the hospital to say that she was in labor and waiting for her parents to come from Pawtucket take care of Susan. By the time Hedy and Walter arrived in Medford, I barely had time to get her to Saint Elizabeth's. For a while, I thought I would have to deliver the baby myself. Jan could not walk up the few stairs to St. Elizabeth's because she was crowning. She went by wheelchair to the obstetrical floor, where she delivered David in about ten minutes. Dr. Kavenaugh was furious that we waited so long. Delivery was uncomplicated, and David was fine.

During my time in residency, I was part of the "Berry Plan" which allowed physicians to stay out of active duty in the Army until they finished training. I was a 2nd Lieutenant in the Army Reserve. We met at the Boston Navy Yard once a week. It also meant going to National Guard programs for two weeks at Fort Devens in the summer, where I was assigned as communications officer for a mock attack. The soldiers declared dead in this "war" were carried back on stretchers to the hospital. There were so many casualties that I had to announce that the "dead" would have to become "walking dead" and walk back to the hospital. The final requirement in the Berry Plan was two years of active duty in the army.

At the end of my 4th year at Saint E's, I was ordered to report to the army hospital at Fort Jay, N.Y. which is on an island in Manhattan harbor. Our furniture was packed up and sent to Fort Jay, but we received a telegram informing us that I had been reassigned to Fort Stewart in Georgia. Where in the hell is Fort Stewart, Georgia? To find out its location, I called Greyhound Bus Lines, asking what bus I should take to Fort Stewart. The answer was to go to Savannah and take a second bus 40 miles south to Hinesville, Georgia. Fort Stewart was also known as "Camp Swampy," as featured in the Beetle Bailey comic strip. Hinesville had a town hall with a mandatory statue of a southern soldier. There was one department store selling appliances and household goods. Their advertising on the radio said: "why go all over town when you can do all your shopping at Saunders?" A few small stores made up the town. Fortunately, Sears from Savannah delivered weekly to Fort Stewart. We bought many of our appliances from them.

I drove down to Georgia alone and waited for the availability of housing, and for the arrival of our furniture. Jan and the children flew in a short time later. The night she arrived, we stayed at the VIP quarters on post – not really VIP in my mind. Roaches were everywhere. They even ate into an unopened loaf of bread that night. The children woke up in the morning with a generalized rash looking like chicken pox. I felt it must be some sort of insect bite (bed bugs?) After that night, we moved out of VIP quarters and into our unfurnished duplex, three-bedroom home. We went to Savannah to buy an air conditioner big enough to cool the entire house. In order to air condition with our house-sized unit, we used the circulating fan of the heating system, with the heat turned off. We had two great years at Fort Stewart. There we met the Cohens who became life-long friends. We were friendly with many people who were dyed-in-the-wool southerners "born and bred." We were Yankees and were told by the Southerners that from childhood, sitting on their grandmother's knee, they were told to be leery of Yankees. My position at Fort Stewart was Chief of Surgery. The hospital consisted of a group of barracks, connected by corridors. Each barrack had the capacity of twenty beds. We had at least ten units so we could be at least a two hundred bed hospital. Most days we had about twenty people in the hospital. I decorated my office as best I could with prints of doctor's outfits through the centuries. The office had a desk and an examining table which was always a resting place for a colony of ants. We had a very efficient young woman, Sally, as our secretary. Her husband was an optometrist on the post. I had a surgical assistant with one year of surgical residency. The first year my assistant was White Edward Gibson III, from Birmingham, Alabama. He was a real Southerner from what sounded like a prosperous family. As was the custom of the day, he was brought up by a Negro "mammy" whom I think he considered to be his mother. Apparently, some southern women in those days from the 40s through the 60s preferred not to rear their children. He visited his mammy frequently until her death in a nursing home. He was sure to take a bottle of bourbon to her each time. It was great to work with a very talented and experienced 1st-year trainee. We had a lot of laughs over the year, as well as a lot of work in the operating room.

I was expected to do just about any general surgical procedure, some orthopedics, some urology, and anything else that I felt confident doing. (A reminder) I was the only fully trained general surgeon in the hospital. My second year at Fort Stewart, my assistant was Robert Hoffman who was a very well trained surgical assistant as well.

The only other surgical department in the hospital was OB/GYN – that was Arthur Cohen's specialty. He had two or three other fully trained specialists working with him. He was fortunate that he had coverage when he was not working. I had no coverage except for my assistant. This meant that to go out of the area, even to Savannah, an hour away, I had to call the hospital on a land line from a phone booth to check on emergencies. For my vacations, the army had to assign a surgeon from another hospital on temporary duty.

1962 to 1964, there were no cell phone, no pagers and no electronic devices like beepers. In the hospital, we did a lot of minor surgeries like circumcisions, hernia repairs, as well as major surgeries of the stomach, bowel, and breast. Our nurse anesthetist was very qualified, but he was not allowed to do spinal anesthesia. Whenever we required a spinal, he would calculate the dosage of the medication, and we would inject it. His anesthesia ability was excellent; we had no complications or fatalities due to anesthesia. You must remember that in the 1960s. The great and safe anesthetics of the 80's and 90's had not been developed. Anesthesia machines with digital systems were not available, and small computers had not been developed. Bill Gates was still working on his inventions.

For some complicated procedures, it was necessary to transfer the patient to Walter Reed Army Hospital. Severe burn victims were transferred to Fort Sam Houston in Texas. The burn center there was doing spectacular work. One of my classmates from medical school became director of US Army medical research at Fort Sam Houston. Basil A Pruitt Jr. became the leading expert in burn treatments in the country. A second classmate, William Monafo, also became a world-renowned burn specialist at the Barnes Hospital in St Louis MO.

Back to reality, I did well at Fort Stewart and worked 8-4, four and a half days per week and was basically my own boss with my own department. The big drawback was that I was on call 24/7. Fortunately, off hour calls were rare. Getting off work at 4 pm was frequently complicated by a late afternoon thunderstorm, lightning, and downpours. Let's have a word about the weather in Southeast Georgia - the summers were unbearably hot and humid, especially in the swamps where we lived. Outdoor pools were open April through October and even later than that, so that swimming was available several months of the year at the public pools. Air conditioning was a must for several months of the year. Golf on the post was a year-round sport. Unfortunately, with lightning storms, it could become dangerous – an occasional death occurred by a lightning strike. There were other dangers as well – we had coral snakes in our swamps. They are the famous "red on yellow, he is a bad fellow" snake. A coral snake bite could result in death in as little as 10 minutes. Because of this, we were allowed to stock coral snake antivenom, one of the few places in the country that did stock it. I never got to treat a coral snake bite, but treated several snake bites. Lightning and snakes! What a great place to live.

I can't stop writing about Fort Stewart without mentioning Captain Klickstein, whom I never met. He was apparently a very dominating person and my predecessor. My first few weeks at the hospital were not easy. It didn't matter what I suggested; I was informed that Captain Klickstein would do it another way. Too bad, Captain Gouveia did it his way. To hell with Captain Klickstein.

After two years, Jan, Susan, David and I moved to Taunton in June of 1964. We were supposed to have a house with an attached office completed at 252 Winthrop Street. Unfortunately, legal problems occurred and construction was not even started by the time we got to Taunton. My cousin, Joe Lawrence, was the contractor – his company was Royal Builders and was formerly a coal company named Royal Coal which used to deliver coal to 248 Winthrop Street. John Andrade, my Aunt Esther's husband, and my godfather, Manuel Lawrence, worked on the construction crew.

But we had no place to live, what are parents for? We moved into 986 Somerset Avenue and lived there for seven or eight months before 252 Winthrop Street home and the office was completed. The office was adequate until I became busier. It had two examining rooms, a reception area, and a consultation room. Within a couple of years, it was obvious that I needed more space to handle my practice's demands. One evening while we were vacationing in Miami, Florida, I received a call that a house opposite Morton Hospital was up for sale. Ernie Helides, our real estate agent, described the building, and we bought it sight- unseen based on its location. The architect we contracted with was Nelson Woodard, who presented us with plans for the renovations. When completed, 89 Washington Street would have two offices on the first floor, one small office in the basement, two three-room apartments on the second floor, and one third floor apartment. Jan's Uncle, Jim Preneta

Posing for the family Christmas picture with our dog Captain, circa 1966

My induction to the American College of Surgeons, Chicago, 1967

was the general contractor on the project. He was amazing and knew everything needed to complete the renovations.

The most difficult the thing that Jim had to do was remove a four-story chimney which on the first floor had a brick baking oven. He did this job one brick at a time. The house was a sturdy Italianate-style, late 1800's building with several marble fireplace mantels. Most of this marble is still stored in our current basement at 68 Governor Bradford Lane. In the early 70s, the Perry White house at 248 Winthrop Street, at the corner of High-land Street, was put on the market by Lois King and Catherine Cambell. Only Sol Berk's house separated 248 from 252 Winthrop Street. We agreed on a price for 248 Winthrop and traded homes with the "girls." Much of our smaller furniture was carried across Berk's yard to our new house. 248 Winthrop Street was a dream house wait-ing to be updated. Over the next several years we redecorated it in our style. In my opinion, we had the most beautiful interior in Taunton. Many visitors to our home echoed that opinion. We contracted with Todd Stevenson from Boston, who was a decorator at Paine's Furniture Company. He had great ideas in design, color and furniture placement. Todd also decorated my office consultation room at 89 Washington Street.

Jan in the kitchen at 248 Winthrop Street

On the Collis yacht

Let's talk about our enlarging family. Lisa was born in 1965. John was born in 1970. We now had four children. John was born shortly after we moved into 248 Winthrop Street. Jan was busy being a mother, doing all of the commuting of the children to sports, practices, games, and lessons. Some of the children went to Brick House School through kindergarten. Some went to Our Lady of Lourdes grammar school. John went to Maxham School. David was into great tennis at Taunton High. Sue was a swimmer and co-captain of the Taunton High School swim team. Lisa went to Martin Middle School, where she was busy in school plays, band, and chorus. John was into soccer and lacrosse. Susan, David, and Lisa graduated from Taunton High School. By the time John was a student at Martin Middle School, public education in Taunton had declined. We took him out of Martin Middle and into Taunton Catholic Middle School for grade 6. He later transferred to Moses Brown in Providence. R.I. Susan received her R.N. from St. Elizabeth's, and a BS in Nursing from Boston College. David graduated from Johnson and Wales, and Lisa received her B.A. from Simmons College in Boston. John was in the first male/female class at Wheaton College in Norton Mass. He also attended one semester at the Eugene O'Neill Theatre

Center in Waterford, CT. He received his degree in English and Theatre from Wheaton College.

Family photo, circa 1980

Janice at age 70

In the summer of 1992, we rented a home on Colonial Way in Pine Bay Estates in Falmouth. It was owned by a couple who were using the rental income to pay the mortgage, and who planned to live in the house full-time upon retirement. It was ok, nothing fancy but accommodated us well for the two-week rental. What our family remembers most about the rental is the "skunking." Our dog, Daisy, was with us, of course, as part of the family. I was standing in the kitchen near the screen door, and Daisy was outside the door when an uninvited guest appeared at the screen. It was a skunk, who quickly sprayed Daisy outside and sprayed me through the screen with "skunk juice." It got in my eyes, hair, and clothes, what a stink! The interior of the kitchen was also sprayed. Daisy and I were banished to the outdoor shower where we both used up a lot of soap and water. Lore has it that cleaning up with tomato juice would dispel some of the odor. It didn't seem to do much for either of us, but Daisy did appear to become rather pink from the juice. The kitchen cleaned up quite well because the kitchen table chairs and floor were made of non-absorbing materials. Over the next few days we tried other remedies, but the skunk smell would not go away. For many months, Daisy smelled of skunk anytime she got wet.

John had graduated from Wheaton that May. That meant that we were finished paying for tuitions. I said to Jan that if we could afford to send the kids to college, we could now afford to buy our home on Cape Cod. One afternoon Jan and I were walking in Pine Bay and saw a 'For Sale' sign at 68 Governor Bradford. The house was an off-center entrance Cape with practically no landscaping – just a couple of rhododendrons "red rockets" and a Japanese maple. It had a poorly kept front lawn, and the backyard was basically a trash pit with much garbage under trees, like a wild forest. My comment to Jan was we certainly will not buy this place; it is the ugliest house in the development! Since we liked the neighborhood, especially that the house being located on a cul de sac, we viewed the property with Lisa Kenney from Real Estate Associates. It was basically a two car garage house. There was a small kitchen and eating area with French doors going out to a wooden deck. There was a family room with a fireplace. The rest of the first floor included a small den to the left and a bedroom to the right. There was also a strange two-section bathroom; one section had a tub, toilet and a sink, the other had a toilet and sink with a door between the two toilet areas. The second toilet was accessible from the corridor. A stairway went to the second floor where on the right was a master bedroom and a storage area under the sloping roof. The second bath with shower was off the hallway. The bedroom to the left of the stairs was small but with generously sized closets. Let's go back to the first floor. The kitchen had just been renovated due to a major water leak requiring all new cabinets to be installed, albeit very cheap ones. The house was owned by the Bergman's who had lived in New York City most of their lives and had never had a garden or a yard to maintain. It was quite obvious that they did not need gardening gloves since there was no garden. We made an offer on the house, and after some negotiations purchased it for $220,000. 1992 was not a good year in the real estate market, so we got the house for a good price. The Bergman's who owned the house were not happy with the purchase price. They asked to remain in the house for a short period of time after papers were passed. In order to do this, as required by law, they were forced to pay us rent for those weeks. We generously offered the rental for one dollar. Mr. Bergman was so disturbed that he had to pay that he took four quarters out of his pocket and threw them at Jan and me. What "class!" I look forward to relaying more adventures and misadventures at 68 Governor Bradford after we moved in.

Jan and I would come down weekends as often as possible year round. One Friday night we arrived at the house, and on opening the door, we were hit with the odor of death – a smell I was familiar with after years of being in the medical field. There certainly was "something" wrong at 68 Governor Bradford. "Something" was dead in the house, a quick look around the house failed to show the source of the problem. The odor was so bad we had to return to Taunton. There was no way we could sleep with that odor. On our next visit, the odor persisted, maybe not as bad. However, there was a "tell-tale" sign on the ceiling of the den. There was a large area of the ceiling that was grossly discolored suggesting that something was dead in the storage area on the second floor.

We asked a neighbor and a contractor, to check out the storage room upstairs. Upon moving some furniture, he found a dead raccoon. To get rid of the contaminated floor and the ceiling below, it was necessary to cut out a piece of the floor and ceiling and replace it. How does such a large animal get into a locked house? The answer was: he ate into the wooden vent in the eaves. We replaced the wooden vents with metal vents, and we got no more smelly visitors.

I may have mentioned that we had a deck outside our eating area; we knew it wasn't in good shape, but we didn't know how bad it was. One day while playing on the deck one of our granddaughters, less than four years of age, fell through the rotted deck surface which collapsed from her weight. It was time to renovate and expand, the reason, if we made improvements in later years, we might not have the patience or the strength to tolerate the hassle, because of our age.

Let's talk about renovations and expansions. Peter Levesque's father, Paul, drafted the plans for our first renovation. Based on our needs, we agreed to quite a change in the building. Exterior changes included moving the front entryway to the middle of the house. A covered entryway was added, a wide farmers porch was planned to the right side of the building. Two large dormers were added to the second floor in front, and all new windows were added throughout the exterior, including two front windows on either side of the center entrance, replacing the small windows of the original. All windows were extra-long with the bottom at the legally allowable height from the floor. Major changes also occurred within the interior, one supporting wall in the middle of the first floor was all that remained of the "guts" of the building. A wonderful cathedral ceiling family room 24x26" in dimensions was added to the back of the house. Large French doors led from the kitchen to the family room. A custom kitchen was built by Eric Wing, using a special type of maple wood. Part of two car garage was used to make an entry hallway with a large guest closet, washer and dryer and 3rd complete bath.

The builder we hired was a neighbor. We thought he would provide us with outstanding service. We had been advised not to use him for the project but did not listen to the naysayers. What a mistake! It took almost two years to complete the project. One of our neighbors told us his crew worked on 68 Gov. Bradford only on Fridays. Friday was the day we drove up to check the progress. Apparently, he was not prompt to pay his bills. Sub-contractors were hesitant to take a job with him for financial reasons. We watched his inefficiency many times. His team would arrive between 8, and 9 am, and then leave to buy supplies for the day, so half of the morning was gone before any work was done. One day, I noticed a man working on the porch, I had not seen him before, and he didn't look like he knew what he was doing. I found out that he was a bartender and not a carpenter. Because of his lack of ability to perform his duty, I asked him to leave the property immediately.

We told the contractor that we had to have an occupancy permit by July 4th. We moved in, although the house was not finished, but we had the necessities of running water, toilets and cooking facilities for Jan's birthday party. I won't bore you with some of the many difficulties we had with the house and its completion. To give you an idea of our builder's incompetence as a businessman, I will tell you about his question when we met to arrange final payment. I sat down with checkbook in hand, and he asked: "how much do you owe me?" Fortunately, I had kept good records of payments to him, so I was able to produce an accurate answer.

Car parking was a problem at 68 Governor Bradford. With our first addition, we used part of the two car garage. The remainder of the garage was being used for storage. Attached to the garage was a shed where the smelly garbage cans were kept. Since the time we were married, Jan and I never had a garage connected to the house. As we aged, it became more difficult to clear snow off the cars. It also meant that we were exposed to rain and snow just to get in and out of the cars. We felt it was time to solve the problem of outdoor parking. Paul Levesque to the rescue. Peter's father came to the house to get ideas for another addition which included a two car garage. The old garage was incorporated into the plan as a library and a large pantry. The smelly shed became a very functional office which connected to the two car garage. An addition, to the rear of the new garage was built, a shed, and a potting room. That room is quite large and stores our garden tools, supplies, and fertilizer. An unexpected bonus from this addition was a large room above the garage. Eventually, we finished the upstairs room.

One day, while driving into Pine Bay, we noticed a truck at Dr. Heilser's house. The truck had a sign saying "custom pool tables." We thought that was a great idea - a pool room over the garage. The builder of the pool table told us he used pieces of older tables as well as newly constructed pieces. The table weighed 300 pounds (slate), which was prefabricated and brought up in pieces, and constructed on location. It was very nice, my son David liked it enough that he asked the man to build him a pool table in Mahwah. When Ron, our investment advisor, saw David's pool table, he ordered one for himself. So one stop at Dr. Heisler's house resulted in three new orders for pool tables. The room over the garage is not heated and does not have any plumbing. It is used a few months of the year, even during some mild winter days. Our original hide-a-bed from 9 Wallingford Road was moved upstairs. The room is a good place for our grandchildren to enjoy themselves.

Many pieces of furniture from 248 Winthrop Street are now in the room above the garage. The children's artwork is displayed there. It's a wonderful room for the grandchildren to use. You should hear the noise from the boom boxes. Fortunately, we cannot hear them in the main house.

We have used up as much land for buildings as we can. The past several years Jan and I (mostly Jan) have been very busy expanding our garden. We have added many new plantings of bushes and trees. We now have a circular drive off of our main driveway, which has made parking easier. There are several walking paths in front and in the back that I call "A Walk in the Woods." Our old swing seat has been removed and replaced by a single swing attached to two cedar trees. We have added a very large blue stone patio which is accessible from our great room. The patio accommodates a large dining room table that seats six or more people. Other areas of the patio have several lounge chairs and small tables. It gets plenty of use. It's great for sunbathing, with its southern exposure. There are many tree shaded areas around the patio. One area has a bench to sit on. There is a second dining area under the trees, where we have placed a wrought iron table and four chairs that we bought from Louis and Margaret Stone. The garden has a great variety of plants, bushes, and trees. Janice is always on the lookout for new gardening ideas. There are oak trees, stuartia, red maple, Japanese bell tree, several arborvitae and white pines and a several Hanokis. There are at least ten varieties of bushes, hundreds of perennials including rhododendrons, azaleas, and inkberries.

In the front of the house, there is a climbing hydrangea that climbs up to about 50 feet on a tree trunk. Our landscaping plans were created by Jan and drafted by Hilde Maingay and by Terry Soares.

Every year since we bought at the Cape, our children and grandchildren look forward to the 4th of July parade at Little Island Beach. The day includes a bike decorating contest – the favorite event of the day. All sorts of decorations, red, white, and blue are used for the contest. Crepe paper is wrapped onto the bikes and wagons. Many flags are taped onto the handlebars. The parade starts at the head of Little Island Road at Quaker Road and proceeds to our beach. Participants are dressed in the patriotic colors of red white and blue. I wear the same bathing suit once a year; it has stars and stripes to enhance the patriotic theme. The bikes are then judged for originality and a clever use of decorative materials, etc. Prizes are given to winners in several categories. Everyone wins a prize for participating.

Jan and I have carried the Liberty and Union flag several times in the parade. It results in questions from the bystanders. I enjoy educating the people on the history of the Liberty and Union Flag. (In 1774, in Taunton, the Liberty and Union Flag was the first flag flown against the British. It is also the first flag in the collection of flags at the Hall of Presidents in Disney World).

A sandcastle competition is held in the afternoon. The youngsters, with help from the adults, are very imaginative for this competition. Over the years we have been involved in sandcastles depicting a mermaid, a dragon, a fortress, an armchair, a whale, and several other designs. Each participant is given a ribbon for his or her categories; there are several categories in the competition. So everyone is rewarded for his or her efforts.

Our grandchildren have been wonderful over the years. They now number 10 and are a source of great love and satisfaction. I will list them in the order of their birth:

Sarah Gouveia

Christopher Thomas

Alyssa Gouveia

Kerrin Thomas

Alexandra Gouveia

Catherine Levesque

Paul Levesque

Isabel Gouveia

Jude Gouveia

Matthew Hin Levesque

Included in the deed to 68 Governor Bradford are beach rights to Little Island Beach. The beach is about a mile away. Since there is no parking there, we taxi people to the beach. The driver goes back to the house and rides a bike back. For the younger children, Little Island is ideal, especially at low tide when there are many sandbars everywhere. Children can play on the bars, and adults can sun on them as they watch the grandchildren dig for crabs, and attempt to catch minnows. The beach differs from year to year. Some years it is free of stones, other years there are many stones. It is a long beach, almost as long as Old Silver Beach. About 150 families have beach privileges. The only time the beach is crowded is the 4th of July. Otherwise, about ten or fewer families are on the beach at any one time.

Little Island Beach Association can have use of the beach because it maintains the entire area as a wildlife sanctuary. The property includes some marshes, forests, and a second area to the left that could be used as an additional beach in the future. The property on the left is on West Falmouth Harbor. The beach is on Buzzards Bay and is protected by a rock jetty. Once our grandchildren become teenagers, they prefer to visit Chappaquoit Beach or Old Silver Beach. Those two beaches attract a much younger crowd.

Those two beaches have much more activity for their age group.

Family photo during Jan's 80th birthday party, 2017
(Catherine and Peter Levesque not in photo)

July 4th Little Island Beach parade

Some Musings on Hedy and Walter Such

Marya Litra & Albert Preneta & family

The wedding of Hedwig Marion Preneta
and Walter John Such, 1934

I first met Hedy and Walter Such when I started dating Jan in the late 1950s. There was a feeling of acceptance of me on my first visit with them. The acceptance was mutual. One could not ask for a nicer couple as in-laws. They were generous in many ways. When we needed help with babysitting, they would drive up from Pawtucket at any hour. They stayed with us on weekends, thus allowing Jan to work as a nurse. Our "hide-a-bed" was well used. We also went on vacations together to many locations – Cape Cod, Florida, the Bahamas, Bermuda, and California.

Hedy was born in 1915 and died in 2000. She was named after Queen Jadwiga of Poland. Jadwiga [1384-1399] became queen at the age of 10. Hedy's Christian name was Jadwiga Marian Preneta, but she used the Anglicized version – Hedwig. The second of four children born to Polish immigrants, Marya Litra and Albert Preneta. Her siblings were John Preneta, Eugene James Preneta (Uncle Jim), and Matilda Preneta (Aunt Tillie), who was the youngest child and oldest to pass at the age of 96.

Janice was born in 1937 and lived in the family home at 85 Tobie Avenue in Pawtucket, R.I. until she and I were married. Her home had three bedrooms on the first floor. A living room, dining room, and small kitchen with a dining table made up the remainder of the downstairs. On the second floor were two small apartments – a two bedroom and a one

The Such residence at 85 Tobie Ave, Pawtucket RI.

bedroom. Over the years, the apartments were used by family members, and then later became rental units.

Jan's Uncle Jim did not marry and lived on the first floor most of his life. Hedy was a dedicated worker for many years as a forelady at American Cord and Webbing in Pawtucket. American Cord was owned by Jack Krauss of New York City. Hedy was a symbol of reliability, generosity, and stability. On her retirement, Mr. Krauss gave her a nice retirement party. I am certain Hedy was hard to replace.

Eugene James Preneta

Hedy and Walter at their 50th wedding anniversary

Hedy and Walter had a close group of friends which included her cousins, Kay Preneta and Wanda Pulaski, wife of Frank Pulaski. Other friends included the Nowaks, the Sansones, and Joe and Cora Kraviec. These couples took turns hosting card parties at their homes on some Saturday nights. On occasional vacations, Frank, Kay, and Wanda would pile into the car with Hedy, Walter, and

Janice and travel around to areas of interest. Over the years they went to many locations including Canada, New Hampshire, Vermont and Cape Cod.

Life at 85 Tobie Ave. was similar to that of families at the time. Many families had both parents working in factories for eight hours a day, five days a week. Contrary to today's customs, children were expected to do household chores, which today is not common. Janice was ten years old when her maternal grandmother died of a stroke. After that, she would come home from school to an empty house. The fact that a ten-year-old girl should walk home alone from school, a mile or so from home, is unthinkable now. Janice had family chores on Saturdays. Her routine, with her father's help, included house cleaning, making beds and other household tasks.

On Saturdays, Hedy did the grocery shopping and made several meals to be consumed over the next week. Jan would heat up these meals and have supper ready when Hedy and Walter returned home from work. Supper was a nightly family affair. Family life today is completely different with hectic school schedules and kid's activities. Many mothers can be compared to taxi drivers, going from one location to another to satisfy after school programs and sports. Although many families today do their best to have a family dinner, there is a tendency to eat in shifts or just grab something rather than sit down to a meal. The intrusion of electronic devices has complicated and changed today's family lifestyles, but that is too broad a topic to discuss in this memoir.

There are many feelings and interesting opinions that come to mind when I think about Hedy. A confirmed saver, she was a believer in systematic deposits into her savings passbooks. Any amount into the bank was good. "A penny saved is a penny earned." Even the smallest deposit would add up to something, as time passed. With Uncle Jim's recommendations, she eventually got into the stock market buying conservative bank stocks. She rarely sold any securities – "buy and hold" was her mantra.

Hedy had certain rules about life that I will try to explain to you:

Remarriage – I would question her as to what is a reasonable length of time for a widow or widower to wait before remarrying? She did not hesitate to answer – "It is at least one year." Any violation of that time-period she would consider in poor taste, perhaps even immoral. I loved to bug her about this rule and asked her many questions about it. "Why not 11 months or 6 months," I would ask. Were there any exceptions to the rule? Would she associate with someone who violated the time-period? Did the survivor's age make a difference? How about a widow of

30 years of age with two young children? Could she be excused of the violation if she married sooner than one year? These questions and much more will forever remain unanswered.

One weekend, Jan, Hedy and I traveled to New Jersey to see Lisa and Peter's "fixer upper home." The house needed work, but with a little effort, it would be quite nice. The visit was pleasant, but their crazy hyperactive Dalmatian was not! At one point he pinned me to the couch with all fours. I had to call for help to get him off of me. After a day-long visit, we decided to return to New England late in the evening. I mention this trip for only one reason – on the five-hour drive, Hedy would not sleep. She was worried I would run out of gas. She sat in the backseat and kept her eye on the gas gauge for the entire trip. Hedy asked many times if I had enough gas. Is there a name for a phobia about running out of gas?

Hedy was an excellent cook. Turkey stuffing was one of her specialties. It had to be made with Jimmy Dean pork sausage as the main ingredient. At our house, we use her stuffing recipe all the time. My niece Joan Mello serves "Hedy Such stuffing" at family gatherings. Hedy cooked mostly American style foods. Occasionally she made Polish foods like kapusta, stuffed cabbage, pieroges and kielbasa. Polish foods were on the table at 85 Tobie Avenue on most holidays. Manhattan cocktails were a common denominator in my relationship with Hedy and Walter.

In 1995, Jan and I planned a surprise party for Hedy's 80th birthday at the Pawtucket Country Club. We thought it was a convenient location for most of her friends. The surprise was ruined by one of her friends who called her to explain she could not attend the party. The thought that everyone knew her age caused Hedy considerable anxiety. I reminded her that Janice was 57 years old, and unless Hedy were a "teenage mother," it would not be a surprise to anyone that she was an octogenarian. Jan and I think she was so upset about the party that she had a stroke, about a week before the scheduled event.

The day Hedy had a stroke, she called our Taunton home, but no one was home. She then called Tillie in Florida. Tillie then called the neighbor who she knew had a key to Hedy's home. He called an ambulance after seeing her condition. When he reached us, he told us that she was taken to Pawtucket Memorial Hospital. After hospitalization and rehabilitation, she had a fairly good recovery. Eventually, she was able to go back home with a First Alert button, which she could use if she needed help (she rarely had it around her neck).

Her last few years were one of gradual decline in function because of additional minor strokes. Her favorite rehab facility was the third floor of Morton Hospital's senior rehabilitation ward where she was treated like a queen. For her last two years, she lived with Jan and me at 248 Winthrop or our home in Falmouth. For her comfort at Winthrop Street, we converted our den into a bedroom since she had a difficult climbing stairs. She had access to the half bath off the corridor.

Another humorous story about Hedy – when living with us on Winthrop Street she asked several times for Polish blood sausage. Her friend Mrs. Nowak visited and brought two large links of blood sausage. She ate an entire link and then asked to eat the second one. Since we were aware of the salt content, we refused her request – lest she go into pulmonary edema (fluid in the lungs).

Hedy's driver's license was to expire, so she asked Jan to take her to the DMV in Pawtucket to renew it. Jan figured it was safe to take her since she thought she would not pass the test. The clerk at the registry asked: "does she still drive?" Jan answered: "no but she wants to keep her license." She easily passed the eye test, because she just had cataract surgery done, and could see every letter on the chart. Hedy got her license renewed with no problem. When she was still driving, she would say that cars kept bumping into her in parking lots – that is how she explained the multiple dings on her car. She was being deceptive about hitting things with her car. Without our knowledge, she once asked Lisa to go with her to a Rhode Island police station after she was involved in a collision. We knew nothing about this incident or the visit to the police station until she gave up her car keys. Her inability to drive became a major problem with her friends. She had been the "taxi driver" for several widows of her age. She took them to church and shopping weekly. Hedy's last car was Goldy, Peter and Lisa used Goldy when they were in the US. Goldy had a formal farewell ceremony, and its obituary is included in another section in this memoir.

In preparation for her eventual demise, Jan asked Hedy what she would like to wear in the casket. Jan suggested a nice fitting suit with short sleeves. Hedy felt the suit was inappropriate. She felt that the arms and hands of an older person were not attractive because of the wrinkling and looseness of the skin. Long sleeves were a must. The dilemma was solved when Hedy and Jan went shopping and found an appropriate pink dress with long sleeves – perfect for the occasion.

Hedy wanted the family to be prepared. She actually wrote her own obituary. She pre-paid her funeral. Jan, Hedy and I went to the Romenski Funeral home in Central Falls to finalize funeral arrangements, including the choosing of the casket. Hedy would have no part in choosing her casket. After Jan and I had picked a casket, we returned to the office. Her first question was "did you buy a Cadillac?" I answered: "no, we bought the Kia." She was not familiar with the low priced Kia car, so my humorous response failed.

Hedy passed away in 2000 at age 85. A few days before her death, she asked if she could be buried in ballet slippers, and not shoes. It became Susan's task to buy her pink satin ballet slippers for her to wear as she climbed the stairway to paradise. At her interment, my granddaughter, Alexandra, placed a flower on the casket and said: "we will miss you, Gramma Such." The priest was impressed with her spontaneous statement, which obviously came straight from the heart of such a young child. Alexandra was only three years old.

Jan and I were present when she passed away. She was lying peacefully in a semi-comatose condition. Suddenly she sat upright-looking straight ahead with a big smile on her face. Was she seeing Jesus? Was she seeing Walter? Was she entering heaven? She lay back and was gone. She has been sorely missed by all who knew her.

Let us talk about Walter John Such. Born in 1909, he was one of eight children born to Joseph and Catherine Such. Both parents were from Poland, met in the US and married. The surname Such can be found in directories in Poland. It is not a name that has been shortened or Americanized by leaving 'ski' or other endings off it. We were asked many times if the name had been changed.

Polish immigrants were eager to own their own houses. To do this, they pooled their money with other Polish families and bought two or three story homes. Living on the first floor, they rented the second and third floors to help pay the mortgage. Both the Such and Preneta families owned homes with rental incomes.

Walter worked at Pansy Weaving Company in Pawtucket before being drafted into the service in World War II. Janice clearly remembers the day that Walter entered the Army. At age 5, she went with Hedy and Walter to Boston. She remembers the day well. They went to the Boston Public Gardens and rode the swan boats. It was a calming and peaceful trip, the rest of the day, however, was different. The embarkation point was at South Station. Janice says she can still visualize the wives and children kissing their fathers, crying, and waving goodbye as the train left the station.

Walter was assigned to a camp in Missouri in the Ozark Mountains. He was trained as an artilleryman, shooting cannons or howitzers. On duty, he sustained a back injury which occurred when he and several other soldiers were firing a canon. The recoil disengaged and knocked several soldiers on top of Walter, who ended up at the bottom of the pile and suffered a hip injury resulting in his medical discharge.

He returned to his job at Pansy Weaving Company where he worked his entire career as a loom fixer in the textile industry. The noise level in the factory was damaging to his hearing (there were no rules regarding protective wear in the workplace back then). As a result, his hearing, which had already been damaged by artillery fire, worsened. Like many people with hearing loss, Walter rarely used his hearing aids, because of their tendency to accentuate background noise.

Factories usually ran three 8 hour shifts daily. Walter worked the first shift, as did Hedy. Depending on what time he started work, he would take a bus to work. Other times he was able to ride with Hedy. One-car families were the norm in the 1940s and 1950s. At one time Hedy and Walter considered buying a variety store in North Attleboro but decided that running a business was not for them. Having grown up in a family that ran a similar business, I think they made the right decision.

Life was not all work and no play. Weekends were time to live it up. Ballroom dancing was very popular in the post-war period. Walter and Hedy danced the night away on Saturday nights at very busy ballrooms in Providence, Central Falls, and Pawtucket. They were a smooth dancing couple who looked great on the ballroom floor.

Walter loved to sunbathe and loved to swim. On summer weekends, the family went to beaches in Rhode Island, especially Narragansett Beach, Newport's 2nd Beach, or Scarborough Beach. On their one-week summer vacation, they occasionally stayed in Hyannis. Walter especially loved Craigville Beach near downtown Hyannis. He loved to swim long distances and was known to stay in the water for long periods of time. One summer, when Jan and I rented a cottage in Dennisport, Walter and Hedy joined us. The weather was just terrible, not only did it rain, it rained for days and so hard that water was coming into the cottage, under the front door. After several days of rain, the sun finally came out, but the weather was cold. Walter was so happy to see the sun that he went to the beach and dug himself a hole to lay in. He lay there for many hours with a smile on his face. The cold wind did not bother him at all.

He tended to leave his group of people for a "potty break." We lost him twice – once in New York City, he disappeared near St. Patrick's Cathedral and Rockefeller Center. This was long before the days of cell phones so that no contact could be made with him electronically. For a long period, he was nowhere to be found, and we were getting very worried. At last, we had found him, but his wanderlust had caused us all much anxiety. We also lost him once at Boston College during Susan's graduation with a Bachelor's Degree in Nursing. Walter was nowhere to be found for what seemed like an eternity. Magically he suddenly appeared and undisturbed by being away from us for so long.

The Such family enjoyed vacationing and motored to several locations over the years. They visited Tillie and Bob when they were working at Rockingham Park in Salem, N.H. during the summers. Usually Frank and Wanda Pulaski and Kay Preneta joined them for far away vacations. All six of them were packed in the car (Janice sat in the front seat between Walter and Frank). The three women sat in the back. They traveled to spots like Niagara Falls, New Hampshire, and Maine. Travel then was a little less comfortable. Roads were narrow and usually had two-lanes of slow moving traffic. Cars traveled at slower speeds. Air conditioned cars were not the norm. Sleeping accommodations were not as frequent. Many areas had individual cabins, mostly privately owned. Motels and chain hotels were just beginning to appear along highways.

One summer, Susan had spinal surgery at the Massachusetts Rehabilitation Hospital and School in Canton, M.A., where she would be a patient for several months. To allow Jan to visit her, and to keep David busy, we thought he should go to summer camp at Tabor Academy in Marion. There, he would have tennis, swimming, and sailing. We were wrong, after about one week, David asked to come home. Jan went to Tabor and asked him to stay for the rest of the week. If he still wanted to come home, she would pick him up on the following Monday morning. When she and Poppa [Walter] arrived in Marion, David was sitting on the sidewalk with his suitcase ready to escape Tabor Academy. Poppa's comment was so typical of his philosophy. He said: "he really loves his home and family." Poppa was so happy for David.

After Jan and I had married, Hedy and Walter accompanied us several times on family trips. This gave them much additional time with their grandchildren. Our children truly loved Hedy and Walter, and continue to speak fondly of them.

Walter John Such married Yadwiga Marian Preneta on Thanksgiving in 1934. He passed away in 1989 at our home at 248 Winthrop St. The day he died,

Walter spoke to me, as I was leaving for work. He said: "David, I am very sick today." His heart stopped a couple of hours later.

He was a quiet man, a very gentle soul. He was truly religious, and in his bedroom, he kept several religious statues and pictures. The beautifully clothed Infant of Prague statue was my favorite. Under the statue, there was a $50 bill taped – ensuring that he would never be out of money. This statue is now in our bedroom at the Cape, with the $50 bill still attached.

Walter was a believer in the afterlife. He did not want people to go to his grave on a regular basis. He told Hedy not to visit his grave often because he would not be there. He would meet her in heaven instead.

John and Patricia, My Parents

Early photo of my father taken in Connecticut

In several areas of this book, you have read information about my parents. The following pages may have some duplication in presenting multiple ideas and happenings. I hope to give you some additional insight into their lives, starting with the roots of John Figueiredo and Patrocina Alvaro Netto as compiled by my aunt, Mary Marques.

My father was born Joao (John) Figueiredo in 1888 in Portugal, in the village of Moradia, near Fornos de Algordes (a part of Gouveia). His father was Jose Figueiredo, and his mother was Luisa Lopes. He had two brothers and two sisters - Antone and Andre, Maria Lopes and Candida Lopes Alves. Maria came to America and settled in Taunton, Massachusetts. She married Antone Almeida who was from Fall River, Massachusetts, and they lived on a farm on Dighton Avenue. Candida remained in Portugal.

I remember meeting only one of my uncles who stopped at our house, while on his way to Brazil, where he remained the rest of his life. My father never returned to Portugal. He said there was no reason to go there. Being a grocer in the United States was much better than being a shepherd in Portugal. My father had a major stroke in 1971, and passed away on December 8, 1972, after a very rewarding life as a small businessman.

My mother, Patrocina Alvaro Netto was born in 1899 in Villa Franca da Serra in the Gouveia area of Portugal. She was the daughter of Joaquim Alvaro Netto and Purificacoa Lopes. She had three sisters who were born in Portugal: Lucy (Costa), Josephine (Lawrence) and Mary (Marques). A fourth sister Esther (Andrade) was born in the United States. My mother's grandmother was Maria Luiza, who was a French orphan. She came from France to Portugal with Portuguese soldiers who were returning to Portugal, after being involved in the war with Napoleon. (Napoleon attempted to conquer Portugal, but he was not successful). On arriving from Portugal, my mother lived on Dighton Avenue, in

My father in the front row wearing white pants,
at company outing in New Shoreham, CT, August 4th, 1917

My Parents wedding.
Photography by Boutin Studios

A photo of sheperds in Villa Franca da Serra,
1938, photo by Patrocina Netto Gouveia

**The Netto family home in
Villa Franca da Serra**

Mrs. Fonseca's house. Her father, with whom she immigrated to this country, lived two or three houses away at a distant relative's house owned by the Netto family. My mother passed away on Easter Sunday 1971, at the age of 72 of complications of heart valve disease.

As I poured through many legal documents, I found that the couple I knew and loved had a myriad of names during their lifetime - I will cite only a few examples. Their wedding certificate of January 1919 records that John Figueiredo, age 29, a mill operator, married Patrocina Netto, age 20, a mill operator.

I have a mortgage dated November 18, 1927, for the property at 986 Somerset Ave. This included a house (with a grocery store on the first floor), and a large lot of land extending down the hill along Baker Road. No mention of Lawton Street in the mortgage. I can only assume that Lawton Street was not built until later.

The property was purchased from Joaquim F. Pereira and Maria F. Pereira, one of my grandmother's sisters. The purchaser was John F. Gouveia. No mention of my mother in this transaction. The mortgage was $1500. Monthly payments were $15.50 at 6%. A deed for adjacent land on Lawton Street in 1946 listed the sellers as Frank and Amelia Correia (also my grandmother's sister). The buyers were John F. Gouveia and Patrocina Gouveia. No dollar value was recorded, but the tax stamps on the deed were in a mere $1.10.

In 1947, John F. Gouveia and Patricia Gouveia signed a mortgage to the South End Portuguese Club. In 1965 John Gouveia sold Gouveia's Cash Market to my sister and her husband, Daniel J. Rapoza and Constance Rapoza. They ran the business for about eight years. My sister Virginia continued to work at the store on a part-time basis. The business was sold to Cumberland Farms. The store, the barn, and the gas station were torn down. A new larger Cumberland Farms store with a self-service gas station was constructed. There are other transactions that I have, but I think you get the message that their names varied as the years passed.

In May 1946 the probate court of Bristol County approved a certificate of changes of our family names as follows - our legal names became: my father, John

My parents in front of our garage on Lawton Street in their older years

My mother in her early sixties

Figueiredo Gouveia; my mother, Patricia Gouveia; my sister Chris, Constance Figueiredo Gouveia; my sister Jean, Virginia Figueiredo Gouveia; and my name, David Figueiredo Gouveia.

My cousin, Evelyn Costa Roessing, gave me a poster-sized colored print which I think was the cover of an advertising calendar which she found in the attic at her family home on Dighton Avenue - the Netto-Costa farmhouse. I had it framed. It depicts St. Teresa of the Roses. It preceded the building of our store on Lawton Avenue. I've not been able to find the exact date that Lawton Avenue divided our home from the acres of land that my parents owned. The poster has advertising on top "Compliments of John F. Gouveia, telephone 3506. Meats, Groceries, Provisions, Candy, Tobacco and Ice Cream - 986 Somerset Ave. corner Baker Road in Taunton, MA."

I know very little about my father when he was living in a suburb of New Haven Connecticut, before his marriage to my mother. I have several photos taken by a professional photographer showing my father along with other people whose identity I do not know. He seemed to be quite a "Dapper Dan" in the pictures. Att he beginning of this chapter, the photo shows him holding a small musical instrument, some sort of horn. I am not aware that he ever played any musical instrument. He was dressed in a suit and tie, and in the mode of the day, he was not smiling. All the people in the pictures seem very stiff. I think they had to be motionless in order to get a clear photo. One of the photos that

My parents' 50th wedding anniversary

I was given a few years ago is a large panoramic photo of a group of over 50 well-dressed employees of the Hoggson and Pettis Company, at an outing in New Shoreham, Connecticut and is dated August 14, 1917.

Most of the men were wearing suits. My father wore a dark jacket, a white shirt, and a tie. His pants were of a light colored material. He had on white shoes and white socks. A few men were not wearing jackets, but they wore white shirts and ties.

Extensive computer searches reveal that the firm was established in 1849. Many of the products found currently online, were tools used for working on either leather or rubber. Patents date back to the 1890s. I found a more recent patent dated 1968 for a paper punch with variable spacing. The firm also produced some of the early typewriters. Recently, a typewriter produced by the company (only five are known to exist) sold at Christie's in London for $8126. I am not certain if the firm is still in business. I found that it later had an alternate name - Smedley Company Warehouse Number 3 but the building in which this company worked was listed as demolished.

One weekend, while I was on summer vacation from college, my father and I made a trip to Connecticut, more than 30 years after his move to Taunton, Massachusetts. We visited the area where he lived and worked. I wish I had made notes of this trip. Details are not coming back to me. I didn't think of it at the time, that in 70 years or so I would be writing about one of the rare times in my life, that I was one-on-one with my father. Each time we drive 95 in Connecticut on our way to David's or John's house. I think about the rare time I had with my father as he reminisced about his early years in America.

I was told by my mother that most of their courtship was by letters back-and-forth from Connecticut. They had only a few visits together before their marriage. When both my parents came to the USA, they had little formal education. In all probability, the love letters were written and read to them by third parties. Talking about education, my parents were self-educated. Three of my mother's sisters were born in Portugal - Mary, Lucy, and Josephine. They attended the school that in later years was known as Herbert E. Barney School. My aunt Esther was born in this country. An interesting note, all three of my aunts, who were born in Portugal, had Miss Smith as a teacher in the early grades. My sisters and I had the same Miss Smith as a teacher a decade or two later.

The love letters between John and Patricia, however, they were written or read, were successful. They were able to celebrate 50 years of marriage 1969. The 1920 Taunton City census lists John F. Gouveia living with John Netto on Dighton Ave. Apparently, my parents did not have their own place for a while.

In several areas of this book, I have discussed my father's life, his long, hard hours at the store, and his virtual slavery on the farm. He was a man who wanted to be successful. Success he did accomplish.

Although he worked like an ox, he was a very gentle man. As my mother once told my wife, Jan, "he has never hit me." It is unfortunate that some men of Portuguese background were physically abusive to their families. I never saw the trait in my father's actions. I know he was not initially happy that I did not become a grocer. He was a little hesitant in accepting my going to college, but he honored my decision. I know it was the right decision. I was not meant to be a purveyor of foodstuffs.

My mother and sisters were very supportive of my desire to be a doctor. (Did I say that I wanted to be a doctor at age 3?) I've been told many times that I did say it. My parents somehow were able to find the money to pay for college and medical school tuition. I don't know how they did it since profits in the store were not that lucrative.

Let us look into the life of my mother. There've been several references to my mother in other chapters of this book. Some of what I wrote on this topic may be repetitive. She was the major factor in the Gouveia household, the strength of the family. I ask for your indulgence as I reminisce about my mother.

She and her father sailed in steerage to get to Ellis Island. She occasionally would make comments about the perils of the voyage. Neither she nor her father spoke any English. They had very little money with them. She left behind her mother and three sisters who were living in the family home in Villa Franca da Serra. I was fortunate to visit the family home in the mid-80s. The home had a dirt floor. I've been told that the home has fallen down since then. Considering it is 200 and 300 years old, that's a good long time, before its demise. The structure was made of stone. It had one door and one window with a wooden shutter. My grandfather was a shoemaker, whose business was conducted through the only window in the house. The dirt floor remained unchanged in the 80s. There was no running water.

Jan and I met the last relative who lived in the house. He was probably in his 50's. We also visited another home where my grandmother's sister lived. Her daughter was a widow, now living in the house alone. This house was upscale in many ways including a finished floor. She demonstrated how she cooks. There was an open fire pit in the corner of the kitchen which consisted of an exterior stonewall and a stone floor. The cooking surface was depressed several inches, allowing the cook to sit on the lip, holding a skewer on which meat was cooked over burning flames. The smoke from the burning logs escaped through a hole in the ceiling. The house was elevated one-half of a story, allowing her to have a chicken coop under it.

My mother must have felt like a Vanderbilt when she moved in with Mrs. Fonseca from Villa Franca on Dighton Avenue. Mrs. Fonseca probably had a cast-iron stove that used either coal or wood to cook with. The stove was most likely a Glenwood range – a Taunton product.

My mother had the luxury of sleeping in a bed with one or two other women. It was very common to share a bed with multiple people in those days. This custom continued at 986 Somerset Ave. My sisters had one full-size bed in their room. Many times, my aunt Esther had to stay with us, so we had three people to a standard bed - making a total of six people using one bathroom. Somehow we survived.

I don't know where my mother worked. Her marriage certificate said she was a mill operator. City census shows that my grandfather Joaquim Netto lived with a relative, John Netto, on Dighton Ave. Within a couple of years, my mother and grandfather saved enough money to bring my grandmother and three daughters to Ellis Island in 1919.

My aunt, Mary Marques, was detained in isolation in the infirmary at Ellis Island for three weeks because of what sounded like a mastoid infection. She required surgery for this problem. If she had not improved, she would have been sent back to Portugal. My grandmother and her other two daughters were detained until Aunt Mary's infection cleared. They said that they had cots to sleep on, and were apparently fairly comfortable.

My grandfather Joaquim took a train to New York City. He was able to visit his daughter, Mary, at Ellis Island, but could not visit with his wife and children. Traveling to New York was quite a feat for someone who knew very little English.

My Aunt Mary was interviewed for the "Oral History" program sponsored by Ellis Island. More than 50 years later, this interview was narrated by a woman who came to Taunton to record interesting stories about people who went through Ellis Island. These tapes can be listened to at Ellis Island for anyone interested in the stories of new arrivals to the USA in the early 20th century. The recordings are in the American Family Immigration History Center. My confirmation godfather, Joe Fresta, was also interviewed for the Ellis Island archives by the same woman. I have copies of these two tapes for anyone interested in hearing them.

I have some memories of the house at 986 Somerset Avenue which I will share with you. There was a cast-iron stove in the kitchen. The stove was the heater for the house, using kerosene at times, or coal at times. The oven and stove top were used for cooking. The stovetop was also used to heat a clothing iron. Have you ever heated an iron on the top of a stove? Have you actually ironed clothes?

After the 1938 renovations, the kitchen changed completely. The dining table sat 8 to 10 comfortably. The original cast iron stove was replaced with a more efficient one. Eventually, the stove was removed, and a gas stove installed in the pantry. We then had enough room for a good sized refrigerator. Cooking space in the pantry was small. Counter space was no more than 36 inches. There was no dishwasher. Dishes were washed by hand and placed on a rack to dry. There was minimal storage for food. We did not need a lot of storage. The store was just across the street.

As I may have mentioned previously, my mother loved to bake pies and cakes. A good day for her was one in which many pies were baked. You have already heard about her amazing nourishing brownies in other chapters. She

Ellis Island

served family dinners 2 to 3 days a week for her children and grandchildren. She provided nourishment for all. Besides providing meals, my mother was a caretaker for her grandchildren. Young Danny, Patty, Debbie, and Joan were often at the house after school and during school vacations. She was the force that kept her family secure. Other activities for her were as a business woman. She helped keep the books for the store. She cleaned the house, and she did the ironing, as did most women of the day.

I don't think she returned to work in a factory after the death of her first son, Julio, at age six months. One activity that I found fascinating was her knowledge of midwifery. This came in handy next-door. Her cousin, Armand, and his wife, Phoebe, had 12 children some of whom were delivered in their house next door. My mother did some of the deliveries.

When I first started to write about my parents, it was extremely difficult. Over a period of weeks, I wrote down ideas for this chapter. Lo and behold, before I knew it, I had written considerably more than I expected, but not quite of epic proportions. I hope these words have given you an insight into the life early and mid-20th century, and of the lives of many immigrants who came to this country, seeking a life better than they had in Portugal, and of the many other nationalities that came to America, hoping to have a better life for themselves and their children.

Gouveia family photo at 50th wedding anniversary, 1969

Some Final Words from the Author

Now that you have read this memoir, and I hope you found it interesting, I'd like to present some thoughts about this book.

The early chapters embody my impression of life in the 1930s and 1940s during the great depression and its aftermath.

The life customs and celebrations of the Portuguese immigrants are examples of how they adapted to life in a new country where they were a minority. Although they barely spoke English, they made their life as satisfactory as they could by establishing a community of families, friends, and neighbors who came together in good times and bad.

The chapter involving the killing of a pig is an example of how they worked to improve their lives despite their long hours at work, and a minimal salary for five to six days a week of hard labor. Much of this work was in difficult conditions for many years. These years preceded the enactment of labor laws and environmental protection regulations.

The stories of my education are an example of the number of years it takes to become a surgeon. I did not start private practice until 1964 at the age of 33.

I witnessed life in the segregated Deep South while living in southern Georgia from 1962 to 1964. As a "Yankee" from New England, I had not seen the type of human inequality that was common in Georgia. My exposure to people of color was one in which our Taunton "Negro" neighbors were accepted and treated equally and fairly. Some of the stories that I was told regarding segregation policies were quite graphic and not appropriate to be included here.

I have chosen several stories about people whom I was privileged to know and to be involved in their medical and surgical care. These stories are quite varied, and I hope you enjoyed reading them. I have so many wonderful memories of my patients.

My life story would not be complete without an inclusion of my penchant for American history. I have a great desire to make history a living thing, not a boring story. As you can see, I did my share of being involved in the many aspects of life in a Twentieth-century city which unfortunately was undergoing a decline in prosperity. Founded in 1639, Taunton is one of the oldest cities in the country. Many changes in American industry occurred during my time in Taunton. Many businesses closed or left the city - once a location with about 20 silver manufacturers, today there are no silver companies remaining. The last survivor was the Reed and Barton Silversmiths which ceased operations in 2015. There is very little manufacturing of any kind being performed in my hometown.

Being such an old city with an abundance of Victorian and colonial buildings that have survived; there has been plenty of time for people to suspect the presence of spirits and ghosts in some of these homes. Ghost stories have been included for your contemplation. I have left it up to you to decide whether the events in these stories were caused by spirits or not.

Many references were used to authenticate some of the historical data included in this memoir. "A History of Taunton Massachusetts," by William F. Hanna was a frequently used reference. It was published in 2007 by The Old Colony Historical Society.

Although my wife Janice and I have traveled quite extensively, I decided to include only three short stories of our travels. I think the most important story is my visit to Auschwitz and Birkenau. The memories of that day are with me forever. It is my hope that the world will never forget the atrocities which occurred during Hitler's reign.

The last several chapters showcase the people most loved in my life – my wife, my children, grandchildren, and my parents and in-laws. Without these people, my life would have been very different. They were my muses, my guiding spirits, and my inspiration.

Although I have mentioned religion in some of these writings, I have not gone into my involvement with God. I have been a lifetime practicing Roman Catholic, like my relatives who have gone before me. If I am chosen to join them in heaven (Deo volente), then I look forward to the greatest possible family reunion ever.

Roots of Joao and Patrocina Gouveia - compiled by Aunt Mary Marques

Joao Figueiredo Gouveia Mother: Luisa Lopes Father: Jose Figueiredo Brothers: Antone and Andre Sisters: Mary Lopes Almeida, Candida Lopes Alves Joao was born in a small town near Fornos de Algodres.	Patrocina Alvaro Netto Mother: Purficacao Lopes Father: Joaquim Alvaro Netto Sisters: Lucy Costa, Josephine Lawrence, Mary Marques, Esther Andrade Patrocina was born in Villa Franca da Serra (a part of Gouveia)
Joaquim Alvaro Netto Mother: Maria Luiza Father: Joaquim Alvaro Netto Maria and Joaquim had eight children. Maria was a French orphan who was brought to Nespeireira, Portugal at age 12. She went to Portugal with returning regiment which was involved in a war with Napoleon. Maria died when Joaquim was eight years old. He was raised by his grandmother until age 14 when he moved to Villa Franca da Serra to live with his uncle. His uncle taught him shoe making which became his source of income. He married Purficacao at age 33.	Purficacao Netto Mother: Rosario Victorino Father: Antonio Val Lopes Brothers: Jose Val Lopes, Manuel Val Lopes Sisters: Mary Perry, Emelia Correia, Jesus Val Lopes-Alves, Virginia Purficacao was born in Villa Franca da Serra

Curriculum Vitae

David F. Gouveia M.D.

68 Governor Bradford Lane

Falmouth, MA 02540

M: 774-313-0043, E: jandave2@comcast.net

Diplomate of the American Board of Surgery

Fellow of the American College of Surgeons

Education:

B.S., Magna Cum Laude, Tufts University	1953
M.D., Tufts University School of Medicine	1957
Internship, The Ohio State University	1957-1958
Residency in Surgery, St. Elizabeth's Hospital, Boston MA	1958-1962

Professional Affiliations:

Chief of Surgery, U.S. Army Hospital, Fort Stewart GA	1962-1964
Active Staff, Morton Hospital, Taunton MA	1964-2011
Delegate, Massachusetts Medical Society	1966-
Member, Massachusetts Medical Society, Various Committees	1966-
Secretary, Bristol North Medical Society	1975-2015
President, Bristol North Medical Society	1977-1978
President, Medical Staff, Morton Hospital	1983-1985
Member, Board of Trustees, Morton Hospital	1983-1985
Member, Public Relations and Image Committee, Morton Hospital	1983-2000
Member, Massachusetts Medical Society, Ethics and Grievances Cmte.	1996-2006
Chair, Massachusetts Medical Society, Ethics and Grievances Cmte.	2001-2006
Active Emeritus Staff, Morton Hospital	2001-2011
Assistant in Surgery, Falmouth Hospital	2003-
Inactive Emeritus Staff, Morton Hospital	2011-
Former Member, Blue Cross/Blue Shield Physicians Liaison Cmte.	
Former Member, Bay State Health Plan Physicians Liaison Cmte.	

Honors, Awards, Recognitions, Community Involvement

High School Diploma, Magna Cum Laude, Taunton High School	1949
Bachelors of Science in Chemistry and Biology, Magna Cum Laude, Tufts University	1957
Welcome Home Reception, Taunton Community	1964
Recipient, U.S. Army Commendation Medal	1964
Diplomate of the American Board of Surgery	1967

Fellow of the American College of Surgeons (F.A.C.S)	1967
Member, Taunton Historic District Commission	1970s
Recipient, Marian Medal, Fall River, MA Diocese – Our Lady of Lourdes Church	1970s
Member, Our Lady of Lourdes School Committee	1980
Falmouth Historic District Commission	1980s
Recipient, Portuguese American of the Year, Prince Henry Society	1994
Recipient, Community Clinician of the Year, Bristol North Medical Society	2000
Recipient, Ten Year Service Award, Massachusetts Medical Society, Ethics Cmte.	2006
House of Delegates, Fifty-Plus Year Award, Massachusetts Medical Society	2012

Photography

Best of Show in Photography, Newport Outdoor Art Festival

Best of Show, Falmouth Art Association

Photo Contributor, Falmouth Chamber of Commerce Visitor's Guides

Photo Contributor, Pilot Press Travel Book Series

Photo Contributor, Feldene 1991 International Calendar – Moscow Circus

Honorable Mention, 1990 Feldene International Calendar – Beach at Nazare, Portugal

Ethnicity Estimate

Region		Approx %
Africa –	Total 6%	
•	Northern Africa (Morocco, Tunisia, Algeria, Libya)	6%
Europe –	Total 88%	
•	Iberian Peninsula	46%
•	Europe West	12%
•	Great Britain	12%
•	Italy/Greece	11%
•	Ireland	4%
•	Israeli	2%
•	Scandinavia	1%
West Asia -	Total 6%	
•	Middle East	6%

*Approximate Estimates for the DNA of David Figueiredo Gouveia complied by Ancestry.com

http://dna.ancestry.com/ethnicity/8FB0A8C9-E3D4-4527-A93B-9B26BEDF154F

About The Author

Dr. David F. Gouveia is a well-known surgeon and physician and was educated and practiced medicine in Massachusetts for over 60 years. In addition to his surgical and private patient practices, he has been a member and delegate of the Massachusetts Medical Society and Chair of its Ethics and Grievances Committee. He was formerly President of both Bristol North Medical Society and Morton Hospital and is currently an active surgeon at Falmouth Hospital. In addition to various other regionally based medical committees, David is a fellow of the American College of Surgeons and Diplomate of the American Board of Surgery.

Dr. Gouveia is a professional photographer and a contributor to the Old Colony Historical Society, Falmouth Historical Society, and 'A History of Taunton Massachusetts.' He has won multiple regional best of shows for his photography, including the Newport Art Show. Dr. Gouveia is also an active member of the Portuguese community in Bristol County, MA and recipient of The Prince Henry Portuguese American Award for his service to Portuguese families. A former President of the Old Colony Historical Society, Dr. Gouveia currently is a Board Member of The Falmouth Historical Society.

In addition to his traveling and photographing the world, Dr. Gouveia lives in Falmouth, MA with his wife Janice, and is the parent of four grown children, ten grandchildren, and two Labradoodles, Luke and Abby.

CPSIA information can be obtained
at www.ICGtesting.com
Printed in the USA
BVHW04s2319130718
520756BV00005B/4/P

9 781457 559457